CHICAGO'S PROGRESSIVE ALLIANCE

CHICAGO'S PROGRESSIVE ALLIANCE

LABOR AND THE BID FOR PUBLIC STREETCARS

Georg Leidenberger

NORTHERN ILLINOIS UNIVERSITY PRESS / *DeKalb*

© 2006 by Northern Illinois University Press

Published by the Northern Illinois University Press,

DeKalb, Illinois   60115

Manufactured in the United States using acid-free paper

Design by Julia Fauci

Library of Congress Cataloging-in-Publication Data

Leidenberger, Georg.

Chicago's progressive alliance : labor and the bid for public streetcars /

Georg Leidenberger.

p.   cm.

Includes bibliographical references and index.

ISBN-13: 978-0-87580-356-2 (clothbound : alk. paper)

ISBN-10: 0-87580-356-3 (clothbound : alk. paper)

1. Labor unions—Illinois—Chicago—Political activity—History—20th

century. 2. Electric railroads—Illinois—Chicago—History—20th century.

3. Chicago Federation of Labor and Industrial Union Council—History—

20th century. 4. Transportation—Illinois—Chicago—History—20th

century. 5. Progressivism (United States politics)—History—20th century.

I. Title. II. Title: Labor and the bid for public streetcars

HD6519.C44L45 2006

388.4'2097731109041—dc22

2005029739

CONTENTS

ACKNOWLEDGMENTS

This project has trodden a long path, along which I encountered most valuable teachers, colleagues, professionals, and friends who provided guidance, assistance, and support. The writing of history certainly is a solitary craft, but no doubt represents a collective effort as well.

My greatest acknowledgments go to my dissertation advisor, colleague, and friend, Leon Fink. As is appropriate for a good historian, Leon first inspired me through his written work, which prompted me to pursue graduate studies with him. Ever since then, I have been most fortunate to receive his intellectual and personal guidance. Besides his keen and profound insights as a scholar, Leon has served as a model of somebody able to integrate the exigencies of an inspiring professional with all of life's pleasures and challenges. Salutations go to the whole Fink-Levine family in that regard.

Many other teacher-scholars have directly or indirectly contributed to this manuscript. It was my undergraduate teacher and advisor Peter Rachleff whose passion for the history of working people converted me to the field in the first place. Other key professors during my formative years were (in order of appearance) Ingrid Ittel, Emily Rosenberg, Norman Rosenberg, Emil Slowinski, Judith Bennett, and Jacquelyn Hall, among others. My thanks also go to fellow students at Chapel Hill: Cindy Hahamovitch, Scott Nelson, David Shaw, Jeff Cowie, Laura Moore, Gary Frost, Robert Tinkler, and especially Margaret Swezey. Here in Mexico, I am indebted to friend and colleague Ariel Rodríguez Kuri.

During a difficult moment of this project, Lois Parkinson Zamora appeared as a rescuing angel, infecting me with her enthusiasm and astute advice. Most generously, she undertook a thorough revision of the entire manuscript. I also wish to thank the anonymous peer reviewers for their constructive criticisms, and I extend particular gratitude to Jim Barrett for backing this project.

ACKNOWLEDGMENTS

At Northern Illinois University Press, first Martin Johnson and, for over a year now, Melody Herr have been diligent and highly professional editors. Thanks go especially to Melody for her painstaking work and patience during the book's editorial stage. Residing in Mexico for some years now, I have depended on the gracious aid of several errand runners, especially of my always-traveling brothers-in-law Saúl, Arón, and Álvaro Bitrán. Aaron Berkowitz at the University of Illinois at Chicago did a wonderful job of gathering the visual materials, which, in turn, Robert Medina of the Chicago Historical Society (CHS) most kindly facilitated; and Alejandro Dionicio expertly designed the book's maps. The research for this book was greatly enhanced by more than a few archivists. My special thanks and memories go to Archie Motley, deceased head of archives at the CHS, for rendering the Society's manuscript division such an agreeable place to work in; he always was ready to offer hints on sources and inspired one with his lived enthusiasm for the history of that wonderful city. I am also much obliged to CHS staff members Linda Evans, Theresa McGill, and Ralph Pugh, as well as to Ingrid Schulz of the Illinois Regional History Archives.

This work has benefited from important financial backing. At the University of North Carolina at Chapel Hill, several Mowry graduate fellowships from the History Department as well as two research and writing fellowships from the Graduate School provided key aid for completing the dissertation. Several institutions in Mexico, the Universidad Autónoma Metropolitana—Azcapotzalco, and the Sistema Nacional de Investigadores and a stipend from the Consejo Nacional para la Ciencia y Tecnología (CONACYT-2002-C01-39653) allowed me to dedicate time to the revision of the manuscript. Two other institutional backers of this book are the Chicago Historical Society and, last but not least, Northern Illinois University Press.

I am indebted to my parents, Hanne and Freimut, for their love and manifold backing. My wife, Yael Bitrán, has been a wonderful companion during this journey, at both its brighter and darker moments. I thank her enormously for her support, advice, and, always, for her presence. My no less amazing children, León, Samuel, and Clara, arrived at distinct moments during this odyssey; they have done a great job of putting things in perspective.

CHICAGO'S PROGRESSIVE ALLIANCE

, , ,

HALSTED STREET CAR

Come you, cartoonist,
Hang on a strap with me here
At seven o'clock in the morning
On a Halsted street car

     Take your pencils
     And draw these faces.

Try with your pencil for these crooked faces,
That pig-sticker in one corner—his mouth—
That overall factory girl—her loose cheeks.

     Find for your pencils
     A way to mark your memory
     Of tired empty faces.

     After their night's sleep,
     In the moist dawn
     And cool daybreak,
        Faces
     Tired of wishes
     Empty of dreams

—Carl Sandburg, *Chicago Poems,* 1916

A STREETCAR NAMED DEMOCRACY

Labor and the Search for the Common Good

How better to get to know a city than by riding its streetcars? Today, we can take tourist rides through historic downtowns on board of fake combustion-engine versions. Today they are quaint relics of the past, but one hundred years ago streetcars exemplified the progress and conflicts of the modern city. In the pre-automobile city, trolleys (as electrically run streetcars were known) provided the most important means of getting around. Their routes defined the central growth axes of the rapidly expanding metropolis, with new townships and suburbs being incorporated into the old walking city. Critical to the city's functioning and development, trolleys came to be recognized as a vital public interest by a broad segment of the urban population. Yet, given that they were owned and operated by private investors whose motives appeared to clash with public concerns, city after city witnessed the rise of an intense debate over the public regulation of this essential urban service. Seeking to assure good streetcar service but also to fight the corruption reigning among company leaders and aldermen, an immense number of citizens and civic associations involved themselves in the streetcar question.

One key constituency of this movement was organized labor, which spearheaded campaigns for the public ownership of transportation in many U.S. cities and thereby offered a radical solution to the need for public regulation. Streetcar politics offer a unique window on the democratization of reform politics during the early twentieth century and on urban trade unions' participation in those politics.

Inviting the reader to board a streetcar in a turn-of-the-century metropolis, this book offers a historic tour of the ways trade unionists and middle-class activists shaped municipal reform politics during the Progressive Era in the United States. Like today's touristic trolley rides, the tour contains a dose of nostalgia, for the way organized labor managed to assume center stage in municipal reform politics of the period appears an age gone by, given its marginalization in today's mainstream politics. Back a century ago, however, the workers' presence in public discussion exemplified the democratic opening of politics, where trade unions pushed for far-sighted policies in the realm of urban services and many other issues, such as education. By examining the intersection of labor and reform within the political debate concerning streetcars, I wish to raise an enduring concern: how to negotiate and promote the common good within a genuinely democratic framework.

No other place offers a better case study of the intersection of working-class mobilization and reform politics than does Chicago, a city exhibiting a fertile mix of astonishing progress and deep social chasms. Arising from a swampy military outpost on the western shore of Lake Michigan in 1830 to become a metropolis second in size only to New York City by 1900, Chicago constituted the archetypal industrial city. Located at a central node of the country's railroad network, it became the grand distributor and processor of the goods emanating from the plentiful Far West basin: grains, wood, and cattle entered the grand machineries of Chicago's storage houses, cereal processors, breweries, timber yards, and meat-packers, only to continue their way eastward to feed the insatiable demands of the Atlantic world. Chicago was a site of tremendous human labor. In "Big Shoulders," manufacturers, financiers, engineers, inventors, and architects converged with a massive, mainly immigrant, working population of artisans, mechanics, bricklayers, and factory operatives, sustained by the immense reproductive and domestic labor of working-class women. From 1860 to 1900 alone, Chicago's population increased from 100,000 to 1.7 million. It was a city where the logic of industrial capitalism held sway, and travelers left impressed by its stunning contrasts of wealth and poverty—by the juxtaposition of the world's most luxurious districts, such as the Gold Coast, with the most abject agglomeration of materially deprived human beings, in Back of the Yards, for example.

Given such contrasts, it was not surprising that Chicago became the site of the country and western world's most severe industrial conflicts. If the disaster of the Great Fire of 1871—when over three and a half square miles of the city lay in ashes—could be branded as a phoenix-like opportunity for a new beginning, the Great Upheavals of the late nineteenth century provoked fears that the nation was headed for another civil war, this time to be fought between labor and capital. In the first nationwide railroad strike, in 1877, Chicago exhibited some of the worst rioting, human slaughter, and destruction of property. A decade later, on May 1, 1886 (commemorated as May Day in most of the world), the explosion of a bomb in Haymarket Square led some to forecast an anarchist revolution while others, with an eye on the severe repression and hysteria that followed, felt they lived in an autocracy rather than a free republic. The trilogy of late-nineteenth-century industrial confrontation found its completion with the Pullman Railroad Strike of 1894. Originating just south of Chicago during the Great Depression, this conflict ceased only through federal military intervention.

Beneath these upheavals lay not only an irrational and desperate mob (as the elite pictured it) but also a solidly organized and firmly rooted labor movement. Chicago trade unions ranged from the city's skilled workers, especially the printing and building trades, to most sectors of Chicago's economy (with the great exception of some of the most important industries such as meat-packing and steel) and found expression in citywide labor federations and short-lived political labor tickets. By the turn of the century, Chicago witnessed a heyday of trade unionism, whose ranks increased from one hundred thousand to three hundred thousand members between 1900 and 1903 alone. About every sixth unionized worker of the United States lived in the midwest metropolis, and no other city, with the possible exception of San Francisco, matched its unionization rate of 50 percent.[1]

More than a mere quantitative leap, trade unions infiltrated new sectors of the urban economy, most notably the teaming trade. The teamsters union, first formed in 1902, many times either seized or threatened to seize the flow of goods throughout the city, in order to assist the unionization of unskilled workers from other trades of the city's service, retail, and manufacturing sector. Such intertrade solidarity found solid backing from the labor central, the Chicago Federation of Labor (CFL), founded in 1896. At a time when trade unions tended toward a vertical structure, where every trade responded to its national headquarters, Chicago labor forged unprecedented horizontal and locally oriented ties among the city workers. Another key agent of this metropolitan unionism were the female elementary-school teachers, who pushed organized labor toward a citywide political outlook and forged ties to an avid reform community of middle-class women. It is workers such as the teamsters and the teachers, who defy any neat categorizations of class identity, rather than workers in the more studied Chicago industries, such as meat-packing and steel, who constitute the protagonists of this story. Their activism illustrates how American Federation of Labor (AFL) trade unionism did provide room for un- and semi-skilled workers and women workers.[2]

If Chicago acquired fame as the labor capital in the world, it also became known as the nation's municipal laboratory of social reform, which grew out of the same late-nineteenth-century social crisis that gave way to trade unionism.[3] In no other U.S. city did reform-oriented journalists, college-trained professionals, and social-minded millionaires confront the ills of their society with greater fervor. Historian Frederick Jackson Turner set the stage when he proclaimed the end of the western frontier, in his 1893 address to the American Historical Association, only to argue that its spirit of expansion and renewal would now be directed inward, toward the improvement of the nation's cities.[4] Beginning during the Great Depression of 1893, reformers exposed poor housing conditions of immigrant wards, child labor in dangerous industries, the lack of sanitary services, as well as the corruption of Chicago's public institutions. Chicago became the site of numerous settlement houses (including Jane Addams's Hull House, Graham Taylor's Seventeenth Ward Commons, and Raymond Robins's Municipal Lodging House) and originated a host of reform organizations, such as the Civic Federation of Chicago, the Municipal Voters League, and the Chicago City Club, all of which heralded nationwide reform associations. Chicago also produced major intellectual advances, including John Dewey's pragmatist philosophy and the Chicago School of Sociology's urban ecology, a model of urban growth that grew out of the city's political turmoil.

Yet how did these two Chicago traditions of labor militancy and social reform relate? Did they coexist in the midwest metropolis and acquire unprecedented strength out of sheer coincidence? The answer is no. Both of these civic impulses, rooted in the country's predilection for forming voluntary associations, entered Chicago's public deliberations and transformed its political culture. It was the fruitful exchange between the two that generated what I describe as the progressive moment of Chicago's history, which lasted from 1902 to 1907 and reappeared briefly in 1911. I argue that progressivism in Chicago rose and fell with the ability of labor and middle-class reformers to enter into coalitions, in which each side acted out of its own interest while also pursuing a singular common good. Progressives thereby forged a unique moment that consisted in the hope and project of affirming the public good through and by a civic and democratic revitalization, which included trade unions in its fold. This insertion of new social actors into the public sphere did not ipso facto lead to pluralism. Rather, pluralism constituted an ideological reaction to the democratization and reaffirmation of the public ideal of the progressive moment.

The notion of the public sphere serves as a key concept in this study and therefore requires some explanation. Jürgen Habermas described the public sphere as a space that serves as a buffer between civil society and the state and in which publicly relevant opinion can be formed. It constitutes a conceptual space that allows for citizens to engage in rational thought and exchange with the goal of formulating a public interest. The public sphere conceives of the political process beyond elections and policy making to include the mechanisms of opinion formation, where a host of ideas compete upon the basis of unwritten rules, or scripts, of appropriate forms of exchange. This concept also pays attention to the social and organizational basis of the agents of opinion making. Finally, the public sphere can also operate in terms of the specific, physical places and institutions in which public deliberation occurs, including saloons and salons, cafés, civic meeting halls, and the street, as well as, and perhaps most important, the city press.[5] By centering on the unfolding of the public sphere, we invariably generate a broadly conceived social and cultural history of politics, one that also pays attention to its spatial setting.

In Chicago, the streetcar certainly constituted one of those places of public interaction. As the main mode of transportation in this rapidly growing city, the trolley provided an essential service to the vast majority of residents who found their places of home and work at ever greater distances. Sitting or, more likely, standing inside a trolley, any passenger was surrounded by a diverse population stemming from different backgrounds that social scientists like to categorize by gender, class, ethnicity, and race, and which our hypothetical passenger must have registered as an amalgam of different clothing, smells, attitudes, and habits. By watching through the window of the streetcar a film of passing pedestrians, horse-drawn vehicles, crowded streets and squares, sumptuous buildings, modest wooden row houses, and so on, this passenger was also reminded of living in a city that constituted an interconnected whole, notwithstanding the specialization and fragmentation of urban activities—be they related to residence, work, consumption, or leisure. The streetcar, then, meant a tool not only for moving from one place to another but also for picturing and imagining the city's population and landscape.

No wonder that the streetcar became a central object of political deliberation. By the late nineteenth century, Chicagoans recognized urban mass transit as a crucial element of the public interest. Worrying that streetcars were run by private companies, Chicagoans spent a great deal of their energies arguing over how urban (and, to a lesser extent, state) government ought to regulate this service and how that government should be held accountable to the citizenry. The narrative of this book unfolds around the debate beginning with the first popular civic upheavals against the streetcar companies—run by supposedly evil magnates—during the late 1890s, continuing with the rise of a movement for their municipalization and the attempts by a mayor elected on that platform to enact the corresponding legislation, and ending with the unfolding of Chicago's transit policy and political culture from 1907 to World War I.

Municipal politics in cities all across the nation centered on streetcars, but in Chicago the confluence of a highly developed labor militancy, on the one hand, and of civic reform, on the other hand, generated a particularly intense and therefore interesting debate. The labor question proved central to the streetcar struggles. For one, streetcars were run by unionized conductors and operators. When these workers struck, city traffic was brought to a halt. Streetcar strikes constituted moments of urban—in addition to industrial—crisis, where the need to confront the issue of streetcar regulation proved imminent. It was the 1903 streetcar strike that propelled a municipal-ownership movement composed mainly of CFL trade unionists and a host of radical middle-class associations. By then, organized labor became a key player in Chicago's public sphere. Important questions to be addressed are how and why trade unionists engaged in reform politics, how they gained and eventually lost allies among the city's middle class, and how they shaped the city's political universe.

Chicago's streetcar struggles are an example of the democratization of early-twentieth-century political life and of a corresponding expansion of the public sphere in the U.S. city. When trade unions along with women's clubs, radical newspapers, settlement house reformers, and ethnic- or neighborhood-based associations participated in Chicago reform politics, they broadened the social basis of the public sphere. They also raised the stakes of debate by postulating that matters such as urban transportation formerly considered private in nature were in fact public concerns. This labor-led movement also premiered in Chicago's political universe a variety of measures associated with so-called direct democracy: citizen's law suits, petition drives, referenda, and political mass meetings. The unions widened the range of spaces considered suitable for political debate; the streetcar question was fought out not only in city hall, at the ballot box, or in Chicago's newspapers but also in a great variety of public and semi-public buildings, such as schools and concert halls, as well as union headquarters, saloons, and settlement houses. The most important site of conflict proved the street itself, where numerous strikes and demonstrations took place and where an enlarged public sphere made itself most visible. If the uses that ought to be made of Chicago's through-ways formed a central object of the streetcar question, the streets also provided the forum where such debates were carried out.[6]

This public and political mobilization provoked a counter reaction by an elite eager to delimit the public presence of certain social agents, especially of trade unionism. On the industrial front this meant a major offensive, known as the open-shop drive, against the city's most powerful trade unions, especially the teamsters union. On the political front it took the form of a functionalist and pluralist ideology that was to take shape by the 1910s. Essentially, this ideology acknowledged a broader social basis of the urban polity but reduced the function of citizens to that of narrow-minded (that is, functionally oriented) recipients of urban services. At the same time, pluralists abandoned the search for a singular public interest and conceived the political process as a mere reconciliation of multiple group-based interests. This shift toward pluralism related directly to a revived class conflict in Chicago and must be understood as a closing in on the expansion of democracy and the widening of the scope of public administration, which was characteristic of the early progressive period.

This study illustrates events that were occurring in cities nationwide. In urban centers all across the country, streetcars provoked some of the fiercest battles of early-twentieth-century urban politics, and regulatory matters frequently spilled over to the level of state government. Especially in the midwestern region where technological innovations in mass transit (for example, the electrification of streetcars) coincided with the take-off phase of industrial cities including Toledo, Detroit, Cleveland, Milwaukee, as well as Chicago, streetcar struggles formed a central element of progressive politics.[7] Many of our story's protagonists—Frederick Howe, Clarence Darrow, William Randolph Hearst, and Walter L. Fisher, among others— proved active in cities other than Chicago and in national-level progressive associations. The local debates over public utility regulation informed the work of national reform organizations such as the National Civic Federation (NCF) and the Municipal League. In numerous U.S. cities, streetcar strikes provided the catalyst for public-ownership campaigns, usually led by local trade unions and citywide labor federations.[8]

Yet Chicago proved unique in the way its politically oriented metropolitan unionism coalesced with a widespread reform fervor. In part this is explained by the city's political framework, whose fragmented nature and lack of partisan political machines allowed for cross-class coalitions to transform into viable political campaigns. In contrast, San Francisco, another "labor town," saw organized labor and progressives take separate paths, partly because trade unions entered partisan politics in the form of a labor party, which did not have to rely on middle-class allies. Thus, when progressives took control of the mayor's office in San Francisco, they did so in opposition to organized labor.[9] To the east, in New York, a well-established political machine and a consolidated reform-oriented patrician elite rendered it difficult for an independent labor and middle-class progressive coalition to take the fore. There, ambitious public projects, such as the construction of the first municipally financed subway or the drafting of a new metropolitan charter, were initiated and orchestrated by the city's commercial elite.[10]

After all, Chicago is Chicago. Many contemporaries considered the midwest metropolis, with its vivid public life and relative fluid class structure, to be the vanguard of democracy. Located between the civilized East and the expanding West, Chicago appeared to combine the best of both: a strong sense of the country's republican tradition and the energy and will to experiment that was associated with the frontier. "If Christ came to Chicago" (to cite a leading muckraking exposé), he would indeed encounter the extreme depths of civilization, but here, too, he would encounter a marvelous "spirit for democracy."[11] Yes, the city was class-ridden, violent, even brutish, but it did not exhibit the classist structures of a European city or, for that matter, Boston or New York. These, of course, were all myths, but myths develop out of communally held belief systems, and for this reason they can be a powerful source of political culture. How democratic, how progressive the city really was and what social forces stood behind these attributes will be considered in the pages that follow.

In reassessing the interrelation of labor and progressivism, by way of Chicago's debate over streetcar regulation, this work, of course, is indebted to a large body of historical and some theoretical literature that has served as an essential empirical and conceptual backdrop. It is necessary to acknowledge these works and situate my own argument in terms of previous characterizations of progressivism and labor politics during the early 1900s. This book's contention that the progressive moment occurred previous to—and indeed provoked—the advent of pluralism differs from works on the Progressive Era that have sought to explain the nature of progressivism by focusing on the agenda of a particular social group or class, therefore interpreting this age of reform within a pluralist or Marxist framework. Was progressivism the product of Richard Hofstadter's "old middle class," anxious concerning the rise of a corporate economy and the wave of immigration of Catholics and "wets"? Or did it conform to the hegemony and search for order by a new corporate elite? However different these two interpretations, both tend to neglect the ideals put forward by progressives and underestimate the democratic and unifying potential of the period.[12] Even quite recent works, although shifting focus from a social or class analysis of progressivism toward an institutional or political-cultural one, affirm pluralist arguments.[13]

This study attributes a central role to organized labor in the unfolding of municipal politics, and it thus contrasts with most studies on progressive-era politics, which describe workers and trade unions either as opponents or as passive backers of reform. Historian George Mowry, for instance, acknowledged occasional, if what appeared to him unusual, alliances between progressives and labor leaders, but he argued that "such co-operation was almost invariably a one-way street . . . work[ing] only if the progressive rather than the labor politician was in the drivers' seat."[14] Implicit in his argument is the assertion that a far-reaching and disinterested reform perspective could stem only from a middle-class person. The problem, I insist, lies in the historiographical tendency to categorize workers and other social groups in terms of a singular, usually job-related interest.

Functionalist accounts of the urban boss and machine politics, for example, situated worker immigrants as loyal constituents to ward bosses, who provided for their material and emotional needs (jobs, housing, and a sense of belonging). Studies that recognized workers as key constituents to progressive legislation nevertheless viewed them as a passive force, motivated by their material needs and immediate concerns about working and housing conditions.[15] Studying progressive politics in Milwaukee, David Thelen found that workers were deeply concerned about the quality of urban services, especially the city's transit system, but the conclusion he drew from this fact was that workers were acting solely as consumers, not as wage earners. Thelen's identification of consumer or urban-service issues as a basis of the progressive reform upheaval signified a key historiographical contribution, and one that is picked up by this study.[16] Yet in pigeon-holing wage earners (or any constituency, for that matter) according to singular and ultimately narrowly defined interests, the point is missed about the integral—even if at times messy and contradictory—quality of a citizens' agenda. When workers in Chicago entered politics by way of their unions, they had a variety of concerns in mind, concerns related to their work, their neighborhoods and services, and their political community, all of which need to be taken into account.[17]

The tendency to attribute to workers an overly narrow or fixed interest is shared by labor historians. When it comes to politics, and especially to twentieth-century politics, trade unions' engagement is considered in terms of their work-related agenda. Earlier characterizations of narrowly job-centered and apolitical workers have been thoroughly corrected by several works that show how craft unions, especially on the local level, actively pursued laws on workmen's compensation and limitations on hours, as well as anti-injunction and anti-immigration measures. Labor politics that addressed matters going beyond the workplace, the issue of urban services, for example, are treated with skepticism, especially when it comes to assessing cross-class alliances.[18] The repressive features of the cross-class project of the NCF, which sought to harmonize industrial relations and imposed a straight jacket on militant labor practices, has served as a powerful precedent for questioning any attempt by labor to search for allies beyond its own class.[19] Yet again, workers and trade unions' concerns proved complex and multifaceted, especially when they circulated within a broader political sphere and especially during the Progressive Era when these workers, like middle-class residents, formed part of an age that sought to harmonize collective group interests while upholding the ideal of the common good.

When Chicago trade unionists allied themselves with segments of the middle class, they did so in pursuit of a (class-) specific interest, certainly, but they also entered such alliances as citizens who shared with middle-class reformers a concern for the public interest.

This held especially true for workers whose class status, be it in economic or cultural terms, came close to the fringes of the middle classes—a condition that applied to the protagonists of this story: the skilled or "white-collar" workers who made up the CFL leadership. Moreover, class-based identities and interests are continually reshaped by the very process of engaging in politics and thus in coalition building. Public deliberation was not only the result of social interests as such; it helped define the identities of those partaking in it—a point forcefully drawn home by two recent studies of urban progressive politics.[20] In the following discussion, I use the notion of cross-class alliances with this caveat in mind and seek to evaluate such projects without adopting a rigid definition of any "class'" previous interest. This is a crucial endeavor, given that these alliances stood at the heart of progressivism.

Our streetcar is about to leave its depot, so here is the itinerary. The first stop in chapter 1 delineates the surge of a citywide metropolitan trade unionism centered on two crucial groups of workers, the teamsters and the teachers. The next two chapters will focus on the streetcar question as a key debate of urban reform. Chapter 2 establishes the importance of streetcars to urban development and reform and describes the first political campaigns on their behalf during the late 1890s. Chapter 3 discusses the entrance of organized labor into Chicago reform and the rise of the municipal-ownership movement from 1902 to 1905. Chapter 4 then shifts focus back to the industrial scene to describe the 1905 offensive of the employer organizations against the teamsters and against a broad-based trade unionism in general. Chapter 5 describes how this backlash and other developments affected plans for a public takeover of the streetcars from 1905 to 1907. A final chapter discusses the legacy of the 1907 referendum on mass transit and urban development in Chicago and assesses broader shifts in the city's political culture. The journey ends with concluding remarks that situate the story of U.S. class relations and reform in a comparative, intercontinental context. So, please board this streetcar named Democracy, and enjoy the ride!

SERVICE WORKERS AND THE NEW METROPOLITAN UNIONISM

For years the power of trades unions has been growing in that city [Chicago],

until it is now regarded as the strongest labor center in the world. The Teamsters

Union and their support of strikers in other lines have brought the matter to a crisis.

—*Iron Age*[1]

Near the end of the twentieth century, on the morning of April 13, 1992, Chicagoans experienced a rude, and rather wet, awakening. Many basements of downtown office buildings flooded with water from the Chicago River, causing major disruptions in utility service and damages costing millions of dollars. How could this happen? A piling recently driven into the river bottom had caused a leak in one of the city's underground freight tunnels. Water streamed throughout fifty miles of the tunnel network and flooded all downtown buildings connected to that system. Hardly anybody remembered the existence of these tunnels. For a good part of the century they had been out of use. The disaster suddenly reminded Chicagoans of their city's underground past.

The flooding of 1992 brought back into public memory the heyday of modern Chicago at the turn of the century. When the tunnels were constructed in the early 1900s, they constituted the newest advance in the city's infrastructure, the latest sign of the modern city. Forming a grid of sixty-two miles in length, they served as an underground delivery system to downtown buildings, which received coal and merchandise transported in lorries through the tunnels. Modern technology had left its mark on rail transport not only underground but above ground as well, where streetcars, powered by the magical new force of electricity, moved in a strangely silent manner amidst the newly erected skyscrapers of Louis Sullivan and Daniel Burnham, among others. The city's traffic arteries thus extended in all directions, with streetcars across the plain, elevators toward the sky, and tunnels down below. The city of Chicago appeared to have solved one of the maxims of modern urbanism: to create an infrastructure enabling the free circulation of goods and people throughout its area.

Yet the flooding of the underground tunnels in 1992 might also have brought back less celebratory memories. Were the tunnels signifiers of progress? Ever since their construction, they had led a clandestine life, invisible and unknown to most city residents. Their contractor, the Illinois Telephone and Telegraph Company, disguised them with the claim that it was laying underground cables. It came as a big surprise when it turned out that the cables required tunnels sixteen feet in width. Yet why hide from the public such an accomplishment of urban engineering, such a feat of modernization?

Indeed, the secrecy of the tunnels' construction reflected major social struggles over the use of Chicago's streets, specifically battles between unionized teamsters, their employers, and the police. As teamsters repeatedly succeeded in blockading the city's downtown streets, business organizations sought to move the flow of goods below ground, to be undisturbed by bothersome union drivers. All tunnel operations were to be run by non-union men only. As a visiting journalist noted: "when it is in full swing, it may go far toward clearing the streets of forty thousand turbulent teamsters, and toward making Chicago the handiest city in the world." Indeed, at the height of their operation the tunnels eliminated five thousand unionized truck deliveries daily.[2]

The tunnels constituted a direct response to the unionization of the city's horse-cart drivers. Forming their first trade unions in 1902, the teamsters would come to form the backbone of a new metropolitan unionism that encompassed practically the city's entire transportation and service sector. Teamsters' collective control over the flow of goods in the city yielded them enormous bargaining power with their employers. Moreover, through the teamsters' assistance in the form of sympathy strikes, thousands of formerly unorganized workers, largely in the service and retail trades, formed their own trade unions for the first time. Organized labor reached white-collar employees as well, most notably the schoolteachers, who formed a unionlike organization in 1897 and affiliated with the city's central labor organization, the Chicago Federation of Labor (CFL) in 1902. Through the action of the teachers and the teamsters, Chicago trade unionism not only expanded in numbers but also reached out to a broad section of the city's working class. Already in the 1890s, organized labor's ranks had doubled from fifty thousand in 1893 to one hundred thousand by the turn of the century. Within the next three years that number tripled to three hundred thousand; some even claimed it reached four hundred thousand. The CFL could now claim to represent almost every other wage earner in the metropolis, that is, 50 percent. On the national level, in contrast, trade union membership rates ranged from 3 percent in 1900 to 5.6 percent in 1910.[3]

New trade unionists conceived of their movement differently from traditional craft organizations, especially the powerful building trades unions, which betrayed little solidarity with workers outside their own industry. The more recent organizational wave of Chicago labor envisioned a broad-based recruitment within a trade-based structure, including workers from a variety of skills and of both sexes. Although several key industries such as steel would remain, for the time being, outside the orbit of Chicago labor, a broad cross section of Chicago's workforce found a place in organized labor long before the rise of the industrial unions of the 1930s.

The workplace-centered and politically limited union strategies of the building trades unions form the subject of the first part of this chapter, followed by an account of the innovative approaches of the new unions such as the teamsters and teachers. A third section is devoted to the CFL. The teamsters and the teachers attacked political corruption among labor leaders and pushed for the CFL to adopt a broader, more public, more politicized vision. Echoing attacks on the city government by progressive reformers within the city at large, these workers adopted the rallying cries of "Democracy!" and "Reform!" in support of their claims.

THE CITY'S BUILDERS—THE BUILDING TRADES UNIONS

Until the turn of the twentieth century, labor power was in the hands of the building trades. Construction workers were essential to a booming city, and their unions, among the best organized and most powerful, had commanded Chicago's labor movement throughout the nineteenth century. By the late 1890s, all but a handful of the thirty thousand Chicago building trades workers were members of a trade union. They enjoyed closed-shop agreements with contractors that permitted only union men to be hired with more than decent wages. Most unions explicitly defined a day's work and restricted the use of labor-saving machinery. Any foreman "using abusive language to, or rushing the men under his supervision," the plumbers' union declared, "shall be fined not less than $10.00 and ruled off the job." Even President William McKinley experienced the meaning of a union town when in June 1900 he was practically compelled to join the bricklayers' union, as an honorary member, before laying the cornerstone of Chicago's new post office building.[4]

Such union power was facilitated by the nature of the building industry, which was labor intensive, confined to a local market, and carried out by numerous small and large contractors. Prior to 1899, contractors were divided among themselves and lacked a central organization, but with the building boom following Chicago's Great Fire of 1871, they nonetheless flourished. Such urban growth, coupled with the 1893 Colombian Exposition and technological breakthroughs in construction such as the steel frame, resulted in a boom that continued even through the depressed years of the 1890s.[5]

Yet it was the effective organization of the Building Trades Council (BTC) that assured closed-shop conditions in Chicago's construction industry. This council united a total of three hundred delegates from all thirty-two different trades of the industry, ranging from skilled and relatively independent craftsmen such as bricklayers, to tradesmen such as carpenters whose skill and autonomy on the job were threatened by technological innovations, to unskilled laborers such as hod carriers. The BTC's business agents—also called walking delegates—ensured compliance with union work rules at each building site. Every union member had to show his union card to the walking delegate upon request. The unfortunate contractor found in violation of union work rules usually faced immediate work stoppages orchestrated by the BTC's board of business agents. Through the BTC, Chicago construction unions managed to "rule the building trades with an iron hand."[6]

Building trades workers defy such categories as "labor aristocracy" or "bread-and-butter-unionism," given that they were neither concerned with wages alone nor focused exclusively on organizing their separate trades. The BTC's objective was to "remove all unjust or injurious competition" and to maintain workers' control over the production process, as well as to improve working conditions. Through the assistance of carpenters and bricklayers, for example, unskilled hod carriers managed to gain greatly increased wages not received among "other labor of the same class." The first BTC was founded by Knights of Labor leader James Brennock in 1887 and resembled the mixed assemblies of his organization. Notwithstanding the decline of the Knights by the late 1880s, industrial councils endured among the building trades.[7]

Intertrade solidarity did not extend outside the industry, however, at least not after the 1890s. Prior to the waves of anti–labor union repression in the late 1880s and 1890s (especially the destruction of Eugene Debs's industrially organized and Chicago-based American Railway Union in the 1894 Pullman strike), construction unions engaged in sympathy strikes with workers who were not part of the building sector. For example, the

BTC supported the Pullman strikers in 1894. Thereafter, the more privileged and conservative tradesmen within the industry took hold of the
BTC and directed it to cease such actions. Bricklayers, for instance, were
skilled craftsmen who were hardly threatened by technological changes,
and they demonstrated relatively little sympathy with workers of lesser
skill, except those employed within the construction industry.[8]

Such an industry-focused orientation did not imply distaste for politics.
In fact construction workers proved eager to gain political power. By supporting councilmen and mayors with a favorable attitude toward organized labor, building trades unions obtained vital benefits, including employment in the numerous public works projects and control over public
inspection jobs. Perhaps most important, the promise of union votes made
mayors think twice about using police force to break a strike. In Chicago,
such a political bargain meant an alliance between the building trades and
the ruling Democratic Party. At first, during the 1880s, the building
trades—disillusioned with third-party politics after the failure of the
Greenback labor tickets—sought political influence by endorsing pro-labor
candidates of either of the two major parties. Such nonpartisan political
bargaining quickly yielded to an informal alliance with the Democratic
mayors Carter Harrison Senior and Junior. Positioned outside the relatively
weak regular Democratic machine, Harrison Senior through his personal
charisma and effective fence straddling forged a broad coalition, incorporating organized labor, Irish nationalists, German liberals, and some leading Chicago capitalists. He ruled as mayor from 1879 until 1893 and was
succeeded four years later by his son Carter Harrison II (1899–1905,
1911–1915), who continued to enjoy close ties to organized labor and especially to the building trades unions.[9]

Such political dealings paid the price, however, of limiting labor's militancy. When trade union action spilled outside its own trade or industry,
these alliances reached their breaking point. During a streetcar strike in
1885, one of the "largest and most violent mass strikes since the 1877 riots," labor action suffused entire working-class communities.[10] Faced with
such a publicly visible battle on Chicago's streets, Mayor Harrison appointed Captain John Bonfield—later to become notorious for his involvement in the 1886 Haymarket riots—as police chief, instructing him to
break the strike by force. Alienated by the mayor's move, the building
trades unions joined a short-lived labor party campaign, only to return to
the fold of the Harrison Democracy after the general repression of labor militancy in the wake of Haymarket. As these events revealed, the BTC's political
tactic was useful for strengthening unionization among its own ranks, but it
proved incompatible with efforts to unite Chicago workers across trade lines.
As historian Richard Schneirov aptly describes it, the "Harrison Democracy
served both as a safety valve and as a surrogate for working class power."[11]

Surrogate or not, by the end of the nineteenth century, in the midst of an unprecedented construction boom, building trades unions held considerable economic and political power. Employers complained bitterly about the unions' capacity to restrict the amount of work and even to prevent the use of labor-saving technology. According to contractor Edward M. Craig, the stonecutters immediately ceased "work in a yard where machinery of any kind was used"; and bricklayers habitually sent apprentices to the nearest saloon for beer during the morning break.[12] Labor's political ties assured union power over the building site. Mayor Harrison had appointed the BTC president Edward Carroll as head of the Civic Service Commission, which generated hundreds of jobs for building trades workers. Unionized inspectors not only enforced building codes but also assured that all workers on a given site carried a union card. The BTC had further leverage in securing a union monopoly in Chicago; no contractor hiring nonunion labor could hope for an inspector's approval. Two-thirds of the BTC's three hundred delegates held city jobs in 1900, and "at least twenty-two laboring men," an employer charged, occupied important offices in city hall. Most of labor's political ties were with the Democratic Party. According to the Norwegian newspaper *Skandinaven,* sixty-eight of the BTC delegates were Democrats holding well-paid positions with the city and only two delegates were Republicans.[13]

Faced with these conditions, in November 1899 over two thousand employers, united in the Building Contractors' Council (BCC), launched an unprecedented offensive against building unionism in Chicago in what came to be known as the Great Lockout. As the BCC made clear, it did not "question the present rate of wages, hours, or the principle of legitimate unionism"; rather it fought for what it considered employer prerogatives such as control over working hours and the use of machinery, and it bitterly opposed workers' engagement in the sympathy strike. In order to return to work, trade unions would have to adhere to these "cardinal principles" of the contractors. Really at stake during the dispute was the intertrade, industrywide strategy effected by the Building Trades Council.[14]

Around the annual peak of the building season, in April 1900, forty thousand union workers found themselves on the street. At first, it appeared that the unions' political ties to city hall would pay off: the police's hands-off approach prevented employers from hiring replacements to the locked-out union workers. As a result, 90 percent of Chicago's construction activity ceased, and thousands of workers left the city in search of employment elsewhere. The state's neutrality manifested itself in other forms as well: despite frequent outbreaks of violence (which in March and April alone left five people dead and one hundred sixty injured), the police arrested fewer than twenty people. A demand by the contractors to allow private detectives to join the municipal police was voted down by the city council. And the local courts pursued only four cases out of thirty grand jury indictments.[15]

In the eyes of the city's business and financial elite, such governmental leniency with the strikers proved unacceptable. Chicago's leading banks sent a letter to the mayor threatening him to cease all credits to the city unless the municipal police intervened more actively and unless Harrison fired BTC president Carroll from the Civic Service Commission. Harrison got the message, promptly fired Carroll on May 1 (May Day, of all days), issued a decree limiting the number of pickets per building site to two people, and assured "vigorous enforcement" of the ruling. Indeed, the police from then on swiftly dispersed strike-related gatherings; "the rioting stopped instantly," a contractor reported, "and since that time there has not been one-tenth part of the assaulting that there was before." Capital in Chicago had organized and prevailed. Deprived of their ability to restrict "scab-labor," demoralized by the lack of public support, and worn out by over three months of involuntary idleness, the bricklayers, followed by plasterers and engineers unions, broke with their trades council and signed no-sympathy-clause agreements with contractors. By February 1901, carpenters and painters abandoned the BTC as well, and the lockout came to an end.[16]

The Great Lockout proved a watershed in Chicago trade unionism. It sent a clear message to construction unions as to what constituted legitimate organizing practices. During the next five years of economic growth, building trades unions enjoyed growing membership, but they restricted their organizing to their own trade, refused to join a central council, and denounced sympathy strikes. Individual trades would occasionally back the strike of another trade, but without the coordination of an effective trades council these acts of solidarity came to no avail.[17] With regard to politics, the building trades lockout revealed the severe limitations of labor's partisan political strategy. As soon as trade unionists pursued more militant and class-based organizational strategies, their friends in city hall let them down. The teamsters, appearing on the labor scene for the first time on the eve of the Great Lockout, were bound not to trust in such political bargains.

THE CITY'S MOVERS—TEAMSTERS AND TEACHERS

By 1901, the organization of two new occupational groups—the teamsters and the public-school teachers—signaled a major departure in the history of Chicago's trade union movement. Just as the building trades unions were finding themselves eclipsed after the Great Lockout, a new star arose in labor's sky: the teamsters. Like construction workers, teamsters worked in hundreds of different trades across the city. Moving goods across the entire city in their horse-drawn wagons, the teamsters formed a vital part of Chicago's infrastructure, and as they assisted the organization of workers outside their own industry, they became the heart of Chicago's labor movement. For example, when milk drivers, meat deliverers, or ice wagon drivers struck in sympathy with a group of service workers, a small industrial dispute quickly escalated into a citywide ordeal. Operating in the streets, the arteries of the city, the teamsters became the human lifeline of Chicago's internal trade and the main force behind the city's new unionism.[18]

Prior to forming their own unions, teamsters were described as the "roughest scrappers of the working classes." With a working day that lasted up to fourteen hours, teamsters appeared to interact more with their horses than with their families; a former teamster named Sharkey recalled: we "knew each [horse] so well . . . more lovable than human beings! Only 10 hours at home in which to sleep and eat. Figure it out. Horses won easily!" Truck drivers like Sharkey, reported a labor journalist, "belonged to the high chest . . . low brow era. Wages $16.00 per week on a three-horse team. You had to like work to do the job. Five loads, . . . one hundred 135-pound coffee sacks to a load. You carried each sack from tailboard, 17 feet to the front of the wagon . . . that's 67,000 lbs. on, 67,000 lbs. off— 134,000 lbs. per day with which to wrestle."[19]

Union organization resulted in a substantial improvement in living conditions for teamsters and their families. The formation of the first independent truck drivers union—with "truck" still referring to horse-drawn carts—in February 1901 signaled a departure in the industry, for earlier "unions" had consisted largely of team owners who displayed little interest in the concerns of wageworkers. Once joined by the newly organized coal drivers' union, wageworkers quickly seceded from the employer-dominated Team Drivers International to establish the Teamsters National Union, which proceeded to grow with "marvelous rapidity" and by 1903 turned into the International Brotherhood of Teamsters. Within five years, teamsters formed forty-six separate locals with a combined membership of thirty-five thousand workers.[20] By mid-1902, teamsters had markedly improved their wages and working conditions through a substantial reduction of working hours, the elimination of work on Sundays, and increases in wages. Teamsters' wages now stood above those of common laborers such as stablemen, but they were still below those of the blue-collar elite such as bricklayers (see table). Equally important, the union helped raise teamsters' pride in their job and general awareness of the skills involved in their trade. Teamsters proudly stated the qualifications required of them: "he must read and write and know the city thoroughly [and] . . . he must know what to do in an emergency if anything happens to his horse or wagon." In fact, "a driver gets to know his wagon . . . just as a locomotive engineer knows his engine."[21]

TABLE I WAGES OF SELECTED TRADES IN CHICAGO, ca. 1901

occupation	wages/hour	wages/day	wages/week	wages/year
Bricklayers	$0.50	$4	$32	$1,152
Carpenters and Joiners		$3.40		$918
Stablemen	$0.20			
Hod Carriers		$2.98		$805
Teamsters	$0.27		$16.21	$843
Streetcar Conductors		$2.25		$702
Glove Makers		$1.50		$405
Janitresses			$3.40	
			$10 (union)	
Garment Workers			$8	$360
Department Store Clerks				$520
Elementary-school Teachers				$825
CFL Organizer			$35	$1,820

Sources: *Twelfth Biennial Report of the Bureau of Labor Statistics of the State of Illinois 1902* (Springfield, Illinois, 1904); Don T. Davis, "The Chicago Teachers Federation and the School Board," boxes 1, 35, CTF Papers. On Fitzpatrick's salary, see CFL Minutes, November 1, 1903.

As in the building industry, the nature of the teaming trade facilitated workers' organizational efforts. The industry operated in a local market, was labor intensive, and allowed only loose supervision of the driver. Teaming, like construction, was done by thousands of small-scale competitive firms whose leaders held an interest in stabilizing wages through contracts with their employees and in diverting the costs of such agreements to the public. These "bilateral monopolies" signed by the unions and the team owners guaranteed that the latter would hire only union members while the union would work only for employers belonging to the teaming association.[22]

Teamsters revived—and greatly extended—the very organizing strategies employers had attacked in the building industry, especially the use of the sympathy strike. In May 1902, just as the BTC was becoming insignificant, the teamsters' first citywide council, the Shipping Trades Federation, orchestrated a walkout of tens of thousands of teamsters in order to aid the strike for union recognition by packinghouse drivers. What might have been a small strike of a few hundred workers in the city's South Side turned into a city-wide ordeal that challenged one of Chicago's leading industries: the great meat-packing firms, including Armour and Swift. Restaurants no longer received meat from the union drivers, and establishments daring to purchase "scab-meat" soon found themselves without coal to heat their buildings. The struck meat-packers hoped to wait out the dispute and keep the meat on ice, but to no avail: the ice wagon drivers' participation in the strike caused $180,000 worth of meat to rot in the stockyards. And delivery wagon drivers at Chicago's nine leading department stores engaged in a one-day warning strike. "Hotels will have to substitute oatmeal for porter-house steaks," the *Inter-Ocean* observed wryly.[23]

Whereas construction work was confined to individual building sites, the teamsters traversed the streets of the entire city. Disputes over their working rights easily became struggles over the control of the streets and often involved entire working-class communities. During the 1902 drivers' strike, for example, the attempt by strikebreakers to deliver meat to city shops was met by large pro-union crowds, including many women. The ensuing battles with the police caused "three days of the worst rioting and mob violence and terrorization Chicago had experienced since the ARU [American Railway Union–Pullman] strike of 1894." The crowds, at times compounding over twenty-five thousand people, overturned streetcars and blockaded the streets with the horse wagons: a veritable "civil war" ensued in Chicago's streets.[24] The notable presence of women in the battles further reveals the communitywide nature of teamster strikes. Chicago's chief of police considered these protesting women "the most dangerous persons with whom the police have to deal." The police "would charge upon . . . infuriated amazons . . . with drawn clubs, but then hesitated when it came to rapping them over the head as they would have done in the case of dispersing a mob of men." In general, the police proved ineffective in protecting strikebreaking teamsters who had to traverse wide areas of the city.[25]

The crowds' actions had the desired effect. The packinghouses "were made almost as inaccessible to the Chicago public as if they had been in China." Teamster president Alfred Young threatened to tie up stockyards in Kansas City, St. Joseph, and East St. Louis as well, and the strike was settled within three days, yielding the meat-packer drivers a solid victory. Quick sympathy strikes by most of the city's teamsters and the actions of pro-union crowds provided a small group of drivers with a victory over a powerful group of meat-packer employers. In the eyes of a journalist, the teamsters were ruling Chicago "with the grasp of a tyrant," turning it into an "industrial hell." By 1905, the teamsters had made Chicago the bastion of their movement: of forty-five thousand union teamsters nationwide, thirty thousand lived in Chicago.[26]

Street scene from the 1902 teamsters strike, which affected large portions of the city. The overturned horse cart is lying on top of streetcar rails. Since teamsters' industrial disputes took place in the city's public thoroughfares, and not at the factory, they were public events, rendering visible industrial violence and causing the halt of traffic often across the entire city. Chicago Historical Society DN-514

The teamsters used their industrial power to aid workers outside their industry, enabling unionization among a large segment of Chicago's service workers. In February 1903, coal drivers added a powerful edge to the strike of elevator men by refusing to deliver coal to the fifteen struck skyscrapers, thus leaving the buildings without heat in the middle of a Chicago winter. The dispute was quickly submitted to arbitration and brought union recognition to the striking workers. Tailors, rubber workers, glove makers, janitors, and janitresses also benefited from the teamsters' sympathy strikes.[27] And teamsters' command of the streets enabled streetcar conductors to win a strike in 1902, an event (discussed below) that would play an important role in the movement for municipal ownership. A "strike epidemic," an *Inter-Ocean* reporter wrote in May 1902, "seems to have struck Chicago. . . . It is confined almost entirely to unorganized workers, or those who have recently formed unions."[28]

The year 1902 had been a good year for Chicago trade unions. Most union workers enjoyed substantial wage increases, and the labor movement managed to double its constituency to reach 250,000.[29] "Labor's Phalanx, 60,000 strong, Takes Chicago Willing Captive," the *Inter-Ocean* commented on that year's Labor Day Parade. Labor's new kid on the block, the teamsters, presented the "greatest showing ever made by an organized body of working men in this country, it taking their division one hour and ten minutes to pass a given point." The teamsters did not head the parade but granted that privilege to a small group of as-yet-unorganized messenger boys who, aided by the teamsters, were seeking to gain union recognition from the Illinois Telegraph and Telephone Company—the same firm that soon would begin digging tunnels beneath a now-unionized asphalt.[30]

Concurrently with the teamsters, a quite different group of workers made its appearance in the halls of union labor: the public-school teachers. The affiliation of the Chicago Teachers Federation (CTF) with the CFL signified great inroads into the organization of the city's female workforce. Embracing the principle of intertrade solidarity, teachers—most of them being female—identified with other women workers in the service and manufacturing sector and aided these other women in their organizational efforts. As white-collar (if low-paid) workers, teachers occupied a crucial position within Chicago's class spectrum and thereby aided the formation of broad-based, cross-class, and often women-led reform coalitions that extended beyond the workplace. Albeit for different reasons, both teachers and teamsters abhorred the politics of partisan alliances as had been practiced by the building trades, and they pushed Chicago's labor movement to new heights in urban politics. Unlike the building trades unions, which had allied with the Democratic mayors since the 1880s, female teachers, deprived of suffrage, engaged in politics from outside the electoral process and sought to reform entrenched partisan political practices. Initially concerned primarily with their salaries and pensions, teachers gradually amplified their agenda and became part of progressive-era efforts to reform municipal government.

Although granted white-collar status, female elementary-school teachers enjoyed salaries and working conditions far below the standards of many skilled blue-collar workers. Elementary-school teachers' maximum yearly salary of $825 from the 1880s until 1901 was considerably lower than the yearly incomes of workers such as bricklayers, who earned over $1,000 per year, or carpenters, who received about $900. Even semi-skilled workers such as the teamsters enjoyed slightly higher wages in 1901 ($843). In fact, elementary-school teachers made about as much per year as did unskilled hod carriers ($805). Yet, when compared to other women workers, the teachers commanded relatively high salaries. For example, a teacher on the maximum salary schedule earned about twice as much per year as a glove maker or a garment worker, and about 1.5 times as much as a department saleswoman. Positioning women schoolteachers in terms of social class and status is thus a difficult undertaking. Although teachers did indeed form the "aristocracy of women laborers," they fared far worse than most male craft workers.[31] It was precisely this ambivalent position occupied by the teachers that would render them likely candidates to forge unusual alliances within Chicago's new reform universe.

In 1897 the teachers adopted a strategy that had never before been employed by their peers: through the initiative of Margaret Haley and Catherine Goggin, they formed a trade-union-like organization known as the Chicago Teachers Federation, which five years later affiliated with the CFL. Recognizing the distinctive grievances of teachers working in elementary schools, the CTF excluded higher-grade teachers from membership. Indeed, the mainly female elementary school workforce received far lower wages than their almost exclusively male high school colleagues. By 1902 the CTF counted over four thousand members, representing 80 percent of the elementary school workforce and well over 70 percent of all of Chicago's schoolteachers.[32] In 1902, the CTF became the main founding institution of the National Federation of Teachers, an organization that still exists to this day.

Given the nature of their work (public school instruction) and of their employer (the state), teachers' work-related concerns quickly spilled into the public realm and right to the center of progressive-era reform debates, especially concerning the question of education. Marjorie Murphy's study of the Chicago teachers describes how the CTF resisted the efforts at centralization and professionalization of school instruction. Under the leadership of University of Chicago president William R. Harper and other educational reformers, the city's board of education sought to assume control over curriculum, hiring standards, and teacher supervision, the kind of professional standards typically applied during the Progressive Era. Rather than characterize the teachers as being opposed to progressivism as a whole, as Murphy does, I would consider the teachers' posture as an alternative variant of reform. Teachers did not so much resist professionalism, efficiency, and centralization as offer their own versions of these concepts and, in so doing, placed the question of democracy at the heart of debates over progressive reform.[33]

In opposing attempts to place control over education into the hands of a few (university-trained) experts, the leaders of the CTF proposed that they themselves should be considered the experts in their field. For example, teacher leader Margaret Haley considered school authorities' attempts to control the selection of textbooks "distasteful to a great majority of the rank and file of the teachers, [who] . . . must be considered and trusted." Rather, she argued, "a text book commission [ought to be] made up of the best grade teachers from each of the eight grades of the ten best schools of Chicago—excluding school principals."[34] Here we have indeed a white-collar version of the argument for "workers' control": a restatement of the adage that "the managers' brain lies in the worker's cap." Yet Haley was not opposing the notion of expertise as such, nor was she hostile to the idea of centralization; after all, she proposed the establishment of a textbook commission. Likewise, the CTF would promote the idea of a central council of all teachers for advisory purposes on all educational matters, in order to enhance communication between the city's board of education and public school instructors.[35] It was not over the existence of central planning as such, but over who was to be involved that Haley clashed with the reform efforts of Harper's school board.

When Harper invoked the need for efficiency as an argument for educational reforms, the teachers replied with their own version of this concept. Organized educators resented what they considered the arbitrary power of their supervisors—as manifested, for example, in a nebulous system of performance evaluation, which rendered salary raises and promotions "subject to dubious evaluation schemes and dependent upon the whim of principals." For instance, school instructor Mary P. Squier, attributing her low markings to the personal dislike for her on the part of the principal, filed a formal complaint against the State of Illinois. Upholding standards of efficiency and objecting to arbitrariness, the CTF demanded that the evaluation of a teacher occur promptly, be undertaken by the immediate supervisor, and be stated in terms as specific as possible.[36]

The teachers saw the key to effect greater efficiency and coordination of education in direct democracy. The CTF consistently worked to defeat the so-called Harper, or "one-man-power," bills, which sought to enhance the superintendent's authority over matters of curricula, promotional examinations, and methods of dismissal, and which appeared on several occasions from 1893 to 1909. Again, the teachers were not opposed to placing authority over school matters into the hands of the board of education, but they demanded that the board be a directly elected rather than appointed body. This would assure greater popular input in decisions on education by allowing the general public, rather than partisan interests, to directly shape educational policy. In the realm of education at least, the teachers formed part of a voting public, for under Illinois law, women had the right to elect educational boards.[37]

In their argumentation, the teachers thus interwove a defense of their working conditions with a reform of the schools and the securing of the health of democracy more generally. For Haley, "the work of securing better conditions for teachers . . . can go along with, [indeed] . . . is an essential part of," broader efforts to render "the public school . . . a more potent, conscious and recognized factor in the civic life of the large communities."[38] The outcome of this struggle, in the eyes of the teachers, would determine whether the public school was to be a democratic or an autocratic institution. In a letter to settlement reformer Jane Addams, Haley summed up the CTF's ideological underpinnings: "For seven years, Miss Addams, I have led the teachers in a struggle to prevent the last institution of democracy, the public schools, from becoming a prey to the dominant spirit of greed, commercialism, autocracy, and all the attendant evils. . . . If you could know how deeply I feel that the perpetuation of our democratic republic depends on the success of this struggle."[39] In drawing widely the boundaries of their engagement, the teachers were to confront unusual opponents, one of them being Chicago's streetcar companies; these the teachers blamed for not paying their taxes and thus depriving the city's public coffers of much-needed funds, which could be used for an improvement of the schools and instructors' salaries.

The teachers' broad-based understanding of their mission was reflected also in their decision to affiliate, in November 1902, with the CFL.[40] Many of the teachers considered themselves part of the city's working population. Like manual workers, they were contributing to the welfare of the nation. Exposing the nineteenth-century notion of the labor theory of value, Haley considered "that the wealth producing power of America and her power of sustaining the higher ideals of civilization are due chiefly to the general intelligence of the American people. That the greatest factor in producing this element is the Public School, and that the teacher is the school."[41] Like other workers, the teachers were not receiving a just share of the public wealth they helped produce. Teacher leader Catherine Goggin described teachers as the intellectual counterparts of manual labor: "they are but workers in another field."[42] In fact, half of all primary-school teachers in 1900 were daughters of skilled workers and had grown up in working-class communities. At the same time, however, efforts to professionalize education, in part by increasing entry requirements for beginning instructors, led to a greater proportion of teachers with white-collar backgrounds: thus, from 1880 to 1900, the proportion of teachers from white-collar backgrounds increased from 24.6 percent to 50.8 percent.[43]

One of the main arguments to affiliate with organized labor concerned the immediate tactical considerations necessary to advance the CTF's reform agenda. Being excluded from suffrage, the teachers needed male voting power, which an organization of two hundred thousand men would provide.[44] When the teachers described their union with organized labor as "the most important . . . step politically for the people since the Emancipation

Proclamation or the Civil War," they had a broad reform agenda in mind.[45] Here the teachers' mission clearly went beyond a working-class identity. As Goggin explained: "Belonging, as we do, to the so-called intelligent class, we ought to be the pioneers and leaders in all movements for the betterment of the conditions under which all classes of labor exist."[46] Whereas Goggin saw no contradiction in promoting a vision of transcending class interests and affiliating with the CFL, another CTF leader, L. S. Rowe, objected to the idea "of teachers allying themselves with a class in the community rather than trusting the whole people to right the evils which affect the schools."[47] In fact many teachers fearful of an affiliation with organized labor could be persuaded only by the argument that the CFL had no authority to order a strike. Publicly as well, teachers assured the public that they had no intention of taking recourse to the strike weapon.[48]

Such concerns clearly reflected the teachers' ties to a number of Chicago middle-class reform organizations, especially those composed of women, such as the Federation of Women's Clubs and the settlement houses. In fact, it was after Jane Addams addressed CTF members on "sociology" that these voted in favor of affiliation with the labor federation. Haley frequently spoke to middle-class audiences, and teachers worked with these constituencies to procure educational bills desired by the teachers. The CTF also frequently donated money to orchestra funds. Gender-based interests clearly played an important role, as in the teachers' cooperation with middle-class organizations on behalf of improving the conditions of other female wage earners, especially in efforts to pass legislation on behalf of working women. Teachers knew that their working conditions were related to their sex. As with most female wage earners, teachers' demands for decent wages were met with arguments justifying women's low wages with their supposed temporary work status as future housewives. Although the average teaching career in Chicago was eight years, many teachers worked for up to thirty years; the CTF, along with the Chicago women's clubs, fought attempts by the board of education to prohibit married women from working in the schools. The CTF would also form an active part in the women's suffrage campaign. For their part, middle-class associations backed the CTF for a variety of reasons, some of which proved specific to the cause of women; thus the women's clubs supported Haley in her fight against the Harper bills not so much out of concern for their centralizing tendencies as for their "masculinist language."[49]

The teachers' unique positioning between the working and middle classes, along with their strong intellectual and political commitment, rendered them prime candidates for the pursuit of progressive reform in Chicago, whether in the realm of education, protective legislation, or urban transportation politics. Indeed we might think of them as a type of working-class settlement reformer. Like Jane Addams or Florence Kelley, many CTF members worked in the poor industrial districts of Chicago, and certainly the requirements placed upon them in the classroom went beyond the instruction of reading and writing. In terms of pay and cultural affinities, we can consider teachers "working class"; yet as women, "white-collar" workers, and intellectuals, the teachers clearly moved outside the universe of regular craft unionism.

Rather than considering their multiple ties as conflicting phenomena, we should consider that flexibility as a necessary condition for their political agenda—and in keeping with the spirit of the Progressive Era more generally. Historian Marjorie Murphy has revealed the socioeconomic backgrounds and nature of teachers' work as well as their attempt to fight "managerial" control measures stemming from the county's board of education and the superintendent of schools. While thus convincingly locating the teachers' movement within a working-class universe, she neglects or views with suspicion teachers' alliances with middle-class reform groups. Yet it was precisely because of their cross-class links and flexible alliances, especially among women reformers, that organized teachers could assert such a prominent role in the city's public affairs. Thus, at the same time as Haley advocated the affiliation with Chicago's trade union central, she considered her own association a central forum of urban reform: "The part which the Teachers' Federation will take in the civic question is a matter of as much interest and inquiry as is the attitude of the Federation of Labor, the Civic Federation or the Municipal Voters League."[50] As the teachers' statements reveal, the question of their precise class identity was beyond the point. In fact, through their affiliation with the CFL, they would help transform craft unionism itself and thus render these distinctions less important. If it is misleading to impose a rigid roster of class on our interpretation of the teachers' engagement, the same holds true for other categories of social analysis. Historian Maureen Flanagan, in a provocative reinterpretation of Chicago progressivism, considers gender to be a basic divide in explaining the city's early-twentieth-century reform politics and considers that female activists, including the teachers, were motivated essentially by concerns and visions specific to their identity as women and in opposition to a male-based agenda. Yet, in doing so, Flanagan downplays the teachers' and other working-women's class-specific concerns, making bare mention, for example, of the CTF's alliance with the CFL.[51]

Although gender issues help explain the ties between the teachers and other women-led associations, clearly the logic of their engagement proved more complex, including working-class-specific concerns as well as an interest in political reform based on a vision of direct democracy and progressivism. Whatever their motivations, the affiliation of the teachers with the CFL, as well as the rise of the teamster unions, their militant use of sympathy strikes, and the defeat of the building trades in the Great Lockout a year earlier, all served to reshape the contours of Chicago labor toward a more inclusive and reform-oriented movement. It was through the city's trade union central, the CFL, that these changes found expression.

THE CFL AND THE NEW UNIONISM

With the rise of the militant teamsters and the teachers, the CFL assumed a new role in organizing Chicago wage earners, promoting solidarity among its affiliates, and coordinating action of the numerous and diverse trade union locals. Through the sympathy strike action of the teamsters and other trade unions and the effective leadership of CFL organizer and later president John J. Fitzpatrick, the CFL between 1901 and 1904 more than tripled its membership, from about 100,000 to 350,000 wage earners. Between 1896 and 1903, it also increased the numbers of affiliates from 34 to 427. Representing almost every second wage earner of Chicago, the CFL moved to assume a stronger political role in Chicago's affairs.[52] In a city swarming with voluntary associations, the CFL stood out as one of the largest, perhaps the very largest, not considering religious organizations.

Since its founding in 1896, the CFL played an important role as the central forum of Chicago trade unions, especially with regard to political matters. Almost all trade union locals of the city sent their delegates to the CFL's biweekly meetings on Sunday afternoons, when 300–500 delegates attended. The CFL endorsed sympathy strike actions and boycotts, established strike funds, financed a legal defense company, and through its organizer aided in the formation of new unions. Through a monthly journal, the *Union Labor Advocate,* and occasional strike bulletins, the CFL also served as the trade unions' public relations organ, and its meetings received consistent coverage in Chicago's main daily newspapers.[53] Given the voluntarist nature of the AFL, which left most decisions in the hands of the affiliated International Unions, the CFL's jurisdictional authority over its affiliates proved quite limited. Each of its local affiliates responded directly to their national headquarters, not to the CFL. As a result, the federation enjoyed little to no direct control over unions' decisions regarding membership dues, work rules, or strikes. Still, it served as a forum in which organizational matters could be debated and where moral pressure could be exerted upon its affiliates to act in ways transcending narrow trade-based interests. Above all, the CFL functioned as labor's public organ, since it was the logical place where Chicago trade unions could formulate their political responses and coordinate actions, especially with regard to local politics.

As the teamsters and the teachers rose to the fore, the central organization of the city's trade unions was still in the hands of the building trades. With the decline of the Knights of Labor and the weakening of unions associated with the Pullman strike and the depression of the 1890s, the building trades, somewhat less hit by the crisis, had come to dominate the CFL's forerunner, the Trade and Labor Assembly. Resenting the construction unions and their leader William Pommeroy's hegemony over the assembly, in 1894 Socialist and Populist-leaning trade unionists broke away to found the Chicago Trade and Labor Congress, which two years later was renamed the Chicago Federation of Labor. Yet within a short time the BTC, now under the leadership of the notorious Martin B. ("Skinny") Madden, regained its dominance over the city central and soon occupied most of its executive positions.[54]

Under the rule of the building trades unions, the CFL had pursued a narrow economic and political strategy. Recalling their defeat in the 1900 Great Lockout, most unions in the construction industry resisted strategies directed at fostering intertrade solidarity and concentrated instead on organizing their own ranks. Such an organizational approach went along with a political tactic designed to further the building trades unions' interests and little else. Even after Democratic Party Mayor Harrison's hostile stance during the 1900 lockout, Madden and cohorts continued to align the CFL closely with the Democratic Party. During the spring 1902 election campaign, Madden endorsed all Democratic candidates for county offices, with several union members among them: James Bowman, a pressman, Timothy Cruise, a carpenter, and James E. Daley, a steam fitter. The 1902 November elections proved a success for the CFL and the Democratic Party; all three CFL-endorsed candidates for Cook County were elected. According to the *Tribune,* "the labor unions return to the Democratic Party and vote its ticket with accustomed zeal and thoroughness."[55]

Yet by 1902, the BTC's grip on the CFL came under attack by the new unions of teachers and teamsters. Together, these uncommon allies helped dislodge the CFL's old guard and pushed the organization to the forefront of a municipal reform campaign. Recently formed unions, both the teachers and the teamsters lacked inside political clout with the Democratic Party. As women, the teachers found themselves excluded from politics-as-usual. For them, an issue-based nonpartisan approach proved the logical course of action. Only by reforming partisan politics and by streamlining funding and taxation, they argued, could public funds be used for important ends, including good public education with a well-paid staff. The teachers also held a concrete grievance against the building trades. The graft and favoritism surrounding construction unions' links to city hall Democrats, they felt, were responsible for the high costs of schoolhouse construction, which in turn drained their salary fund.[56]

Teamsters shared in the teachers' reform outlook on labor politics. They, too, lacked a tradition of political clout with city hall and frequently clashed with the mayor's police force. So frequent were injuries or deaths of teamsters during strikes that teamsters used to wear double-sided buttons, one side to indicate union membership, the other side, framed in black, to mourn the death of fellow workers.[57] These new service sector unions followed a reform logic that in many ways would prove compatible with the issue-focused and nonpartisan agenda of middle-class progressives.

Shortly after joining the CFL, the teachers set out to shatter the building trades' grip on the labor federation. During the executive committee elections of November 1902, they had to convince delegates to vote for the "reform faction"—made up of a group of teachers, teamsters, and a few representatives of other trades. They also had to overcome the construction unionists' practice of intimidating voters and stuffing ballot boxes. A tumultuous riot erupted in Bricklayers Hall, the site of CFL meetings, when Haley of the CTF and other reformers insisted on attending the vote counting. Haley, recalling the teachers "housekeeping" of the halls of labor, described the scene:

> Finally, the protestations grew so violent that our friends among the delegates, who had previously asked us [the teachers] to stay, came over to warn us to go. I walked up to the table upon which stood the ballot box.
> "There's going to be trouble," men shouted at me.
> "If there's going to be trouble, I shall be right here." I could see dozens of guns and I could see, too, the looks on the faces of some of those men. I thought that the next moment would bring bloodshed and so I attempted to speak. Someone in the crowd shouted, "Hats off!" Men took off their hats. Someone gave me a chair to stand upon, for otherwise I could not have been seen or heard.

Haley then begged "those men to think of the organizations which they represented and the thousands of men, women, and children for whom they were acting" and successfully pleaded for calm and a smooth unfolding of the elections. The building trades leader was not pleased with the election's results; with none of his gang elected, Skinny Madden found himself ousted from control of the CFL. Haley exultantly recalled the event: "the look in Madden's face when he caught [a teacher's] eye was worth all the trouble. . . . He could not conceal his disappointed rage." The election of the reform faction, led by horseshoer John J. Fitzpatrick, initiated a new era in Chicago's labor movement.[58]

Just a few years prior to the foundation of the Industrial Workers of the World (IWW) in Chicago in 1905, the CFL sought to forge a broadly based, inclusive movement within a trade-based form of organization. The house of labor would be open to "all toilers of whatever craft, class, or caste," including workers of both sexes, of various skill levels, and, to a limited extent, of all races.[59] Acts of solidarity with trades that lacked the economic clout to unionize on behalf of skilled workers were required to assure such inclusivity; "where there is no agitation among the organized," Fitzpatrick pointed out, "the unorganized working in close conjunction to them are dormant." This new militancy acquired a missionary zeal: to the *Advocate*, trade union solidarity was indicative of "working people . . . [being] the most truly Christian class in society." Yet labor's religious leanings had their limits: when Presbyterian ministers applied for membership in the CFL, that body's delegates soundly refused them.[60] Following the teamsters' lead, sympathy strikes formed the core of the CFL's strategy. Countering the mounting efforts of employers to prohibit such actions, Fitzpatrick insisted: "It will be either union men and women or non-union men and women and we will not be bound by a 'no sympathetic strike' clause." By July 1903, all CFL member unions were obliged to refuse contracts with employers that included "no-sympathy strike" provisions: "By engaging in sympathy strikes," Fitzpatrick declared, "we prove that the cardinal principle of organized labor (that the injury of one is the concern of all) is not a myth but a reality."[61]

Aided by the CFL's coordinating action, many affiliates besides the teamsters turned this principle into action. Skilled butchers assisted the organization of thousands of unskilled meat-packers, many of whom had just recently arrived from eastern Europe or southern Italy. Like the teamsters and the building trades unions, the meat-packing unions established a central council, the Packinghouse Trades Council, which promptly threatened employers with a general walkout should they dare to cut the wages of any of the affiliates, whether skilled butchers or stockyard laborers. In the fall of 1904, this militancy provoked a major, if ultimately failed, packinghouse strike that sought to achieve an across-the-board unionization of workers in one of Chicago's leading industries.[62] Similar actions of solidarity, such as the boycott, occurred in the metal industry. The description of one Chicago machine manufacturer illustrates how unions' activism could affect every single aspect of a firm's dealings:

> The unions had so boycotted our place that we could not buy a pound of castings in any shop in the United States; they had watched the railroads so that we could not ship tools out of the city. They had so picketed us that when we brought a load of men . . . we built a restaurant and fed them, and we could not buy bread or food; they would not sell any member of our company . . . a newspaper. [Moreover, the unions] went around and said, "If you sell anything to this house, . . . we will withdraw our patronage and you will have to go out of business."[63]

The union label campaign constituted a less coercive consumer-oriented strategy. A specially designed committee of the CFL promoted the purchase of union-made products. Union waiters and waitresses asked workers to eat only in restaurants where they were served by personnel wearing green buttons. When mail clerks complained of being overworked, the federation promptly asked its members to refrain from mailing letters early in the day and on Sundays. CFL organizer Fitzpatrick set an example. About to be married (to a schoolteacher), he went out of his way to obtain a union-made wedding ring.[64]

Although the CFL's militancy took place in the context of a nationwide boom in trade unionism, its intertrade policy contrasted with the national federation's stand. By the turn of the century, AFL leaders opted for a conciliatory stand toward a group of corporate employers mildly tolerant of trade unionism. The NCF grew out of employer, trade union, and progressive reformers' attempts to avoid the violent industrial disputes of the previous decades. In order to be recognized as "legitimate" organizations, however, trade unions had to refrain precisely from those radical organizing strategies, such as the sympathy strike and the boycott, which were continually practiced in Chicago. At least in this city, as well as in many others, the NCF's project received little adherence by local trade unions.[65]

Employers in Chicago and elsewhere adopted aggressive means to stem the tide of unionization. Especially small-scale businesses operating in competitive sectors of the economy saw little use in the NCF's conciliatory stand and sought to mobilize all economic, political, and legal means to fight trade unionism. They organized on a nationwide basis, as in the American Anti-Boycott Association, which orchestrated legal campaigns against labor's solidaristic trade union practices. Learning their lessons from organized labor's strategies, employers coordinated their actions on a citywide basis. So-called employers' associations or citizen's leagues sprang up in cities all over the country and affiliated with the national, Indianapolis-based Citizens' Industrial Association. The latter's most important affiliate was the Employers' Association of Chicago, formed in 1903 by a remarkably united front of small and large Chicago businesses. Its new president, F. W. Job, having just left a position as lawyer on a state arbitration board, abandoned a conciliatory approach: sympathy strikes, he declared, "shake the belief of business men in the stability of the trade union movement."[66] His new association set out to launch a militant anti-union campaign in Chicago, which would culminate in the teamsters strike of 1905.

Given such pressures, it was only natural that some trade unions resisted an engagement in sympathy actions. The 1900 lockout weakened the building trades unions' taste for such militancy. Other unions, especially those composed of skilled craftsmen with a relatively secure position in the labor market, also opposed Fitzpatrick's policies. The cigar makers

union, for example, insisted that the decision about whether to sign contracts with "no–sympathetic strike clauses" be left with the individual
unions. Their petition was rejected by a vote of ninety-eight to sixty-three.
Other union delegates claimed to uphold the principle of intertrade solidarity but complained of the rashness with which recently organized
unions called strikes: "Men organize in one week, come here the next, and
we indorse a strike," carpenter Harry McCormack lamented, and he demanded, again without success, that the federation support only strikes of
unions that had been CFL affiliates for at least a year.[67] Speaking for many
middle-class reformers with a favorable disposition toward union labor,
Jane Addams confirmed the carpenter leader's claim: "the older unions,
which have reached the second stage . . . of business dealing are constantly
harassed by the action of the younger unions which are still in the enthusiastic stage." Occasionally, the rank and file walked out against their leaders' orders, as proved the case with strikes of stable workers in August
1902, rubber workers in January, waiters in June, and streetcar workers in
November 1903. Again and again, union leaders complained of undue
rank-and-file militancy. Hugh McGee, president of the truck drivers, for instance, exclaimed that he could no longer "hold his men in check."[68]

Ironically, it was the inability of the CFL to impose its sympathy-strike
policy on its affiliates that prevented more permanent factional rifts over
the issue. The leader of the cigar makers' union, George L. Thompson, explained: "the C. F. of L. has neither the right nor the power to in any way
interfere in the settlement of affiliates' decision over sympathy strikes."
Thompson was right; CFL affiliates were, at least in theory, bound to their
national unions' policies. Fitzpatrick and other reform leaders lamented
this fact, demanding that city labor centrals be authorized to call and enforce sympathy strikes within a given industry. "We have been a voluntary
organization [for] too long, . . . it is a waste of time to get together every
two weeks and 'resolve'—which is about all we can do with our present organization."[69] Yet given the AFL's voluntarist structure, not only were such
demands unrealistic; they might have been self-defeating to the CFL's goal of
forging a broad-based and inclusive labor movement. Had Fitzpatrick's federation gained the power to enforce sympathy strike action, many conservative
locals would certainly have seceded from the organization. Moreover, it was
the CFL's lack of jurisdictional power, especially with regard to calling strikes,
that convinced hesitant locals such as the teachers to join. Certainly Fitzpatrick must have had these considerations in mind when he rejected the Socialists' demand that the CFL be authorized to call general strikes. The CFL's
voluntarist advocacy of an "industrial consciousness" within a trade-based
form of organization was thus the most prudent and effective means of effect-
ing intertrade solidarity within a highly diverse workforce, varying greatly in
terms of skill level, organizational strength, and strategic outlook.[70]

John J. Fitzpatrick, horseshoer by trade and chief organizer and president of the Chicago Federation of Labor from 1905 to 1946, was a key figure in furthering metropolitan trade unionism and progressive labor politics in Chicago. This portrait dates from 1919, the year he ran for mayor of Chicago.

New Majority, March 22, 1919

Given the CFL's weak jurisdictional powers, informal factors such as an effective and charismatic leadership became crucial to its success. John J. Fitzpatrick, the federation's most prominent leader and its president from 1905 until his death in 1946, provided just that. Born in Ireland in 1871, "Fitz" arrived an orphan in Chicago in 1882. There he began work on Chicago's killing floors at one of the major meat-packing plants and soon became a learned horseshoer, a trade whose workers lacked the kind of economic leverage enjoyed by labor aristocrats. These experiences affirmed his conviction of the need for intertrade solidarity; "every wage worker, no matter what his occupation," he insisted, had to be brought into the ranks of organized labor.[71] Following several years of organizing without compensation, and overcoming a controversial nominating process that led to frictions with AFL headquarters, the Irishman became the CFL's first paid organizer in May 1902.[72] Every other week, Fitzpatrick reported on the formation of new locals, such as cooks, glove makers, waitresses, even hospital workers. During the last quarter of 1902 alone, he managed to organize more than one hundred unions, with a combined membership of seventy-five thousand. A year later, Fitzpatrick proudly reported the establishment of fifty-one new locals, incorporating an additional eighty thousand new workers.[73]

Group of streetcar conductors in uniform and equipped with coin dispensers. Streetcar workers were unionized by 1902 and actively campaigned on behalf of municipal ownership. Their strikes provoked major halts in Chicago traffic and brought to the fore the question of the political regulation of mass transit. Chicago Historical Society IChi-24058

Turn-of-the-century trade unionism gained greatest strength among people who moved the city's goods and serviced the city's infrastructure: teamsters, freight handlers, streetcar drivers and conductors, elevator operators, as well as retail clerks and building cleaners. In the spring of 1902, employees of Chicago's streetcar companies—the South Side's City Railway Company and the North Side and West Side's Union Traction Company—organized for the first time since their defeat in the 1885 streetcar strike. These locals participated in the founding of the national Amalgamated Association of Street and Railway Employees (AASRE), which by 1910 counted twelve thousand members in Chicago.[74] As the trolley workers were to recognize, the question of unionizing street-based work was closely related to the politics of regulating street-based services, not the least because these unions were among the most vociferous in demanding the public ownership of public transportation.

The most impressive and important advances in unionization occurred among women workers. Employees in a great variety of consumer-goods-manufacturing trades, including paper-box makers, cracker packers, candy dippers, feather-duster makers, boot and shoe workers, glove makers, and ladies' garment workers formed unions for the first time. Female service workers such as retail clerks, telephone operators, waitresses, janitresses, laundry workers, and of course schoolteachers followed suit. Other women's trade unions in Chicago included canning-room employees, can makers, ticket agents, elevated-railroad employees, bindery girls, twine workers, suspender workers, knitters, dyers, cleaners, woven-wire-mattress workers, picture-frame makers, horse-nail makers, curled hair finishers, and core makers. Unionization resulted in reductions in working hours and substantial increases in wages; union janitresses, for example, managed to decrease night work by 2.5 hours and to raise their weekly earnings from $3.40 to $10.00.[75] In 1903, the city counted twenty-five unions composed entirely of women, with a membership of over thirty thousand, comprising half of the national membership in women's unions. Adding to this figure another thirty thousand women who belonged to mixed craft locals, women comprised almost 20 percent of the city's unionized workforce. This boom in women's unionism was rendered visible in the 1902 Labor Day parade, where women workers marched for the first time.[76]

Women also breached the leadership ranks of trade unions, especially among all-female locals. Margaret Chilton headed a union of five hundred waitresses, who first organized in November 1902; Elizabeth Maloney led another waitress local. Agnes Nestor was head of the glove makers' union and leader of the Chicago branch of the Women's Trade Union League, a nationwide organization founded by middle- and working-class reformers to promote the unionization of women workers and to educate the public on labor concerns. Two women served on the CFL's executive board: CTF leader Margaret Haley led the legislative committee and shoe worker Sophia Becker belonged to the finance and label committee.[77]

These advances proved far more notable, however, in trades and unions of female workers than in those of their male counterparts. Within the CFL, women's activism continued to prevail only in functions that related to what were considered female-specific areas, such as the sphere of consumption. The union label committee was run by women. Always dedicating one page to its activities, the *Advocate* assured its readers that "ladies

A group of waitresses and waiters posing with the "tools" of their trade during a strike in 1903. The unionization of service workers such as these represents the way organized labor in Chicago expanded its social base during the early twentieth century.

Chicago Historical Society DN-637

were more successful as label agitators." Many women were active in their role as "wives, daughters . . . sweethearts, and . . . sympathizers" in the CFL's Auxiliary, which also entertained a junior organization for nine- to eighteen-year-olds.[78] When women transgressed into traditionally male leadership roles, they might well encounter opposition. For instance, the president of the carpenters' union lashed out at Haley and the "feminine domination in the central labor body." Nonetheless, the advances in women workers' unionization and the assumption of leadership roles by female working-class organizers in Chicago was unprecedented and contrasted sharply with the national AFL. In Chicago and other cities, craft-based unionism proved more flexible and open to women workers than historians have assumed.[79]

Plying trades in which they had little leverage over their employers, women workers relied on sympathy strikes. The teamsters proved crucial in this regard. Thus, an organizing drive by forty-one waitresses in March 1902 turned out successful in great part because milk wagon drivers ceased deliveries to the affected restaurants. Out of that germ sprouted one of the most successful women locals, Local 484 of the Hotel Employees and Restaurant Employees International Union, which a month later counted over fifteen hundred members.[80] Laundry workers, garment workers, and telephone operators benefited from similar acts of teamster solidarity.

Women themselves furthered a variety of solidaristic practices and generated a sphere of female labor activism that infiltrated the middle class as well. Forming an aristocracy of women workers of sorts, the teachers assumed a clear leadership role in this regard. Although teachers could not paralyze Chicago's downtown traffic, they could organize fund-raisers for women on strike; they could walk picket lines and demand the right to use school buildings as meeting places for striking workers.[81] The teachers federation proved particularly supportive of female textile workers in the form of financial and moral assistance, and through union label campaigns. Thus, eager for union customers, businesses such as the Henrietta Skirt Company sent unsolicited letters to the CTF assuring the federation that all their goods were union made.[82] The boom in female trade unionism in turn-of-the-century Chicago would have been unthinkable without the support received from middle-class women. Settlement reformers such as Graham Taylor, William English Walling, and Jane Addams helped found the Chicago Women's Trade Union League (WTUL), which was led by glove maker Agnes Nestor, and which effectively assisted union organizing among women and lobbied for protective legislation for working women. The WTUL congregated weekly at Hull House and was financed largely by private donations from middle- and upper-class patrons. Still, the league's leadership was remarkably egalitarian, with both trade unionists and the so-called allies of the middle class being represented. Other organizations run almost exclusively by middle-class women such as the Federation of Women's Clubs also provided important moral and financial assistance to the unionization efforts of working women.[83] Chicago and midwestern cities in general seem to have been unique in their experiencing a new spurt of trade union engagement combined with a substantial portion of pro-labor and reform-oriented middle-class activists. In contrast, West Coast cities lacked active middle-class support for labor, while East Coast cities failed to exhibit the kind of worker effervescence characteristic of Chicago.[84]

The CFL's inclusive organizing policy met its greatest challenge and limitation when it came to the unionization of African American wage earners. Already by the early 1900s, as the black population of Chicago barely approached 2 percent (30,150 residents in 1900), the Chicago labor market was a thoroughly segregated one. Excluded from virtually all industrial employment, blacks found jobs primarily in the city's service sector. About 50 percent, mainly women, worked as servants in private homes. Other jobs held by black workers included waiting, elevator operating, building maintenance, and vigilance. Although employers unwilling to hire blacks bore part of the blame, most white trade unionists actively excluded blacks from working in their trade. In trades where African Americans formed a significant part of the workforce, such as waiting, whites insisted on the formation of separate black locals. Tension between white and black workers, still relatively rare during the early 1900s, erupted during strikes, when black workers offered their services as strikebreakers. In the building trades lockout of 1900, the street railway strike of 1903, and the teamster strike of 1905 (just to mention the strikes discussed in this book), blacks formed part of the strike-breaking forces. African Americans' logic for doing so was crystal clear. Black strikebreakers during the building trades lockout of 1900 declared: "You don't let us into your unions and then you don't expect us to work; what shall we do—shall we starve?"[85]

Knowing of subsequent racial conflicts in Chicago such as the 1919 race riot might lead to overstating the racial divisions among Chicago wage earners during this earlier period, when in fact limited attempts to include black workers in organized labor did take place. While the presence of African American strikebreakers in industrial conflicts, beginning with the 1905 teamster strike, would be followed by open racial conflict, earlier disputes still offered some room for negotiation. White construction-trade unionists allowed blacks into their unions, albeit into separated locals. For example, black hod carriers, working in one of the lowest-skill trades in construction, united in Hod Carriers Local No. 4; one of its delegates, I. T. Smith, even went on to praise his Irish colleagues for having raised the laborers' wages in the city.[86] Signs of interracial solidarity can also be seen among elevator operators, whose spokesman deplored employers for firing "our colored brothers" and accused them of purposefully wishing to create "antagonism between the colored men and the white men." In certain service trades, black and white locals seem to have coexisted successfully at certain times; for example, white and black waitresses temporarily organized in the same local. Above all, it was the CFL leadership that promoted racial tolerance. Thanks to John J. Fitzpatrick's insistence, the CFL constitution declared that "the trade union movement knows no race or color."[87] In practice, this meant that Fitzpatrick opposed the formation of separate black locals—a policy encouraged by the national AFL—as discriminatory.

The CFL's efforts to integrate black and white workers notwithstanding, most local trade unions either excluded blacks altogether or insisted on the formation of separate locals. Black workers themselves did not necessarily oppose the idea of forming their own locals, but they did protest the general lack of support from white unions, especially during industrial disputes. During a strike against a major Chicago restaurant in 1903, for example, African American waiters, who formed the largest black local in the city (about two thousand members), criticized white waiters for signing a separate contract with the employer. For years to come, black waiters would remember this as an act of betrayal by white waiters.[88]

In sum, without denying the pervading discrimination in attitudes and practices of the white Chicago trade unionists, it is important to recognize that early efforts were made by the CFL leadership to foster interracial cooperation, that within the service sector some cooperation occurred, and that, finally, open racial conflict erupted only when blacks, usually encouraged by employers, sought to challenge the segregated labor market. Until the Great Migration from the rural South to the industrialized North, which began in 1916, such efforts occurred during strikes only and remained temporary. Moreover, the relatively small proportion of African Americans in turn-of-the-century Chicago's workforce assured that racial tension would prove far less prevalent than during the World War I years. Or—to put it in terms recently stated by historian James Barrett—how racial divisions and a certain degree of interracial cooperation affected the fate of the U.S. working class must be understood in terms of each specific historical moment.[89]

By 1903, then, trade unionism in Chicago had acquired the character of a broad social movement that included an unprecedented number and variety of wage earners. Although many workers—especially in mass production industries such as steel—remained unorganized, the high level of unionization in the city was unmatched anywhere in the country, with the exception of San Francisco, the "labor town" of the West. With such a strong organization behind them, trade union leaders claimed a voice in Chicago's public affairs. A teamster in 1903 expressed labor's new sense of power: "Who is the public? In Chicago most of the people in the last three years have joined labor unions, and the rest—the hundred thousand clerks—they are coming, too. And the middle-classes? Didn't you notice that thirty-five hundred teachers have joined the American Federation of Labor? If most of the people is the public, then the public is the labor union."[90] Like many middle-class progressives, trade unionists now claimed to speak for the interest of the public while struggling to maintain their class-based interests as well.

Construction workers of the 1890s exhibited strategies that foreshadowed the rise of a new unionism. The building trades and other principally craft-based unions, already in that decade, pursued a great variety of organizational forms designed, in part, to promote solidarity across craft and skill lines.[91] Certainly, the raison d'être of the Building Trades Council consisted in promoting concerted industrywide strategies and actions between highly skilled trades (such as the bricklayers) and unskilled laborers (such as hod carriers). Nonetheless, it was the organizational boom of the early 1900s and the rise to power of new unions, such as those of the teamsters and teachers, that constituted a departure from past practices. The increase from under one hundred thousand organized workers to three hundred thousand signified an immense leap in the economic and political power of organized labor in Chicago. Moreover, the trade unionism of the 1900s constituted a citywide not merely an industrywide movement. Although the building trades displayed an industrial consciousness of sorts, they naturally restricted intercraft and interskill solidarity to their own industry. In contrast, the labor movement under guidance of the CFL promoted intercraft and interskill solidarity across a host of different industries and thus helped generate a distinctly urban trade union network whose several trade unions exerted control over the flow of goods and people in the city.

Chicago's new trade unionism gained an unprecedented public visibility. Its organization addressed not only workplace questions (the nature of the industry, the strength of employers and workers, etc.) but also questions that surged in the context of a new reform-oriented public discussion. To put it another way, workplace questions acquired public significance and were debated in a broad public context with workers taking part in the debate and offering their own version of reform. As teamsters, teachers, and streetcar conductors organized, the services they provided became the target of general urban reform efforts. And the impressive increase in the unionization of women workers would have been unthinkable without the public sympathy displayed by a host of middle-class reformers for the plight of female wage earners.

Trade unionism in Chicago was class specific and at the same time often transcended class identity. Many of the new unions that formed in sectors of the urban economy lacked a clear class status. The teamsters, for example, stemmed from an industry of the petty bourgeoisie, organized in a host of small family-run teaming businesses. Here the line between a horse-cart owner and driver proved thin, and until the turn of the century, horse-wagon drivers and owners shared the same trade organizations. Likewise, elementary-school teachers spanned the line between blue- and white-collar work: their supposed status suggested membership in the latter but the reality of their working conditions (pay, hours, etc.) proved similar to the lot of a bricklayer. When teamsters and teachers decided to unionize and affiliate with the city's labor central, they asserted an identity as workers. Chicago's three hundred thousand trade unionists abandoned the identity of producers and the language of the nineteenth-century labor movement, seeing themselves increasingly in class-specific terms. Nonetheless, the CFL and several of its key trade unions managed to integrate themselves into the progressive, liberal, public sphere, where they managed for some time to speak as workers and as citizens without any apparent contradiction.

By 1903, the new metropolitan unionism would confront head-on the central political question in turn-of-the-century Chicago: the streetcars. In fact, by 1903, the CFL would launch a mass-based movement for the municipal ownership of the trolleys, nominate a mayor on that platform, and get him elected by 1905. The trade unions were to become prominently involved in transportation politics, but first let us explore how streetcars shaped the physical growth of the city and became the target of an intensive political debate.

PRIVATE STREETCARS, PUBLIC UTOPIAS, AND THE CONSTRUCTION OF THE MODERN CITY

Transit is today the very gateway to business, to employment, to recreation. . . .

Nothing has been so phenomenal during the last twenty years as the development

of street-car service. . . . It is not visionary to say that here is the key to the municipal

development of the next two generations.

—Chicago Federation of Labor, 1897

The transportation problem is perhaps the most serious that has confronted the city

in the whole period of its existence.

—*Scientific American*, 1907

Perhaps it appears surprising that a journal dedicated to the natural sciences would share with a labor union such concern for the issue of transportation, but this speaks to the centrality of the matter in urban politics during the early twentieth century.[1] The emergence of a militant city-wide trade unionism in Chicago and the founding of the CFL occurred in the context of a vast expansion of the city's industries, commerce, and population—an expansion that would have been impossible without the streetcar. By facilitating travel over considerable distances, the streetcar

boosted the city's physical growth and shaped its qualitative development, which took the form of a specialization of activities within the metropolitan area. Chicago's urban spaces were becoming increasingly specific to the distinct functions of industry, commerce, and residence.
Moreover, the uses of city spaces, especially with regard to housing, became increasingly defined by social class and race, thus leaving the city
fragmented in both functional and social ways. While such segmentation,
typical of any modern city, reflected a great variety of causes (land speculation, cultural preferences, immigration, etc.), it was the trolley that constituted its primary technological tool and main visible symbol. Streetcars,
unlike telephone wires or underground pipes, operated on the city's public thoroughfares and provided a constant visible reminder of modernity's
arrival in Chicago.

Streetcars constituted the means to reunite the urban tissue while at the
same time contributing to its fragmentation. Faced with a city vastly expanded in size and specialized in its activities, a Chicago resident could
best experience the city as a whole by criss-crossing it on board a streetcar,
or perhaps by viewing it from the top of one of the new skyscrapers. The
flâneur of the early-twentieth-century city no longer traversed the city's
boulevards on foot, as in the Paris of Baudelaire, but now enjoyed the possibility of an "elevated voyeurism." Riding in an elevated railroad or in a
trolley, the urban observer might have been flabbergasted by the dazzling
diversity of people, activities, and material expressions, but at the same
time might have sensed a chance to overcome these social and spatial divisions, simply by boarding a train and gazing out of its windows.[2] The
streetcar constituted a central place in public discussions over urban development, where it served as symbol of both the evils and the possibilities of urban life.

Streetcars were more than mere physical means of intra-urban transport.
They were also vehicles for generating an entirely new discourse about the
city. Provoking a new awareness of the city's dismemberment and fragmentation, they also generated an unprecedented citywide consciousness. The interior of a streetcar in itself constituted a new public space, which temporarily
united a microcosm of the city. But the streetcar also became the focus of a
new public awareness over the need to act on behalf of the city as a whole, a
disposition that would include a vastly expanded segment of the urban population. The streetcar thus both defined the physical development of
Chicago and generated an incipient reform discourse over urban renewal.
Both Populist and good-government political forces placed the question of
mass transit at the center of municipal politics. In so doing, they expanded
the scope of public policy and acknowledged the political relevance of new
social forces, especially organized labor. The streetcar became a central vehi-
cle in the transformation of the modern public sphere.

STREETCARS AND URBAN GROWTH

Transportation had always been the lifeline of the great midwestern metropolis, given the fundamental interdependence between the city and its hinterland and its critical location at the nodal point of the nation's infrastructure. By the 1840s, the new city that grew around Fort Dearborn tied the country's eastern region to its southern and western ones: water routes, both natural and man-made, allowed freight ships to travel from New York up the Hudson River, through the Erie Canal, into the Great Lakes, and to Chicago, where they could enter a river (and soon a man-made canal) to connect to the Mississippi River and proceed on south to the Gulf of Mexico. During the 1840s and 1850s, waterways were replaced by rail lines so that, by the outbreak of the Civil War, Chicago formed the central hub of a nationwide railroad network transporting grains, cattle, and wood from the midwestern "heartland" to the East and returning people and manufactured goods back to the West.[3]

Chicago's centrality to the nation's commerce was felt within the city itself. During the 1890s the country's first department stores, specializing in nationwide retail, reached for the skies (quite literally) in Chicago's downtown. Many of the products sold by Marshall Fields, Montgomery Ward, and Pirie Scott were made in the city, which had also become a leading manufacturing center, specializing in the processing of agricultural and forest goods (for example, meat-packing and lumber) and in the production of agricultural tools and machines (the most famous being the McCormick reaper). New industries, including steel and chemicals, also found it profitable to locate in this great entrepôt of the Midwest. By the time of the 1893 Colombian World's Fair, Chicago was known as the Second City, second in manufacturing and commerce only to its eternal rival, New York.[4]

With regard to people, however, Chicago was second to none. No American city's population grew as rapidly during the second half of the nineteenth century. Shortly after its incorporation in 1837, the still swampy outpost housed a little over four thousand people. Twenty years later, they had been joined by over a hundred thousand additional inhabitants. By 1880 that number had increased fivefold, and by the turn of the century sixteenfold, so that in 1900, 1.7 million people resided in Chicago. Within the next decade this number swelled to 2.2 million. Most of this growth reflected immigration. While natural population increases hovered around 20–30 percent between 1860 and 1900, the increase due to foreign immigrants ranged from 48 percent in the 1860s, to 29 percent in the 1870s, 49 percent in the 1880s, and 23 percent in the 1890s, and returned to 49 percent in the first decade of the twentieth century. "Hog Butcher for the World / Tool Maker, Stacker of Wheat / Player with Railroads and the

Nation's Freight Handler / Stormy, husky, brawling / City of the Big Shoulders"—with this stanza Carl Sandburg captured the size and power, as well as the blue-collar workers that backed the rise, of this new industrial center of the world.[5]

It was a city in constant movement: "Dust of the feet / And dust of the wheels / Wagons and people going / All day feet and wheels," Sandburg noted. Yet it was the advent of the electrically powered streetcar—the trolley—that proved of key importance, given the great expansion of Chicago's metropolitan area that it effected by enabling larger numbers of Chicagoans to commute into outlying suburbs. Until the appearance of the trolley, only a small elite had been commuting via costly railway transport to and from the city. The growth of new suburbs and the annexation of outlying townships greatly increased the city's physical size: between 1870 and 1910 the Chicago area swelled from 35 square miles to 190 square miles; in six years alone, between 1887 and 1893, the metropolitan area tripled in size (see map 1).[6] Chicago's tremendous growth during the second half of the nineteenth century thus reflected dynamics internal to the city as well as an unprecedented interaction with its regional hinterland. It is in this sense that we should understand reformer Frederick Howe's observation: "through the electric streetcar, the city is being ruralized and the country is being urbanized."[7]

A vast streetcar network underwrote such expansion. By 1897 Chicago had 605 miles of streetcar track, of which 84 percent was already operated by electric power. In 1904 total track mileage had increased to 703 miles, with 87 percent being operated electrically. (On a national scale, during roughly the same time period, from 1890 to 1902, total track mileage increased from 5,783 to 22,577.) Streetcar ridership far outstripped population growth: the number of annual streetcar rides per capita increased from 200 in 1900, to 229 in 1905, to 300 by 1910.[8] The electric streetcar did not initiate collective travel, which had begun with omnibuses, a cart pulled by a horse or two. By the 1860s, horse railways serviced the downtown's recently widened State Street and initiated its role as the commercial artery of Chicago. Horsecars, however, had little effect on the size of the city. Running at a speed of a mere four or six miles an hour and competing with thousands of carriages for space on the often muddy, unpaved streets, they barely provided an alternative to walking. In the 1870s, machine power first replaced horses as the engines of urban travel. At first, the cars weré pulled by underground cables, powered by stationary steam engines located at the end of the lines. Operating in San Francisco until this day, cable cars in most cities including Chicago were soon replaced by electrically powered cars.[9]

Where in the city people lived and how they lived had a great deal to do with the appearance of the electric streetcar. Streetcar networks helped

I. GROWTH OF THE CITY OF CHICAGO, 1837–1899

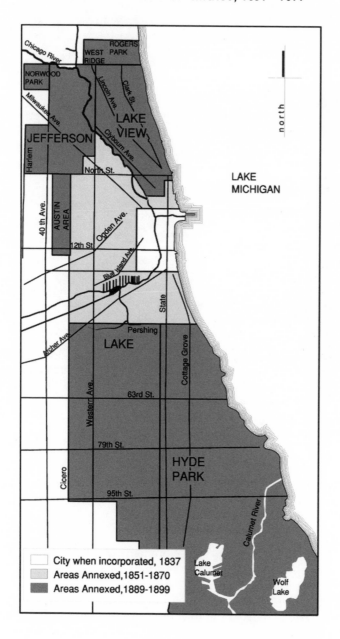

Chicago's major downtown State Street, ca. 1910, filled with electric trolleys, horse-drawn streetcars (riding on the central lane), horse carts, parked automobiles, and pedestrians. The street is framed by office buildings constructed in the Chicago Style.

Chicago Historical Society IChi-24401

define the nature of Chicago's development by generating an urban area whose functions and patterns of residence were spatially divided and arranged concentrically. In 1925 the Chicago sociologist Ernest W. Burgess described a model of urban growth, based on his observations of Chicago's development at the turn of the twentieth century (see map 2). Burgess's work, emblematic of the Chicago School of Sociology, acquired fame as a general theory of urban growth, known as urban ecology. The political implications of this model and how it must be considered itself

2. CONCENTRIC GROWTH MODEL OF CITIES (BASED UPON CHICAGO)
by Ernest W. Burgess

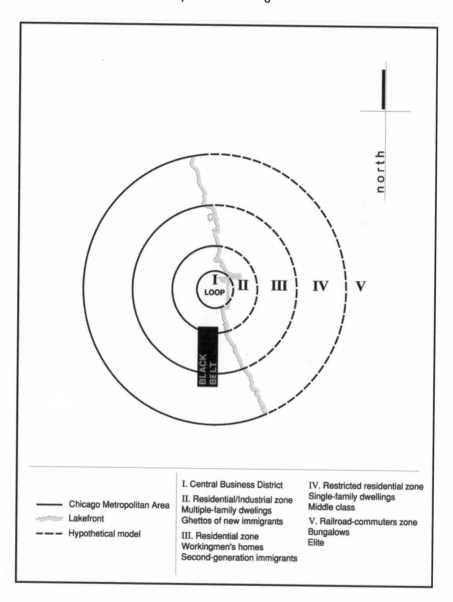

——— Chicago Metropolitan Area	I. Central Business District	IV. Restricted residential zone
～～ Lakefront	II. Residential/Industrial zone Multiple-family dwelings Ghettos of new immigrants	Single-family dwellings Middle class
– – – Hypothetical model	III. Residential zone Workingmen's homes Second-generation immigrants	V. Railroad-commuters zone Bungalows Elite

a product of Chicago's political debate over urban transportation will be discussed below. Here it is used more as a characterization of the city's sociospatial development.[10]

Improved urban transit in the late nineteenth century, Burgess demonstrated, facilitated what he considered a natural evolution of the city's geography into functionally and socially distinct spaces. By allowing people to move with relative ease from the old walking city to the outlying areas, urban transportation contributed to the rise of a city core that specialized in commercial and financial activities, while expelling residential and industrial uses. This transformation was reflected in the steep rise in land costs in what became known as the Central Business District (CBD), which rendered residential and industrial uses there increasingly prohibitive. By concentrating the city's commercial and financial activities, the city center would prove the logical focal point of almost all intra-urban transit lines. A large number of private streetcar companies lay their track in order to provide transportation to and from downtown to a specific sector of the outlying city. Streetcar transportation thus made possible the rise of concentrically arranged residential rings around the downtown area. A later model of urban growth, by Chicago School member Homer Hoyt, gave even greater importance to the streetcar lines, which constituted the central axes around which these sectors—now in the shape of wedges, not rings—evolved. Here the social prestige of an urban residential area was marked directly by its proximity to a given streetcar line.[11]

Returning to Burgess's original model, the ring immediately surrounding the downtown core consisted of cheap apartment and red-light districts. Given its suitability for industries and its proximity to the city center, land here was very expensive and thus encouraged dense tenement settlements. Located within walking distance of Chicago's main industries, this area proved the logical point of settlement for most recently arrived immigrants, unless they settled in outlying industrial towns such as Packingtown or Pullman. The type of housing they chose reveals the intra-urban mobility of the modern city: many of the tenements were former mansions, whose inhabitants had abandoned the area, now haphazardly converted into multifamily dwellings.[12] Moving outward from the central slum and tenement region, the next ring encompassed the major industries along the north and south branches of the Chicago River. Here lived families of more skilled workers, usually those of English, German, or Irish descent who, during the last several decades, had moved away from the near-downtown zone and managed to construct single-frame dwellings. It is in this area that our protagonists lived: construction workers, teamsters, teachers, and a variety of service and craft workers. Unlike the residents of the tenement districts, these families frequently relied on streetcars for their commute to work. It was then the upper and middle classes who

Uniformed motorman and conductor posing in front of a streetcar from the Union Traction Company, which served the southern region of the city. Electric trolleys and their operators provided the most important and most modern means of intra-urban mobility in the turn-of-the-century city. Chicago Historical Society i38765

could afford to reside in the outlying ring, which was far removed from the unpleasant industrial environment, and which provided the city's streetcar network with its characteristic imprint. Closely tied to real estate investors, Chicago's streetcar companies designed their track in order to serve these outlying "streetcar suburbs," for this is where Chicago's professional and economic elite commuted to and from the CBD.[13]

Thus from the outset, streetcars placed their stamp on the social and functional geography of Chicago and many other American cities. More than just enabling expansion, they helped create cities with a functional class-based arrangement of urban space. Whereas the residential settlement of the old

Passengers stranded during an accident in 1902 on the Elevated Railway line. The "El" was mainly used by middle-class commuters. Chicago Historical Society DN-3361

walking city of the 1870s still equaled a relative jumble of rich and poor, immigrant and native, the "industrial metropolis came to be arranged in a systematic pattern of socio-economic segregation." For example, by the early twentieth century, over seventy thousand people, mainly Italians, Poles, and Russians, shared one square mile in a Near West industrial district, whereas half that number resided in eighty-eight square miles in Chicago's suburbs. Traveling out of the city on the streetcar usually meant moving up the social scale, though there were exceptions to this rule, such as Chicago's northern lakefront, which remained a wealthy residential district even after the introduction of electric transit.[14]

It was primarily class, not ethnicity, that accounted for residential location. It is true that by 1900, Americans of Irish and German origin lived farther away from the immediate industrial areas than recently arrived immigrant families from eastern and southern Europe, but this reflected mainly the fact that German and Irish workers had more skilled and better paying jobs than did Italians or Slavs. Concentrations of residents based primarily on nationality did (and still do) exist in Chicago, but they occurred in small clusters and rarely defined entire regions (in fact, urban geographers describe these as "anomalies"). In his study of the South Side Packingtown community, James Barrett documented a remarkable heterogeneity of ethnic groups living within the same neighborhood and even block. Class thus proved the determinative factor in segregating Chicago's living spaces, at least until the 1910s when racial differences began to carry increasing weight. Thanks in great part to the streetcar, "Chicago's residential pattern by class had been fully set by 1894."[15]

This narrative of urban development, whereby the streetcars shaped the form of urban development, suggests a degree of technological and cultural determinism. As soon as technologically feasible, so the story goes, Americans living in cities moved away from industrial locations and as far out of the city itself as possible. (Urban historians, in fact, define the main periods of the United States city in terms of transportation technology: the "walking city" until the 1870s, the "streetcar city" from the 1880s to the 1920s, and the "automobile city" from the 1930s onward.)[16] These residential preferences thus inscribed onto the urban landscape a systematic pattern of socioethnic segregation (albeit one that remained in constant motion), whereby each newly arriving immigrant generation pushed the previous one further outward, geographically, and upward, socially. To be sure, Burgess's model considered transportation a mere tool that rendered possible a quasi-natural, or "ecological," unfolding of social and geographic mechanisms and placed this public service outside the realm of political negotiation. Burgess and his colleague Robert Park assumed that a centrally oriented transportation network predated the very process of centralization they sought to explain. Burgess considered it a "*natural tendency* for local and outside transportation to converge in the CBD."[17] Thus neither the Chicago School nor most models of urban growth (or subsequent historical interpretations) have considered the political process that underlies Chicago's and other cities' social geography worthy of consideration. They all continue to treat transportation change as an independent variable.[18] Even when they do acknowledge political action as a necessary prior step to technological change, they view it in functionalist terms, circumscribing the parameters of politics to the extent to which government provides an urban service to an essentially passive consumer-oriented citizenry.[19]

In fact, when electric streetcars made their first appearance in Chicago during the 1890s, they were considered anything but natural facilitators of urban growth. They provoked a profound society-centered political debate over how this new mode of mass transit ought to shape the form of the city. What the Chicago School would later postulate as a natural process of segregation and fragmentation, urban critics during the 1890s had decried as an unacceptable sign of decay.

STREETCARS AND URBAN REFORM

Nowhere perhaps was urban fragmentation, in both spatial and social terms, as apparent as in late-nineteenth-century Chicago. In 1893 the Columbian International Exposition opened its doors to visitors and reporters from all over the world, presenting the glamorous vision of the White City, an assemblage of neoclassical buildings and landscapes displaying the era's technological and scientific breakthroughs and celebrating the unity of progress, nationhood, and social order. Yet the Great Depression of that same year rendered visible another city, one of poverty and congested, unsanitary neighborhoods. Although destitution itself was nothing new, its extent was unprecedented and its potential results appeared explosive. The next year, in 1894, as employees of the Pullman Sleeping Car Company in Chicago's South Side, one of Chicago's outlying industrial towns, walked out on strike, Chicago once again (after the Great Upheaval in 1877 and the Haymarket Riot in 1886) became the site of violent class conflict. Chicago more than any other U.S. city rendered visible the dire conditions that resulted from rapid industrialization and urbanization.[20]

More than these social problems themselves, it was an acute public awareness of the same that raised the specter of violent social fragmentation and confrontation. It was in Chicago that muckrakers did indeed excel in raking muck, publicly exposing the city's ills. In his *If Christ Came to Chicago,* first published in 1894, the Englishman William T. Stead castigated the city for its immoralities and vice ("the cloaca maxima of the world") and its political corruption.[21] Upton Sinclair's *The Jungle,* published a decade later, completed an array of widely publicized exposures of poverty, congested living conditions, and outright starvation. The gravity of the situation in Chicago fired the imagination of other writers as well, including Theodore Dreiser. In fact, the model of Chicago defined the period of Naturalism in American literature. During the period spanned by the writings of Stead and Sinclair, the press acquired a central role in public discussion. Whereas, during the 1880s, Chicago's newspapers had functioned as the guardians of elite notions of order (fervently attacking its main threat, anarchism), by the 1890s, many newspapers had assumed the role of advocates of the public interest. This held particularly true of the new "yellow press," which offered sensationalist exposés of the city's social and political ills, especially concerning the corruption that surrounded urban services such as transportation.[22]

In the eyes of reformers and intellectuals, Chicago became the Manchester of the New World. European visitors especially expressed intense reactions to the Midwest metropolis. "It . . . stands on the same sort of soil as Calcutta. Having seen it, I urgently desire never to see it again. It is inhabited by savages," the Indian English writer Rudyard Kipling declared; "Its water is the water of the Hugli, and its air is dirt." The *New Republic* picked up on this metaphor: Chicago "is not merely inured to dirt. It would feel naked and indecent without it." Somewhat less categorical, the German sociologist and U.S. traveler Max Weber viewed the city as a material manifestation of the country's soul, where ostentatious new wealth, bluntly expressed in "monumental . . . erections of marble and gilded bronze," contrasted with ragged poverty. To Weber, the city represented a cacophony of restlessness, "a flurry of a jumble of races . . . [and a] breathless hunt for bounty."[23]

Yet within "this monstrous city," Weber discovered a beacon of hope, "gentle traces of loving force, goodness, justice, a firm will to achieve the beautiful and profound," which manifested itself, above all, in the work of one "determined and faithful" woman—an *"Engel von Chikago"*—"who erected in the desolate streets of a working-class neighborhood her famous settlement."[24] Weber was referring to Jane Addams, founder of Hull House in Chicago's West Side. She and several other settlement reformers, including Florence Kelley and Graham Taylor, formed part of a reform movement that approached social problems in new ways because they considered the urban environment as the principal cause of poverty. Desolation did not reflect a failure of individual character or will power (the classic argument during the laissez-faire period of capitalism) but the physical and moral conditions under which people lived. Under the banner of "municipal housekeeping," women living in the settlements fought congested living conditions and demanded paved streets, garbage removal, improved sanitation, as well as better police and fire protection for the immigrant tenement districts in which they resided.[25]

Ironically, this focus on the ills of the urban environment generated a new faith in the city as a force for social and moral improvement. Infused with new energy, reformers saw in the fragmentary quality of urban society a challenge to urban improvement. Just as Chicago had risen like the phoenix from the ashes of the Great Fire of 1871, now it could experience a social and moral reunification. Addams decried the poverty of immigrants and their working conditions, as well as commercialized vice and amusements, but above all she deplored "the division of the city into two nations . . . broken up into classes."[26] Yet the city, instead of being named the culprit of societal degradation, now became the herald of renewal. Through distinctly urban public institutions such as "night schools, art exhibits, . . . parks, playgrounds, a cheap press," and also through "labor organizations and the church," the city, according to urban reformer Frederick Howe, could become "a tremendous agency for human advancement." Having worked as reporter, social worker, lawyer, and political activist in cities such as New York, Cleveland, and Chicago, Howe considered the city a unique setting in which to effect new forms of social organization, direct democracy, and innovative policy. "Urban civilization is armed with powers such as she has never before enjoyed," he affirmed. Moreover, through the growing interaction between city and country (by means of rural free delivery, expansion of the mail order business, the concentration of publishing interests, as well as the development of streetcar lines), the city became the center of national life, thus rendering urban reform crucial to the health of the nation as a whole. (Howe got to practice these ideas when he was elected councilman in Cleveland and joined forces with radical reform mayor Tom Johnson. Later he served as President Woodrow Wilson's commissioner of immigration and resigned in 1919 in protest over the wartime nativist hysteria.)[27]

In such urban-centered calls of reform, the city assumed the role of a biomorphic, organic actor. Reformers envisioned the city functioning like a perfectly coordinated (sociobiological) organism that, once obstructive forces such as political corruption and social desolation were removed, could blossom freely and in perfect harmony. Howe described the city as a body "capable of conscious and concerted action, responsive, ready, and intelligent." Yet these reformers regarded the city in terms that differed from the later Chicago School's ecological view: Howe and others utilized the organic metaphor precisely to counteract what Burgess and colleagues would come to consider as perfectly natural—urban fragmentation; and they located the main tool of city renewal in the political sphere, which in turn would be renewed through the mobilization of a broad section of the citizenry. Finally, midwestern cities such as Cleveland or Detroit or Chicago were particularly prone to reform, given that they were considered "less aristocratic" than eastern ones.[28]

Reformers heralded the streetcar for its potential to improve the living conditions of the city's poor. Offering less expensive rides in comparison to railroads and omnibuses, streetcars were considered tools for the massive relocation of the urban poor to the suburbs. In so doing, streetcars would improve not only people's physical living conditions but also their character and civic consciousness. Already, according to traction expert E. W. Bemis, a new streetcar extension to the Hull House district had induced five thousand slum residents to "move to healthful suburbs."[29] Labor economist John Commons envisioned a whole series of improvements in wage earners' living conditions directly associated with an efficient and affordable streetcar service. Like other reformers, Commons regarded the streetcar as "the workingman's ticket for escape from the slum." He then foresaw a whole series of benefits that would result: "Laboring people could live in the country, and own their own homes. . . . Tenements would not be crowded. Sanitary conditions would be improved and the death-rate lowered. Men out of work could ride in search of employment, instead of wearily tramping the streets." The key, in Commons's view, was that streetcar service was made accessible to workers. Lower streetcar fares, he felt, would allow working-class families to spend more on vital necessities such as clothing, groceries, shoes, and amusements. With workers enjoy-ing better health and better food, they would do better work, which in turn would benefit city industries as a whole.[30]

Behind reformers' insistence on worker suburbanization lay the hope for a broad civic renewal. By living in the suburbs, workers would become bet-ter citizens. According to sociologist Charles H. Cooley, the improved envi-ronment would enhance the workingman's "social imagination," which, in turn, would lead to the betterment of his morals and allow him to strive for the city's civic ideal. An efficient streetcar network would allow the wage earner to spend less time getting to and from work. This added leisure time, according to sociologist Carroll D. Wright would have "a moral influence, for it betters his condition, helps him to a higher plane [and] facilitates social intercourse."[31]

The link that social reformers drew between streetcars and massive sub-urbanization marks a curious midpoint in the transition from a critical to a more positive view of the city. Progressive-era settlement residents and so-cial scientists celebrated the new potential of the city, but many still saw the solution to be less in improving the slums than in shuffling workers outside the central city into the more "healthful surroundings in the coun-try."[32] Even as reformers entered the urban trenches, their urge to escape the town of Babel lived on. Yet these reformers never associated the sub-urbs with "urban flight" or an escape from the city altogether.

In fact, they asserted the importance of public urban spaces for the fos-tering of a new civic spirit. Again, the streetcar figured as a prominent so-lution. Inside the trolley would reign a "sense of intimacy with the city that we most lack in America," Howe exclaimed. "It is a thing that can only come through constant physical touch with the community." Even the interior of the streetcar itself—along with other uplifting spaces such as schools, museums, parks, and playgrounds—would as-sure the revival of a new civic consciousness. With regard to the ele-vated railroad, constructed in 1898 by Charles Tyson Yerkes, hopes for an uplifted public spirit acquired even a literal sense. Streetcars, then, would not only help the technological growth of a functional modern city but would also serve to integrate its body social. As one settlement reformer put it: "The future rivalry of cities is bound to depend in no slight degree upon the organization of their circulatory systems." By helping to improve working-class residents' physical environment, streetcars would alleviate social conflict and help integrate workers into public society.[33]

When postulating this kind of streetcar utopia, how did middle-class reformers perceive the role of workers? Certainly, their idea to move workers to the city's outskirts by means of the streetcars was motivated as much by considerations of social control as by a genuine concern for the workers' living conditions. It is in this light that one might read the affirmation of a realtor that the suburbanization of the working class was "doing more to put down socialism, in this country at least, than all other things combined." Likewise, the conception of the city as an organic entity, whose parts would work harmoniously in pursuit of the health of the city body as a whole (an ideal in which streetcar arteries played no small part), might well be regarded as a hierarchical model set out to impose social order. Yet middle-class civic reformers also acknowledged the need for greater inclusiveness in public discussion. Perhaps they wanted workers to adopt middle-class standards, but they also granted wage earners a place and a voice in the articulation of the civic ideal. This reflected the reformers' awareness that workers themselves were beginning to speak out on public matters such as urban transportation. Workers not only rode the trolleys but also had a great deal to say about their operation.[34]

Reformers' ideals clashed, in fact, with the reality of streetcar operation. A wave of corporate consolidation during the 1890s reduced the number of streetcar companies from around thirty to three principal enterprises, but even so, the problem of a fragmented transit network persisted. Each of the three main companies serviced routes from downtown to its own respective region, the North, West, and South sides, which prevented integration of the city as a whole (see map 3). Only the elevated railroad provided service across the three regions. Streetcar riders wishing to travel from one of the city's regions to another often faced complicated and costly obstacles, having to travel through downtown and there having to walk several blocks in order to connect from one company's terminal to another. Such a journey also required the payment of two or more separate fares, since most lines did not honor the other companies' transfers. The northern lines, for example, terminated in the northern limits of the city center, with lines moving southward originating several blocks further inside the CBD. Riding the streetcar on Halsted Street (Chicago's main north–south axis, considered one of the longest urban thoroughfares in the world) required traveling on three different cars, walking several blocks, crossing a bridge, and paying two fares.[35]

With almost all streetcar lines converging on the city center, the latter suffered from high traffic and congested streets. The much-heralded electrification of the lines, while in theory speeding up travel, proved ineffective

3. PRINCIPAL STREETCAR AND ELEVATED RAILWAY COMPANIES
OF CHICAGO, ca. 1900

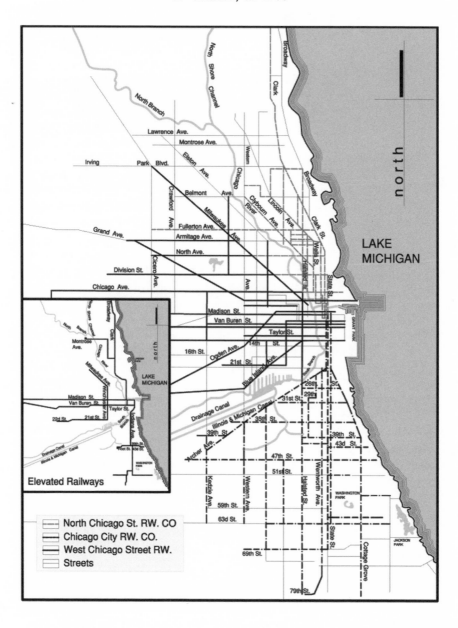

LAKE MICHIGAN

north

Elevated Railways

LAKE MICHIGAN

Legend:
- North Chicago St. RW. CO
- Chicago City RW. CO.
- West Chicago Street RW.
- Streets

against congested downtown streets or against a horse wagon halted on the tracks while unloading boxes. Teamsters' habit of waiting for the push of a streetcar in order to overcome the sharp inclines at the numerous bridges proved especially loathsome to passengers. The practice became so common that some bridges were even equipped with push bars, which helped the wagons get pushed by the streetcars. Thus at the heart of the congestion problem lay the concentric organization of the streetcar network, which in turn reflected the companies' quest for maximum economic advantage. Mass transit and the host of downtown-set commercial and financial activities it served created a city "so geographically centralized . . . that good transportation had become physically impossible."[36]

The conditions that provoked the most protests, however, were the intensely crowded interiors of the trains, in which the passenger "rides a great part of the way hanging to a strap, jammed, jostled and jolted about." Several hundred residents of the Stock Yards district, many of them clerks of the Swift Meat Company, signed "Not a petition but a PROTEST against the abominable treatment given patrons of the 43rd Street car line. The word is not yet coined strong enough," the letter read, "to express the disgust and resentment we feel at the way we are crowded . . . every day of the year, . . . standing and sitting, until it would not be possible to squeeze another one in, and then the conductor is obliged to surge through the car and take tribute." A German pamphlet echoed such sentiments, proclaiming: "The riders can't defend themselves when they are packed inside the cars like herrings inside a barrel." In some cases, passengers even had to travel standing on filthy, week-old straw or, riding in open trolleys, exposed to Chicago's famed winter winds. Overcrowding of streetcars constituted the number one transportation-related violation reported by the police; from May to December 1906, for example, the city's department of transportation received almost twelve thousand complaints.[37]

Rather than providing a dignified space that would foster greater civic spirit, the interior of a streetcar encouraged what many considered morally objectionable behavior, especially with regard to the relations between the sexes. The fact that streetcar operation was infringing upon public decency was highlighted by women's condition of travel. In the streetcars, the city's "wives and daughters," the standard-bearers of public propriety, were being "subjected to conditions so demoralizing as to be absolutely indecent," a pamphlet stated.[38]

Passenger or not, nobody moving in Chicago's streets was safe from the streetcars. Overcrowded station platforms made falling in front of a train a real risk, and with most people still traveling by foot and unaccustomed to the newly electrified high-speed trains of the 1890s, there were often deadly accidents. In 1903, the Chicago Bureau of Statistics

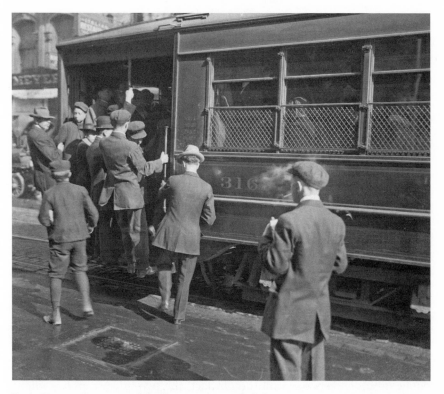

Typical scene of passengers boarding an overcrowded streetcar. Chicago Historical Society DN-60499

reported 2,035 streetcar-related accidents; two years later the number had risen to 2,491 accidents caused by streetcars; the latter year a total of 840 fatalities were reported, most of which were related to streetcars or other railways. In the spring of 1906, during less than a two-month period, 21 people were killed and 86 injured by streetcars.[39] Calls of overcrowded cars, dangerous service, and congested streets filled newspaper columns and conversations in saloons, clubs, and private salons in turn-of-the-century Chicago.

Apart from streetcar service itself, Chicagoans debated the responsibilities of the company to maintain the city's thoroughfares, including street cleaning and paving. This question led to the involvement of a sector of the population that had traditionally displayed little interest in public matters: Chicago's homeowners. During the nineteenth century, decisions of an apparently public nature such as the paving of a street were taken only by the residents immediately affected. Individual residents rather than the city government decided upon public improvements, including the construction of roads, sidewalks, and sewage. In order for a road to be paved, a majority of adjoining homeowners would have to petition city hall, which in turn would finance the project by levying special assessments on all residents affected. Chicago property owners thus fostered a private, particularistic vision and practice toward urban development.[40] The streetcar controversy, however, drew homeowners into a wider public orbit. Their immediate interest began right at their front door. In a street with a trolley line, who should have to pay for maintenance and cleaning, the homeowners or the company operating the streetcars? About two hundred Halsted Street residents, organized in the South Halsted Street Property Owners' Association, insisted on the latter, demanding that the Chicago City Railway Company "pave said South Halsted Street from curb to curb, [and] . . . keep said pavement in good condition and repair." A petition by house owners on nearby Wentworth Avenue voiced the same demand; "in wet weather the street is one mass od [sic] mud and water," they declared. They then added a list of additional tasks to be the responsibility of the trolley company, which they considered the main usufructor of their street: these tasks included street cleaning, the removal of snow "within twenty-four hours after each snowfall," as well as the illumination, "with two-thousand candle power electric light," of the street. In places where streets were already paved, residents complained that the operation of streetcars led to the quick destruction of the pavement.[41]

If homeowners were one important constituency now drawn into a new public orbit, workers were another. In fact, the two interest groups might well coincide, as was the case with the two just-cited petitioners residing in working-class areas of the city.[42] Yet most wage earners voiced their concerns as passengers not as property owners. Streetcars are generally seen as a tool of middle-class suburbanization during the early twentieth century. Real estate agents eager to develop new residential areas procured the construction of a streetcar line in order to drive up lot prices. Indeed, most end points of streetcar routes lay in outlying privileged neighborhoods. While middle-class residents thus relied on the daily streetcar commute to and from work, most working-class residents, so the argument goes, still lived within walking distance of their workplace; their neighborhoods still constituted "almost self-sufficient" enclaves that provided all basic functions, including housing, work, and services.[43]

In fact, working-class Chicagoans relied heavily on urban streetcars. This held especially true for skilled men and employed women. According to a contemporary study of intra-urban travel patterns, the vast majority of trolley riders (about 75 percent) rode a distance of five miles or less. These people did not commute to the more distant middle-class suburbs but traveled within a closer urban perimeter; they resided in the intermediate rings of the city, the typical home location of skilled workers and second-generation immigrants. In fact, middle-class people living in the supposed "streetcar suburbs" preferred the faster nonstop service provided by the elevated trains and "rarely patronize[d] the surface cars of the city." Even unskilled immigrant workers, while generally living in closer proximity to their jobs, relied on urban transportation, if to a lesser extent. Packinghouse and stockyard workers, for example, lived in the area surrounding their job sites yet could still face a daily commute of two or three miles each way, a considerable distance especially during the winter season.[44] Perhaps in single-industry-based cities such as Pittsburgh, working-class residential areas neatly coincided with industrial locations, but in Chicago such proximity proved less likely. This holds especially true for workers who, due to lay-offs and seasonal adjustments, were forced to switch jobs frequently. Also, more and more young women entered the white-collar sector of employment and commuted downtown. For example, of about two thousand female department-store clerks, 82 percent traveled on the streetcar average distances of five or six miles. Female factory workers who lived with their parents also faced considerable commutes to work, as their residential location was determined by their parents' rather than their own workplace. Single women living by themselves lacked the financial means to live near their workplace and were clustered in the only regions with affordable rents, that is, the tenement districts.[45] Although systematic studies of the social background of Chicago streetcar riders are unavailable, it is clear that streetcars had become a vital public service to a far wider spectrum of the city's population than is suggested by the image of the middle-class streetcar.

This is not to argue that trolley service was easily accessible to Chicago's working people. In fact, critics constantly raised the issue of class-based inequities with regard to public transportation. The cost of transportation absorbed a large proportion of workers' budget. The standard streetcar fare of five cents equaled the hourly wage of an unskilled factory worker. Even if only one member of a working-class family used the streetcar on a daily basis, the annual expense (thirty dollars) would almost equal that of annual fuel costs (thirty-six dollars) and could amount to one-third of a family's annual rent.[46] Female operators and department-store saleswomen, for example, in their daily commute to downtown offices spent 7.4 percent and 6 percent, respectively, of their annual income on streetcar fares. The daily expense of the streetcar chipped away at the supposed white-collar status of women operatives. Although telephone operators earned slightly more than women factory workers, the cost of streetcar fares rendered the difference virtually nonexistent.[47] "Self-supporting girls and boys," according to another study, spent ten weeks' worth of their annual wages on streetcar fares alone. U.S. households, in general, had to dedicate a far greater proportion of their income to transportation than their European counterparts; this at least was the finding of a study of consumption patterns during the 1890s.[48]

The geographical layout of Chicago's streetcar lines also discriminated against working-class residents, who often lacked direct access to lines designed to operate between middle-class suburbs and downtown. The city's most advanced transit system, the Elevated, made no stops in the factory districts and catered primarily to the outlying middle-class districts. As a result, working-class residents had to engage in complicated transfers and pay double fares, often paying a greater fare per mile traveled than a middle-class person riding all the way to the city's outskirts.[49] Working-class Chicagoans also faced particularly uncomfortable rides, given that they were forced to ride the cars at times when passenger volume proved greatest and were thus compelled "to pay the same price for a strap or the footboard as the well-to-do, who . . . ride at other times, [and] pay for a reasonable amount of room." Writers such as Upton Sinclair were astounded by the crowding of the streetcars circulating in Chicago's South Side: "the street-car monopoly saw fit to put on so few cars that there would be men hanging to every foot of the backs of them and often crouching upon the snow-covered roof. Of course the doors could never be closed, and so the cars were as cold as outdoors." Nighttime employees might well lack access to streetcars altogether, as service was highly infrequent or suspended at these hours.[50] In assigning cars to different regions of the city, the streetcar companies apparently did not take into account the population density of a given neighborhood. As a carpenters local of Chicago's Northwest Side pointed out, the frequency of cars proved "entirely insufficient to properly carry the people, living in these thickly populated districts." The overcrowding of trains was thus perceived as a service- and class-related problem and was articulated by working-class riders and settlement reformers. George Hooker, one of the latter, set out to document this grievance through photographs and a systematic counting of passengers riding in the cars on South Side Halsted Street, "beginning at 10:42 a.m. and ending at 10:50 p.m."[51] Given the relative high cost, poor quality, and limited access to the streetcars, some workers were indeed forced to walk. Jurgis Rudkus, the hero of Upton Sinclair's *The Jungle,* for example, had to travel several miles to work but, even in deep winter, chose to walk rather than ride the car. Like Jurgis, many a worker found it better "to spend his fare for a drink and a free lunch, to give him strength to walk." Yet this could entail dire consequences. Jurgis's wife, Ona, could not afford to ride the streetcar, so she walked—and caught deadly pneumonia on her way to work.[52]

The series of perceived failures of Chicago's streetcar system—namely, a fragmented, costly, overcrowded, too infrequent, and dangerous service— were mainly attributed to the streetcar companies themselves, which were seen as "applying artificial obstructions to the circulatory system of the

[city] body." The problem, as reformers were quick to point out, lay in the incompatibility between the public interest and the companies operating invariably in pursuit of profit. Thus, critics attributed the fragmented nature of streetcar service to the fact that each company operated within a specific region of the city and failed to look beyond its immediate interest in maximizing the number of passengers.[53]

Political campaigns during the 1890s against the streetcar corporations went beyond service-related issues to the question of the nature of urban government. Poor transit service was perceived as a mere symptom of a far more fundamental problem: the inability of city government to regulate this and other vital public services in the face of corruption. The work of muckraking journalists and a newly militant press during the 1890s made "Chicago" and "graft" virtual synonyms. Any company wishing to provide a public service, such as water, sewage, or transportation, had to acquire a city grant in order to use public land for these purposes. Since public service operations were often not conducive to business competition (one would not want to run streetcars of two different companies on the same tracks, for example), the acquisition of a franchise, in effect, provided a business with monopoly rights over a certain section of the city. "Selling" public rights-of-way to private utility companies was a lucrative transaction for profit-oriented aldermen. Some city aldermen even created their own fictitious paper companies, which, once in receipt of franchises, sold their rights to an existing company. For instance, in 1895 aldermen voted franchise rights to a gas provider existing only on paper, the Ogden Gas Company. Since the contract authorized Ogden Gas to lay pipes at a rate lower than that granted to other gas companies in the city, the new company was immediately bought up by yet another firm, thus generating high returns for the aldermen.[54] Although urban mismanagement became a problem for cities all over the country, the nature of Chicago's political system rendered it particularly vulnerable to graft. Lacking a strong executive and (in contrast to cities like New York) a stable political party machine, the city's decentralized politics harbored an apparently inchoate entrepreneurial form of government, where a city councilman could easily turn his political power into a profitable business undertaking. In a city and county governed by numerous administrative bodies, each with ill-defined and overlapping jurisdictions, hopes to obtain effective government seemed unrealistic indeed.[55]

The decade's most blatant and widely publicized utility briberies centered on the streetcar corporations—and especially their main financier, Charles Tyson Yerkes, who led two of Chicago's largest transit companies. Yerkes began achieving fame and fortune as a corporate investor in 1886, when he purchased the majority stock of the North Side and West Side streetcar lines. Yerkes then financed the costly electrification of the horse-operated lines by dubious monetary dealings, which included the "watering," or excessive capitalization, of assets. The financier managed to increase the corporations' stock value from about eight million to over fifty-eight million dollars.[56] In order to operate a public service, Yerkes depended on franchises from city hall. Based on the 1875 Chicago charter, the Illinois state legislature authorized the city to issue public utility grants for a duration of twenty years. Designed to safeguard public interest in essential yet privately run urban services, these franchises degenerated into attractive sources of corruption. Yerkes, like many other utility providers, paid off city councilmen in return for franchises that failed to stipulate adequate compensation and regulation to the city. As a result, streetcars paid less taxes for the benefit of running on public streets than did the city's dogs: "In 1886 when Yerkes entered the railway business, the dogs paid $27,948 for the few privileges they enjoy, while the street car companies paid $30,530.85, but soon afterwards, the dogs, having less influence in legislative halls than certain financiers, had to bear the larger burden."[57]

When Chicagoans considered such corrupt misdealings on behalf of public utility companies, they invariably thought of Yerkes. "The man's name is very black in the town to-day," muckraker Ida Tarbell noted; "If one believes what he hears, Charles T. Yerkes was without a redeeming quality." Referring to the Great Fire of 1871, the popular columnist Mr. Dooley offered a biting commentary on the streetcar magnate: "We've had many other misfortunes an' they're not cillybrated. Why don't we have a band out an' illuminated street cars f'r to commimerate th' day Yerkuss came to Chicago? An' there's cholera. What's th' matter with cholera?" Yerkes would also inspire Theodore Dreiser to craft his famous trilogy, *The Titan, The Financier, The Stoic,* whose protagonist, Frank Algernon Cowperwood, was based directly on the Chicago investor.[58] Yet, contrary to his popular image, Yerkes was also a city builder who converted most of Chicago's railways to electric power, substantially enlarged its network, and endowed the city with the "Elevated," which still runs to this day and whose downtown loop continues to coin its name. In order to comprehend why Chicagoans were so unappreciative of Yerkes's accomplishments (and this is to put it mildly, for Yerkes would later find himself forced to flee the city), we need to comprehend the broad-based nature of this popular upheaval.

The public attack on Yerkes and the streetcar companies he represented epitomized what historian Richard McCormick has aptly labeled the "discovery that business corrupts politics." Indeed, Chicago witnessed an impressive mobilization of social forces stemming from a variety of class backgrounds. When the English writer William T. Stead, at a mass meeting in November 1893, castigated the city for its political corruption and governmental failures, he spoke not only to business leaders and middle-class reformers but also to populists and trade unionists. Workers themselves not only depended on streetcar travel but also came to perceive it as their right to do so. By the late 1890s, they would emerge alongside middle-class reformers as vocal critics of the companies. As muckraker Tarbell noted, "even humble shopgirls knew something of the rights and wrongs of traction."[59]

STREETCARS AND URBAN POLITICS

During the late 1890s, Chicago witnessed two major political mobilizations over the streetcar question, one of a broad-based and populist nature and one that stemmed more exclusively from the leading middle-class civic reform organizations. Although both campaigns proved quite distinctive in their constituency, rhetoric, and forms of action, they also came to influence each other considerably. As "traction" moved to center stage in turn-of-the-century Chicago politics, it was clear that the city's public sphere indeed had undergone a "transformation" (to refer again to Habermas's concept), and that it would never again be monopolized by a civic elite, a fact that same elite would come to accept.

The Cook County People's Party—an alliance of trade unionists, single-taxers (the followers of Henry George's panacea for the redistribution of wealth), and populists—formulated the first formal political response to the streetcar problem. This short-lived campaign, lasting only from late 1894 until the following year, was torn with factional disputes, hampered by the weaknesses of its constituents, and failed to gain a significant political foothold. Yet early on, the party identified the problems surrounding public utilities and urban government and offered a more serious diagnosis than did most muckrakers. The party's awareness of the close connection between franchise monopoly and urban misgovernment, according to historian Chester McArthur Destler, proved "considerably in advance of the political intelligence of most middle class Chicagoans of the day."[60]

Illinois was one of the few states where populism acquired a significant urban dimension. Given the relative lack of appeal of the populist message to the state's wheat farmers, the movement in Illinois proved eager to enlist workers in the big city. During the 1893 depression, Chicago populists courted the urban unemployed and established contacts with prominent trade union leaders, the Knights of Labor, the Socialist Labor Party, and a myriad of radical groups, including Bellamy Nationalists, single-taxers, and free-silver populists. At the same time, a third-party ticket was of interest to Chicago trade unionists, who echoed the national AFL's call for political action. An intensive anti-labor climate, as manifested in the military suppression of the 1894 Pullman strike and a series of judicial decisions that severely restricted trade unions' range of actions, prompted trade unionists nationwide to consider an independent political strategy inspired by the rise to power of the British Labour Party. In Chicago this resulted in a viable, if short-lived, labor-populist ticket. Its unifying demand was the municipal ownership of the streetcars and other public utilities.[61]

To Chicago populists, Charles Yerkes, leading investor in Chicago's mass transit system and popular symbol of its mismanagement, was only the symptom of a more fundamental condition: the usurpation of special privileges by utility monopolies. Reflecting the U.S. republican tradition that worried about sinister forces seeking to undermine government, Chicagoans feared that public utility companies were coopting their elected government. Franchises, municipal reformer Frederick C. Howe argued, had become the means to obtain special privileges, which enabled their recipients to accumulate wealth without expending human labor and thus to act in parasitical fashion. In contrast to the tirades of muckrakers, the reformers' main targets were the companies themselves rather than corrupt politicians: "my word is not to the Council drunk," Hooker asserted, "but to Mr. Bribe Giver perfectly sober, self-possessed and calculating. . . . My word is to . . . those whose course is parallel to that of the thief who first gets his victim drunk and then robs him; it is to those who first corrupt the manhood of our political agents and then secure from them a capitulation of our rights." Politicians, in that vision, appeared as the emasculated victims of the sinister force of monopoly.[62]

By placing the blame on the streetcar companies, populists offered a radical analysis of urban mismanagement. According to Henry Demarest Lloyd, the charismatic leader of the Chicago populists, it was not sufficient for the people to simply "elect good men"; rather, it was necessary "to abolish the bad system of private monopolies in our streets." Only the People's Party would thus "strike at the root of the boodle."[63] Populists placed their attacks on monopoly within a broad denunciation of the inequality of living conditions and the perceived class hatred, both of which were manifest in the American city.

Yet radical populists also voiced the new middle-class emphasis on the need for civic and moral betterment, and they associated public ownership with the "promise to recover true democracy and civic morality."[64] Hooker, quick to raise questions of social justice, likewise appealed to middle-class concerns by tying the question of passenger and freight transportation to the general "aesthetic and social conditions of Chicago, not to say her morals and politics for the next two generations." The Populist Party also lauded the reform efforts of the Civic Federation of Chicago, a largely middle-class municipal reform organization founded in 1893, and assured the federation of its political cooperation.[65] The populist crusade against the streetcar companies, while clearly positioned on the left side of the political spectrum, included a wide variety of social agents and arguments.

In this sense, Chicago populists combined an anti-monopoly message rooted in nineteenth-century republican thought with a new insistence in the power of civic mobilization in a democracy. To Lloyd, the struggle was one between the people and the monopolies. Recalling the struggle of Jefferson, "the first great social democrat," against "the planter aristocracy of 1776," Lloyd called on his audiences to "demonetize the millionaire." We have here, then, a moment of transition between a vision essentially populist in nature and an incipient progressive argument. What distinguished the two, among other things, was the former's focus on the destruction of monopoly and privilege while the latter offered a more constructive and potentially consensual call for the reassertion of the public interest by means of new civic and administrative mechanisms. Chicago "populist" calls to overthrow monopoly already entailed a "progressive" insistence in the potential of direct democratic measures and coalition building in the unique setting of the industrial city. Lloyd envisioned the possibility of a civic alliance stemming from a broad social spectrum, one that would include workers, consumers, farmers, and small capitalists, all of which by means of a "democratic counter-revolution" would overthrow monopoly capitalism and its "governments of privilege." Lloyd's vision was clearly set in the city and, specifically, in the midwest metropolis: "Here [in Chicago] the workingmen, capitalists, single-taxers, and socialists have come together to join forces with each other and with the farmers, as has been done in no other city . . . . It is the most wonderful outburst of popular hope and enthusiasm in the recent politics of this country," Lloyd acclaimed.[66] The faith expressed in the potential of urban democracy would thus form the bridge between nineteenth-century populism and twentieth-century progressivism.

Yet, this "wonderful outburst of popular hope" fared poorly at the ballot box. In the 1895 municipal elections, the populist party received a mere 5 percent of the votes. With franchise scandals and service problems only just beginning to surface, the populists' agenda of municipal ownership enjoyed only limited public appeal. Organized labor, hard hit by the depression and in dire need of political patronage, returned to the fold of the political party in power, the Democrats. Disputes over the question of socialism also served to fragment the populist coalition, leading to the demise of the People's Party by the end of the same year.[67]

Political efforts directed against the streetcar companies proved more successful on the state level and centered on the Illinois governor John Peter Altgeld. Elected in 1892, Altgeld was the first Democrat governor in thirty-six years. As part of his pioneering progressive legislative agenda (including factory laws and labor arbitration boards, and the pardoning of the Haymarket anarchists), the German American set out to combat the power of public utility corporations.[68] Altgeld's constituency consisted of three main groups: organized labor, middle-class urban reformers, and the state Democratic machine. Early on, Altgeld established close ties to Chicago trade unions. When he first ran for Cook County superior court in 1886 on a Democratic ticket, he received the endorsement of the United Labor Party, a short-lived independent labor ticket in Chicago established during the aftermath of Haymarket. Altgeld also nurtured his labor ties through his friendship to labor intellectuals, most notably Lloyd and lawyer Clarence Darrow, who in turn would be appointed by Altgeld as Chicago's corporation counsel.[69] George Schilling, a Democrat and the leader of Chicago's Trade and Labor Assembly, was Altgeld's main backer among organized labor. Altgeld was championed by middle-class reformers such as Hull House residents Florence Kelley, Julia Lathrop, and Ellen Gates Starr, who assisted the passage of his legislative measures through lobbying and publicity and often became directly involved in his administration. Finally, Altgeld enjoyed the support of influential Democratic political bosses such as "King" Mike McDonald. While the state machine may not have agreed with, or even been aware of, Altgeld's agenda, they were desperate to occupy the gubernatorial mansion after an absence of three decades. When Altgeld took office in 1893, he was considered as much a shrewd Democratic regular as a potential reformer.[70]

However, the governor's confrontational position toward utility interests, along with his famous pardoning of the Haymarket anarchists, quickly secured him the reputation as a radical. Like the populist leader Lloyd, Altgeld sought to contain the "giant corporations" by means of a popular democratic "counter-balancing [of] forces." Law alone, he felt, no longer sufficed to oppose these new combinations.[71] In the spring of 1895, an ambitious move by public-utility entrepreneurs to politically consolidate their investments provided Altgeld with a chance to act upon his convictions. Charles T. Yerkes, facing the expiration of several franchises, sought to gain from the Illinois legislature a ninety-nine-year franchise for his traction lines. At the same time, a conglomerate of Chicago gas companies, under siege by the courts eager to dissolve this so-called Gas Trust, sought to obtain legislation designed to legitimate their activities. Altgeld promptly vetoed both bills and, on top, set up an investigation—led by the director of the Illinois Bureau of Labor Statistics, George Schilling—that documented franchise abuses and tax evasions on behalf of the utility companies. Altgeld, like Toledo mayor Samuel M. Jones, formed part of a curious genre of streetcar investors turned anti-corporate crusaders. In 1892 he had sold his assets in a trolley company in order to finance his gubernatorial campaign.[72] The measures Altgeld took against the companies turned Altgeld into a popular anti-monopolist, but they also resulted in his falling out with Democratic Party regulars, who refused to back him for re-election in 1896. The crusade against public utility companies apparently still enjoyed limited political viability.

Yet the ongoing efforts by the public utilities to secure long-term franchises continued to fuel popular outrage and mobilization. In the spring of 1897, Yerkes, supposedly by means of bribing state representatives, pushed the so-called Humphrey Bill through the Illinois legislature. The bill sought to shift political control over streetcar utilities from the municipality to the state level and increase the duration of franchises from twenty to ninety-nine years. Upon the governor's veto, the house passed a more moderate bill instead, known as the Allen law, which, while retaining city jurisdiction over franchise matters, also permitted—if approved by city hall—the extension of franchises to fifty years.[73] Among the populace, the Humphrey/Allen bill episode confirmed popular fears in the public utility and especially the streetcar companies' sinister, antidemocratic maneuverings. The Allen law now turned the city once again into the main political battle stage.

The possibility that Yerkes might secure a fifty-year franchise through a vote of the city council provoked unprecedented popular furor in Chicago. As rumors spread that the aldermen would vote on a franchise measure, a large "mob—armed with nooses and guns" surrounded city hall. Their broadsides, resolutions, and speeches in opposition to the Allen bill, one observer noted, "surpassed anything Chicago had yet seen in wrathful invective and direful threats."[74] Fearing for "the perpetuity of our . . . present institutions," attendants of a mass meeting in Central Music Hall resolved that "the directors and stockholders of these companies should be exposed to condemnation as criminals and anarchists, in that they are organizing corruption and plotting against the peace and prosperity of Chicago."[75] In the aftermath of Haymarket in 1886 the charge of anarchism had justified the suppression of labor radicalism; now it was applied to public utility companies.

The meeting at Central Music Hall on December 11, 1898, was attended by a stunning diversity of social organizations that would have impressed Alexis de Tocqueville, the early-nineteenth-century French admirer of America's vibrant civic life. The gathering, that December day, included the Mugwumpish Citizens Association, the elite Union League Club, the CFL, ethnic associations such as the Ninth Ward Polish-American Organization, as well as an assortment of trade, professional, and political associations, including (among others) the Chicago Law School, the Milk Dealers Association, the Humboldt Park Improvement Club, the Neutral Social and Literary Club, even the Colored Democratic League of Cook County.[76] United in their opposition to Yerkes, these groups combined defenses of their specific interests with broader civic-minded ones. The Colored Democratic League criticized the streetcar companies for not hiring "working men on account of their color." Workers of the South Side Rapid Transit Company pointed to the hostility of "said corporations" toward their organizing efforts (streetcar workers would not manage to unionize until 1902). The CFL addressed the issue from the perspective of working-class consumers by stressing the high burden imposed by streetcar fares on workers' budgets at a time when wage levels were falling; the labor central pointed out that working children and working women were as much affected as workingmen. Representatives of Chicago's Swedish community spoke as consumers when they expressed their refusal to "by their nickels help to swell the coffers of an arrogant monopoly." Along with the Swedes, almost all groups shared such anti-monopoly sentiments and insisted that any franchise required the direct consent of the people. Not the people as such but the city of Chicago was affirmed as the main counterforce of the companies. Demanding home rule, the CFL opposed "any legislation that takes away from Chicago . . . its right to manage its own affairs" and insisted that the federation wished to uphold the "economical [sic], political and moral interests of this city." Even the Union League Club, an association of Chicago's business elite, could ally itself with labor's urban patriotism; while refusing to condemn Yerkes directly, the club requested that he withdraw his plans for a franchise extension in order to assure the "good name of this city."[77] Workers, consumers, and business interests could find a common language and, for a short time, even a common political meeting ground to voice their protests.

This is not to say that they had reached a consensus over the streetcar question. In fact, the political energies generated by opposition to Yerkes quickly polarized into distinct projects. It is to insist, however, in the city's expanded political universe, which now included labor and consumer groups. To view these newcomers' expressions of broader public concerns as mere rhetoric or as a sell-out of their (class-based) interests fails to do justice to the unifying potential of progressive-era politics. In other words, we should take seriously the moral outrage directed at the streetcar question by a broad cross section of Chicago residents: "Look at the deadly harm inflicted upon the moral sense of the community by these mutual reprisals and corruptions. . . . We tremble for the future of our commonwealth!"[78] Such united trembling, this time around, generated political results. City hall aldermen immediately ceased their flirtations with Yerkes and voted down franchise extensions. Those who had backed the earlier state legislation felt the wrath of the Chicago voters: 80 percent of state representatives were not reelected in the fall of 1898, and the new state assembly repealed the Allen law the following spring.[79]

As the Union League Club's participation in the Central Music Hall event indicates, Chicago's business leaders and civic reformers formed part of the anti-Yerkes campaign. Their efforts reflected less a hostility to the streetcar manager than a repulsion over what they considered widespread corruption among city and state legislators. Thus, in reaction to the franchise scandals of the mid-1890s, various businessmen and reformers of the Civic Federation and elite civic organizations in 1896 formed the Legislative Voters League, which dealt with state legislation, and the Municipal Voters League, which focused on Chicago matters; both associations set out to secure the nomination and election of "honest and capable" men.[80]

In its political strategy, the Municipal Voters League (MVL) followed the lead of settlement residents who, in the early 1890s, had begun to expose corrupt ward politicians. In 1895 Jane Addams nominated a "clean" candidate in opposition to the powerful boss of the nineteenth ward, Jimmy Powers, and exposed his alliances with Yerkes. Posting billboards reading "Yerkes and Powers, the Briber and the Bribed," Addams depicted Powers as the candidate of the railway trust. Yet her repeated efforts to dislodge Powers—aided by Detroit mayor Hazen Pingree, famous for his stand against the traction interests—failed.[81] Equally unsuccessful in defeating the nineteenth ward alderman, the MVL nonetheless continued Addams's efforts and in a more systematized way. With the support of most Chicago newspapers and through massive leaflet campaigns, the MVL exposed the legislative records of all candidates and required its endorsees to pledge specific political planks (many of which related to franchise extensions). In its first trial in the municipal elections of 1896, the MVL managed to get twenty-four out of thirty-four endorsed candidates elected, a success rate that would increase with each subsequent council election and would result in a large plurality of "honest men" in the council by 1900. At least in terms of its own definition of honesty, the MVL was remarkably successful in transforming the city council (as its president put it) "from a den of thieves to a body responsive to public interests." Between 1901 and 1911, 85 percent of aldermen elected to the city council would bear the league's endorsement.[82]

If the MVL represented a strategy for elite control over urban politics, it did so within the framework of a broadened public discussion over reform. The league was led by printing company president George B. Cole and a handful of lawyers, realtors, and other relatively young professionals, and it received the active backing of Chicago's settlement house reformers. Unlike previous middle-class civic organizations, however, the MVL acknowledged the need to rally mass political support for the candidates it endorsed. By dealing with issues of broad public interest that could cut across class and ethnic lines (such as public utility regulation), by adopting what appeared to be simple criteria for endorsing candidates (electing "honest men"), and by eschewing any "Old Stock" nativism characteristic of previous reform groups, the MVL managed to become one of the biggest success stories of the Progressive Era.[83]

Like the populists, the MVL sought to combat civic corruption and to restore sound business principles. It also desired greater regulatory powers for city government over the utility companies. Yet MVL members maintained a strong faith in private utilities. Franchise negotiations with the companies—undertaken by honest politicians guided by transportation experts—ought to be conducted on sound business principles in order to secure the city's interest. Behind this regulatory argument stood a notion of political participation different from that of the populists. As much as possible, decisions over transportation ought to be made by professional experts whose decisions would be merely rubber-stamped by city hall and the electorate. Thus, the MVL had no intention of furthering popular democracy; rather, the (politically educated) masses were simply to approve candidates whose honesty and effectiveness had previously been screened to the standards of the league's experts. As urban reformer Edwin Burritt Smith noted: "there is no attempt by the League to keep up the usual pretense of direct representation of its constituency. It assumes that character and capacity are the fundamental qualifications for useful public service."[84]

Middle-class reform and populist movements continued to center on the question of municipal ownership. In 1899 former governor John Peter Altgeld decided to run for mayor of Chicago and placed municipal ownership at the center of his campaign. Employing the anti-monopoly arguments put forth earlier by the People's Party and demanding a fare reduction of one cent, Altgeld enjoyed strong backing from Chicago's German community, including the Platt Deutsche Gilde von der Waterkant No. 42, the German American Colony Association, and several Turner leagues. The populist Lloyd and labor lawyer Darrow also endorsed his ticket.[85]

Meanwhile, party regulars had taken notice of the new wave of reform politics, including Democrat Carter Harrison II, son of the recently assassinated long-term Chicago mayor, Carter Harrison. With regard to transit politics, Harrison ran a middle course between the radicalism of the Altgeld populists and the sound business approach of the MVL. He ran for mayor in 1897 on a platform that vowed to secure the city's interest during any negotiations with the utility companies and promised to veto all attempts to extend Yerkes's franchises under the Allen law. In line with calls for greater public regulatory powers, Harrison asked the city council to form a special committee on street railway franchises. Composed of leading spokesmen on traction reform, the committee proved the first of a series of municipal agencies that forced the companies to open their financial ledgers and operations to public scrutiny. Unlike Altgeld, who was firmly committed to municipal ownership, Harrison proved willing to negotiate with the streetcar companies under certain conditions, and he paid only occasional lip service to the possibility of a future municipal takeover of the streetcar lines. And unlike the ex-governor, Harrison was firmly backed by Democratic regulars. Partly for these reasons, in 1899, Harrison had little trouble in defeating Altgeld, who finished a distant third, and Harrison managed to get reelected for two additional tenures, until 1905, and again in 1911.[86]

Altgeld's municipal-ownership stance, like earlier ones by the People's Party, thus fared poorly. Despite his popular acclaim as Yerkes's chief rival, his constituency remained small. As his cofighter Darrow noted, with his characteristic sarcasm: "although there was one meeting in a large hall or armory that ran for twenty-four hours . . . [with] the 'Amens' . . . as vigorous at the end as at the start, . . . the same footsore and weary would travel from one end of the city to another and attend meetings night after night." Only a few "weird-looking idealists and worshippers—the poorly clad, the ill-fed, the unemployed, [and] the visionaries gazing off toward the rainbow," in Darrow's assessment, continued to follow Altgeld.[87] Prospects for a radical solution to the streetcar problem apparently vanished from the political scene.

By the dawn of the twentieth century, the streetcar was deeply implanted as an object of Chicago politics. Providing the central means of physical mobility within the metropolis, regarded as a main tool of social improvement and reform, and associated with the nature of urban government and democracy, the streetcar generated a series of debates revolving around service provision: how to alleviate poverty and urban congestion, how to revive a civic consciousness, and how to fight political corruption. This generated a certain consensus on the need to redefine the public regulation of mass transit and other urban services. Settlement reformers and planners, trade unions, ethnic civic organizations, even the city's business elite (excepting Charles Yerkes himself), all agreed on the need for a reform of the franchise system. For the moment, it appeared that populist demands for a municipal takeover had lost their political viability and that the MVL's good-government approach and Harrison's pragmatism had won the day. But both these political responses reflected an important new feature in Chicago's political culture: the inclusion in the public sphere of new political agents such as workers, homeowners, and consumers. In short, a new era of mass politics had dawned in Chicago. By 1902 a new and powerful player would give a radical meaning to that democratic opening: the city's trade unions.

THE MOVEMENT FOR MUNICIPAL OWNERSHIP

Come you, cartoonist,

Hang on a strap with me here

At seven o'clock in the morning

On a Halsted street car

—Carl Sandburg, "Halsted Street Car"

Union Labor is almost unanimous in favor of municipal ownership, but this is

not a class issue. It is the business of the community as a whole.

—*Labor Advocate,* February 1905

Carl Sandburg's portrayal of a morning streetcar riding along Halsted Street (see page 2) is a testimony to the author's empathy for the downtrodden, for the factory girl with loose cheeks, and for a laboring class doing its job, on the brink of exhaustion and devoid of ideals.[1] Whereas the Chicago poet acknowledges the presence of workers in this public space, the CFL's monthly organ, the *Labor Advocate*, affirms their voice in the political debate over their operation. In the declaration by the *Advocate,* (unionized) workers are the subjects, not the objects. They are workers who not only ride the streetcars but also advocate a specific policy regarding the management of this urban service:

municipal ownership. In so doing, they are anything but "Tired of wishes, / Empty of Dreams."

In the early 1900s the new trade unionism under CFL leadership confronted head-on the politics of the streetcars. The "people's" defeat of the franchise maneuvers of streetcar entrepreneur Charles T. Yerkes and the latter's flight from the city in 1899 hardly calmed the waters. Numerous civic groups joined the CFL in calling for immediate public ownership and operation of the streetcars. The solution proposed by middle-class civic organizations such as the MVL, favoring a moderate regulation of the privately operated streetcars, was thus met with a radical alternative. For the 1905 mayoral election, the municipal-ownership movement launched its own candidate on the Democratic ticket. Moving from grassroots mobilization to partisan politics, this campaign altered the dynamics of transportation politics and of Chicago's political culture as a whole.

The vibrancy of this labor-led movement revealed a fruitful confluence of traditional labor concerns with the city's reform climate. Key groups within organized labor such as the teachers, streetcar workers, and the CFL moved beyond their workplace-related grievances toward the streetcar question, and, as the *Advocate*'s declaration reveals, set out to speak for the "business of the community as a whole."[2] Labor thus combined class-specific strategies with a wider reform outlook. It joined in with a variety of middle-class agents, including settlement reformers, club women, intellectuals, artists such as Sandburg, and William Randolph Hearst's influential yellow page press, all of whom not only proved sympathetic to labor's cause but also accepted, to a certain extent, its proclaimed role as representative for the public interest. Two events proved of major importance in cementing this progressive alliance around the streetcar question: the anthracite coal strike of 1902 in eastern Pennsylvania and the Chicago streetcar strike the following year. The presence of organized labor in Chicago's public sphere altered the dynamics of party politics. By 1903 the CFL-led municipal-ownership movement translated its grassroots energies into partisan politics, opting for the age-old alliance with the Democratic Party, but this time with an important difference. Whereas trade unions had previously allied with party insiders who based their power on a network of ward-based influences, this time they managed to nominate a party outsider who formed part of their own movement: Edward F. Dunne, who would run for mayor in 1905.

THE TEACHERS AND THE BEGINNING OF THE MOVEMENT

To moderate reformers, the intensity of debate over the streetcars during the 1900s came as a surprise. With streetcar-magnate Yerkes and his allies removed from city hall and "honest" politicians put in their place, the reformers felt the public interest had been safeguarded. A city administration operating on "sound business principles" certainly could negotiate new franchises to the liking of the streetcar companies and their customers. The companies had even given up their customary intransigence: in response to a request by city hall's new transportation commission, appointed by Mayor Carter Harrison, they opened their books to public inspection. Thus the cry for the alternative solution, municipal ownership, seemed to moderate reformers at best a utopian plan for the distant future and at worst a move toward socialism. What people really cared about, they claimed, was good service, which would be secured through a swift extension of the franchise agreements, most of them scheduled to expire in 1902.

Instead the traction question provoked "a great and swelling tide of local sentiment in favor of municipal ownership."[3] Faced with the possibility that the companies' franchises would be renewed by a vote of city hall, one group of workers and citizens organized one of Chicago's first citywide petition drives, calling for a public referendum on the franchise extension question for the spring 1902 municipal elections. They made use of the 1901 Referendum Law, which authorized any city of the state to hold referenda on a public policy issue, as long as 25 percent of the electorate demanded it. This group was the CTF, which set out to collect the required one hundred thousand signatures. As instructors of Chicago's children, teachers held a central position within the city's communities, and they were well equipped to undertake a neighborhood-based, personal form of political mobilization. With the aid of their pupils, they circulated petitions to thousands of working-class households. Schoolchildren, one flyer advised, should write the invitations for the meetings and circulate them in their homes. Through numerous school-district-based committees, the teachers organization alone secured sixty thousand signatures in support of the referendum. Always outspoken on public policy questions, especially with regard to urban utilities, the teachers' referendum campaign established the CTF "as much [as] an accepted fact of the business of Chicago now as the Board of Trade, the City Hall, or even the Board of Education itself."[4]

The teachers' anti-corporate campaign received widespread backing from a myriad of ward-, ethnic-, and church-based community organizations, and especially from the CFL. Endorsing the teachers, a citizens and taxpayers meeting assembled at Waveland Avenue Congregational Church requested that the board of education permit the use of school halls for public meetings on the traction issue. Other groups that joined the campaign included a group of "citizens and tax payers of the Eighth Ward," various settlement houses, the Bethany Men's Neighborhood League, and the executive board of the Federation of German Societies of Chicago. The widespread enthusiasm for the teachers' initiative resulted in victory at the polls; in the spring elections of 1902, voters overwhelmingly opposed franchise extensions to the streetcar companies. The press rightfully attributed this turn of events to the teachers, who "through the children and the parents of the children, and their own work secured most of the signatures for this . . . referendum."[5] No wonder that after the 1902 elections, the trustee of the Union Traction Company, Downey, asked School Superintendent Cooley to investigate the teachers union.[6]

The referendum campaign was not the first move undertaken by the teachers against the streetcar companies. When, in 1900, the board of education, referring to the city's lack of revenue, rescinded once again a promised salary increase, the CTF found the culprit in Cook County's public utility companies. Drawing on their own investigations and an 1894 report of the Altgeld administration, the teachers charged the Illinois State Board of Equalization with failing to adequately tax the assets of these franchise holders, six streetcar companies among them.[7] Armed with these findings, CTF leaders Catherine Goggin and Margaret Haley promptly sued the streetcar companies of Chicago, along with other utilities, for back payment of taxes. They won the case. The Illinois Supreme Court obliged the state government to properly assess the five public utility corporations of Chicago for the year 1900; and the litigation resulted in a back payment to the county of $598,000 in July 1902. Although it took the teachers federation several additional court cases, now directed against the board of education (which refused to spend the extra revenue on teachers' salaries), the union eventually gained a pay increase for its members. The teachers transformed a fight over the "bread-and-butter" wage issue into a widely publicized attack on Chicago's streetcar corporations.[8] From there it was only a small step for them to assume a leading role in the municipal-ownership movement. Mobilizing under the slogan of "No [Franchise] Extension for Tax-Evaders," they argued that only a company that paid its due share of taxes to the city had the right to service the city's citizens. Through their tax suits and later petition drives, the teachers became a key element in the nascent municipal-ownership movement.[9]

The teachers perceived direct ties between their activities in the classroom and in city politics. Like many progressive-era reformers, Margaret Haley and her colleagues intertwined their professional understanding with a strong sense of public responsibility. According to Haley, when the teachers decided to sue the utility companies, they were simply applying their daily practice of correcting their pupils' errors in the classroom to the city's fiscal system. There "the teaching mind perceived absurdity in the decrease of public revenue from a given source during the most active years in the development of a city."[10] Teachers were especially prepared to undertake one of the progressive reformers' quintessential activities: the accumulation of data. Thus the teachers' tax investigating committee prided itself with having obtained facts pertaining to the tax evasions.

Moreover, teachers—having to apply and adjust pedagogical principles to their encounters with pupils on a daily basis—felt uniquely equipped to relate abstract principles to practices. Echoing Deweyan pragmatism, teachers were most capable, Haley asserted, of "deal[ing] with a condition as well as a theory."[11]

When the teachers entered the orbit of Chicago politics, they spoke as women and as political outsiders. Teachers were active promoters of women's suffrage, but as long as they were being excluded from the vote, they could attack city hall's fiscal policies as a failure of male politics. Somewhat like a wife chiding her husband, or a teacher her pupil, one teacher criticized "[t]his body of unreliable and obscure men [in city hall]" for having "been a protection to the greed of capital and a detriment to the state and city."[12] The teachers' gender identity facilitated cooperation with female middle-class reformers. The CTF established close ties to the women's club movement, as revealed by its permanent membership of the Illinois Federation of Women's Clubs. It thereby procured the aid of middle-class women in drafting legislation on teacher pensions and in securing women teachers the right to keep their jobs after being married; the teachers corresponded by assisting club women's agenda, such as efforts to raise the age of consent for sexual relations for girls, a measure designed to provide legal protection for victims of sexual assault.[13] Historian Marjorie Murphy rightly points to the working-class nature of the teachers organization and emphasizes the tensions between the club movement and the teachers over the latter's educational policies and their ties to trade unionism. Yet, I would contend—along with historian Maureen Flanagan—that the teachers could cooperate quite effectively with middle-class women reformers, especially on issues related to women's economic, legal, or political status; the teachers themselves considered their relation with the federated women's clubs to be "in every sense profitable and educational." My point is not to impose a working-class or a feminist identity on the teachers but, rather, to emphasize the teachers' multiple positioning as workers, professionals, and women.[14]

For, above all, the teachers explained their work, and their move against the public utility companies in particular, in terms of the civic ideals of the Progressive Era. Consider the following statement published in the *CTF Bulletin:*

> During the tax work, . . . the Federation has held strictly to the non-partisan line . . . and has proven that all citizens can work together for the common good, regardless of sex, race, religious or political convictions. It is the aim of the Federation to emphasize the CONSTRUCTIVE rather than the destructive, ever keeping in view the truth that no part or class of the community can be benefited or injured without affecting the welfare of the whole.[15]

Here, the teachers insist in a nonpartisan political strategy, in keeping with progressives' critique of the corrupt practices within the party system. They also put forth the fundamental aim of their engagement: the pursuit of the common good, which in the last instance stands above the interest of any part of the community, whether in terms of class, gender, religion, or otherwise. Rather than consider this a mere rhetorical stand, designed to cloak a "real" class- or gender-based agenda, we should consider it an affirmation of the essence of the progressive ideal. By this logic, the teachers could insert their own work-, gender-, and community-based interests into what they felt was a crucial menace to the good life: the public utility corporation.

LABOR DISPUTES AS CATALYSTS OF THE MOVEMENT

The remarkable public presence of former outsiders such as teachers in the public sphere and their ability to ally themselves with middle-class Chicagoans became especially noticeable during labor disputes. In contrast to past strikes such as the 1900 building trades lockout, several subsequent strikes related to urban service providers received enormous public backing. This remarkable shift in the public's attitude toward organized labor first became apparent in a seemingly unrelated and distant event: the 1902 anthracite coal strike in eastern Pennsylvania involving hundreds of thousands of coal miners. Generally known for prompting the first government-led arbitration proceedings, this strike also affected the political landscape of the city of Chicago.[16]

The news of the strike triggered an astounding wave of trade union solidarity in Chicago. Unions like the teachers and carpenters set up miners relief committees in order to raise funds and public awareness. The 1902 Labor Day parade featured a "money wagon" that collected a "shower of coins" in support of the striking miners; by January 1903, donations had accumulated to a total of thirty-five thousand dollars. And the teamsters relieved the shortage of coal by offering free deliveries, thereby helping to appease potentially disgruntled consumers.[17]

Yet it was the solidarity expressed by a great variety of civic and local organizations that proved most noteworthy, a phenomenon particularly apparent among the city's ethnic communities. Bohemians, for example, collected funds for the miners during lodge meetings and entertainments, and in the factories. The German Turners (ethnic associations organized around gymnastic and other athletic activities but also designed to further a series of community and political issues) and the single-tax clubs set up lectures and fund-raisers on behalf of the miners. Many of Chicago's religious organizations, Irish Catholic parishes among them, backed the coal miners as well. For example, Chicago's carpenters union organized an interdenominational meeting in aid of the miners.[18] Settlement reformers sided firmly with the miners although they were uneasy about endorsing strike action, which they felt violated industrial harmony. Jane Addams, along with her colleague Graham Taylor, considered the event a just struggle of workers against an unrelenting company, not without applauding the strikers' "wonderful self-control." At a mass meeting organized by Addams, Taylor, trade unionists, and others, "a choir of over a thousand voices" performed a newly composed "Song of the Miners." Recalling this and other actions, Taylor wrote: "Chicago was never more a unit than in the favorable attitude toward the miners taken by rich and poor, in press and pulpit, club, shop, and office."[19]

What enabled settlement reformers to endorse the Pennsylvania strike and to celebrate the unity in the city had to do with Chicagoans' anxieties over a threat closer to home: the business practices of the streetcar corporations. The backers of the miners drew direct parallels between the anthracite coal companies in the eastern state and the traction companies in Chicago. Both constituted private monopolies that unduly controlled "natural" essential commodities: fuel and mass transit. According to the CTF, the anthracite strike provided "a concrete illustration of the other equally great danger threatening American institutions today, viz: private monopoly of the privilege of public transportation." Thus strike sympathizers demanded that, just as the federal government ought to withdraw the coal companies' charter authorizing extraction of natural resources, the city of Chicago must cease franchise negotiations with the streetcar companies. Some supporters of the miners went further and called for state control of the respective operations.[20]

Some of the principal players in the coal strike became key actors in the traction debate. The two leading figures in Chicago's campaign for the anthracite miners, Henry D. Lloyd and Clarence Darrow, played an equally prominent role in the movement for municipal ownership. Lloyd, who had led the attacks against streetcar entrepreneur Yerkes's franchise abuses in the 1890s, served as the attorney for the miners union on the arbitration board and published a broadside against the streetcar companies. Darrow, his colleague on the arbitration board, enjoyed great popularity because of his successful negotiations on behalf of the strikers, and Chicagoans elected him to the state legislature on a public-ownership ticket the following November.[21] Later, Darrow would work as an attorney for municipal-ownership advocates and would serve as the mayor's traction advisor.

The cross-class support of the anthracite miners has received, at best, a mixed blessing from labor historians, who point to the ambivalent nature of the victory enjoyed by the anthracite miners (thanks to the intervention of President Theodore Roosevelt). While the United Mine Workers secured a wage increase, they also had to agree to adhere to certain "legitimate" trade union practices such as refraining from sympathy strike actions. The compromise forged in this agreement—toleration of trade unions in exchange for their adherence to narrow job-based goals—would form the basis of the industrial conciliation work of the NCF during the next several years. Arguing that these agreements placed new straightjackets on union labor and pushed it toward an exclusive and elitist organizing style, historians have denounced the virtues of cross-class cooperation of the NCF and, by implication, of the Progressive Era in general. They rightly point out that many who supported the anthracite miners' cause were less interested in strengthening trade unionism as such than they were in pacifying working-class militancy.[22]

In Chicago, however, the broad mobilization behind the anthracite miners forged a political momentum that challenged the regulatory reform vision of the Chicago Civic Federation, the local founding branch of the NCF. Many middle-class reformers in Chicago recognized labor's need to maintain a broad organizational base through measures of intertrade solidarity, including sympathy strikes. They considered trade unions legitimate representatives not only of their constituents' immediate interests but also of their broader civic ones. Moreover, working- and middle-class reformers shared a broad common ground in their agenda of fighting the public-utility corporations.

This confluence of consumer- and worker-related concerns found its greatest expression in the 1903 streetcar strike, which brought into focus a variety of arguments directed against the railway companies. As during the anthracite strike a year before, the work-related demands of strikers blended with widespread anti-corporate sentiments; only this time the adversary was to be found right in Chicago: the streetcar company. For several weeks, the conflict on the public stage—especially the city's downtown streets—displayed popular resentments over the company's labor policies, its provision of streetcar service, and its corrosive political effects. Drawing a direct connection between the company's exploitation of its employees and its customers, trade unionists and their allies advocated a public takeover and prompted the municipal-ownership movement to emerge as a major political force in the city.

One day in early November 1903, a streetcar motorman, fifty-five years of age, reported to work as usual at 5 a.m. He worked his regular eleven-hour day, but because of the split-time work schedule, he did not finish until midnight. With no cars available at nighttime to take him back home and knowing he would have to report again in five hours, the motorman decided, as he often did, to sleep in the car barn instead. This was not an unusual experience, for a motorman's working day could last up to nineteen hours. What did prove unusual in this case was that burglars entered the barn and killed this married father of five children. Chicago's press reported widely on the case, and trade unions were quick to blame the man's death on the company and the excessive working hours it imposed on him.[23]

For at least one year now, a recently formed union of streetcar motor-men and conductors had been negotiating with its employer, the Chicago Railway Company. The length of the working day and workers' right to have a say in the scheduling of cars were the main points debated. The Chicago Railway Company operated the streetcars of the downtown and South Side regions of the city and, along with the Union Traction Company, was Chicago's main streetcar operator. The company included among its stockholders several prominent Chicago businessmen such as department store owner Marshall Field and meat-packer Phillip D. Armour, and it adopted a particularly hostile stand toward trade unionism. Unlike its competitors, the company still refused to recognize the union and readily dismissed the workers' list of grievances: low wages, excessive working days, and harassment by company overseers. When, on November 9, 1903, negotiations over working hours failed once again, the company's car men and conductors voted almost unanimously in favor of a strike.[24]

Three days later, all of the twenty-five hundred employees walked out, causing streetcar service to come to a virtual halt. The company's attempt to use scabs was met with the solidarity of other trade unions, most notably the teamsters, who unhitched the horses from their wagons and left their carts on the rail tracks blockading any streetcar traffic. Teamsters also boycotted deliveries to the Chicago Railway Company, thereby depriving it of fuel for its electric generators and food for its replacement workers. Some teamsters gave rides to stranded trolley passengers; coal wagons filled with office girls proved a common sight. Within a few days of the walkout, the railway company's firemen, stationary engineers, and blacksmiths joined in solidarity with their striking colleagues. The following day, the company's linemen, dynamo-switchboard operators, machinists, and horseshoers followed suit. The CFL levied two special strike assessments on all affiliated trade unions. And the Amalgamated Streetcar Men's Union collected $1.25 per week from each member (the equivalent of a tenth of the weekly income), thereby contributing $8,500 per week to the strikers' cause. The strike committee published a daily strike bulletin.[25]

Given that most of the Chicago Railway Company's lines operated in the city's South Side, a region dominated by industrial districts such as Packingtown, the strike directly involved the residents of mainly working-class neighborhoods. On November 13, for example, fifteen thousand people blockading the South Side's streets stalled attempts by the company to operate cars with strikebreakers. Stockyard workers released flocks of sheep onto the tracks; schoolchildren at Hendricks School left their classroom in protest when they observed their teacher riding in a scab car. "Hack loads" of women residents among the crowds approached strikebreakers in the hope of converting them to labor's cause by more or less coercive means; "the word 'scab' coming from the lips of a pretty girl was worse than a brick from a striker," the *Record-Herald* wrote. Journalists delighted in describing physical attacks by women; one said Katie Quinn led a crowd to attack strikebreakers, shouting "Come on boys, we'll fix 'em. Who's afraid?"[26] The neighborhood crowds and the teamsters would have halted all streetcar traffic had it not been for the intervention of Chicago's police. Mayor Harrison, until then always adopting a tough rhetoric against the streetcar companies, now found himself authorizing the protection of the company's operations by the police. Within days of the strike's outbreak, he stationed hundreds of policemen along the nine-mile car route and ordered an additional battalion to ride on the cars. Notwithstanding the crowds' insults and flying bricks, the police proved able to protect the strikebreakers and the company's property.[27]

Yet these measures to break the strike proved ineffective in the face of a widespread public boycott of the Chicago Railway Company. The only passengers on the cars were the police and a few daring journalists. As many as three hundred thousand riders expressed their sympathies with the strikers by walking or hitching a ride. Settlement house residents provided the strikers with meeting places, spoke at their mass meetings, and advertised the public boycott of the car lines. Even the literary bastion of anti-unionism, the *Tribune*, published addresses to which donations to striking families could be sent. As the Swedish paper, *Svenska Nyheter*, admonished: "Every just and clear thinking citizen must of necessity line up on the side of the workers in the present case."[28]

Greatly inconvenienced by the strike, passengers of all social backgrounds blamed the company rather than the workers for the crisis. For the workers managed to tie their central demand, the reduction of the workday for streetcar motormen, to the public interest in safer transportation. Thus, organized labor attacked the company for failing to "alleviate the stress that is placed upon the motormen and conductors." The company's attempts to blame accidents on the irresponsibility of its drivers were generally dismissed; not the motorman himself, critics charged, but the long hours of work imposed by the company were to blame. In a show of political support of the strikers, the city council resolved that the "cars shall be run by men alert, fresh, vigorous, and not overworked." The central committee of Cook County's German American Democrats even requested the council to impose a legal limit of eight hours on the streetcar operator's workday.[29] (The council also appointed a special committee on municipal ownership.) Furthermore, the company's refusal to submit the dispute to arbitration raised the ire of middle-class reformers such as Graham Taylor, who, especially after the recent anthracite strike, upheld industrial conciliation as the means of achieving harmony between the classes. In a case that affected an essential public service such as transportation, refusal to negotiate was even less acceptable. Even MVL president George

Sikes, generally hostile toward trade unionism, insisted that "a public service corporation . . . ought to stand ready to arbitrate any question that threatens interference with service."[30]

In the end, organized labor successfully represented the streetcar company as the exploiter of both workers and passengers as well as the general public. Charging excessive fares and paying insufficient wages, this "grasping corporation," one union local stated, was harassing and robbing "the citizens while enslaving and starving its employees." In a similar vein, the CFL claimed that the company operated its cars "purely to see how many nickels can be extorted from the people to satiate the greed of men who have no higher consideration for the working class than to consider them a part of the machinery they operate." The labor dispute waged on Chicago's streets thus became a public concern, for not only did the company move its cars with police protection but did so, as the *Tribune* put it, "with no rights in the streets," that is, with no legitimate franchise issued by city government.[31]

During the conflict, municipal ownership lurked as the solution. According to trade unionists, only a publicly run system would improve the conditions of labor, guarantee good and affordable service, and return control over the streets to Chicago's citizens. Under municipal ownership, CFL delegates declared, the profits that resulted from "the operation of the cars upon our highways" would be returned to the citizens of Chicago, in form of better service, reduced fares, and "decent wages to the men who perform the duties as public servants." A publicly operated system would also prevent future strikes and free up the police to fight the real menace to society. As the Swedish paper *Svenska Nyheter* put it: "If the streetcars belonged to the people, we would have no streetcar strike these days, and the policemen of the city would find time to protect the citizens and their homes from those parasites who resemble the corporations." Finally, municipal ownership was presented as the best medicine to cure the ill of corruption. According to the city council's special committee on municipal ownership, corruption continued to thrive in the private utility system, notwithstanding the MVL's campaign to staff the council with impeccable aldermen. In publicly operated services such as Chicago's municipally owned electric light plant, politicians found it far more difficult to procure appointments for their friends. Therefore, the committee affirmed, "the moral and governmental argument" was the strongest justification of municipal ownership.[32]

During the strike, municipal-ownership advocates took their cause to the streets, thus broadening the struggle over "the control of our highways" from an industrial matter to a political one. While trolley workers were picketing, rumors spread of an impending franchise extension vote by the city council. "LABOR TO INVADE CITY HALL," the *Tribune's* headline read on November 14, 1903. Thousands of people followed the call of the CFL, "to go in a body to the Legislative meetings of our City Fathers, and protect them if need be from being drawn into the clutches of these interlopers." The shouts of municipal-ownership advocates forced an end to the council's session.[33] Referring to the imminent expiration of the company's franchise, some councilmen formally inquired by what right the Chicago City Railway Company was operating its streetcars and whether it was appropriate for the city police to be escorting streetcars operated by strike-breakers.[34] The strike witnessed other mass meetings. On November 22, fifteen thousand people paraded through the streets carrying "no-extension-of-franchises" banners along with American flags. Marching from all directions, they gathered in downtown Tattersall's Hall, where crowds sang municipal-ownership songs and wore "M. O. Now" buttons while denouncing Harrison's police force. Trade unionists highlighted their insistence on direct democracy by entertaining innovative "lobbying" strategies. Four o'clock wake-up rallies at the houses of pro-company aldermen were not unusual occurrences. From now on, trade unionists argued, city hall negotiations with the companies would be monitored directly by the public, and the CFL set up a public safety committee for that very purpose.[35]

Trade union solidarity, the backing of the strikers by working-class communities and consumers, and labor's ability to tie the event to the rising sentiment in favor of a public takeover turned the strike into a full-fledged victory for the streetcar workers. After a week of running empty cars and facing insults in the streets, in city hall, and in the press, the company agreed to mediate the dispute through the mayor's arbitration board. It rehired all strikers, and although officially refusing closed-shop conditions and declining to grant the union control over the routing of cars, in effect it recognized the union.[36]

THE MOVEMENT'S ENTRANCE INTO CHICAGO POLITICS

As the dust of the strike settled, the *Tribune* expressed its hope that the momentum for municipal ownership would also cease. But what was essentially a grassroots campaign now moved into formal party politics. Organized labor turned away from its traditional allies, the Democratic Party and Mayor Carter Harrison II, and attempted an independent political strategy. In doing so, it helped transform the city's partisan political landscape. The CFL's break with Harrison was a direct result of the mayor's use of the police during the streetcar strike. A broad section of the CFL, most especially the independent-minded teamsters and teachers, had never backed Harrison, but now even the CFL's old guard, including the building trades, became skeptical. Throughout the strike, the CFL and its affiliates condemned Harrison's orders permitting the police to ride on the "scab-operated" streetcars.[37] Such assistance to the utility company served to undermine Harrison's credibility as an anti-corporate crusader. Rather than work for a public takeover as promised, the mayor, according to the iron-workers union, was "putting this City in a state of siege to bolster up a private monopoly of the public streets."[38] The *Arbeiterzeitung* issued a prophetic warning to Harrison: "the way you acted, you are politically dead. No matter how this streetcar strike ends, you will never be re-elected for office." By the spring of 1904, the CFL had placed Harrison on its Unfair List.[39]

Harrison also failed to keep pace with the radical turn of public sentiment in favor of streetcar municipalization. Ever since the traction issue erupted in 1897, he attempted to ride the tide of public outrage over the streetcar companies. Yet the Democrat remained ambivalent at best. Although he continually vetoed franchise extension plans in the 1890s, he took few concrete steps in pursuit of a city purchase. Worse, from the perspective of municipal-ownership advocates, in 1903 and 1904 he indicated his willingness to support the franchise extension plans worked out by the city's transportation committee, which was negotiating with the companies. Operating within a partisan patronage system, Harrison also proved reluctant to endorse measures of direct popular expression, as put forth by the CTF, for example. Although he approved public referenda in principle, he imposed such early deadlines for the submission of petitions as to render them virtually meaningless. He allowed less than a month to collect the signatures required to place the franchise extension question onto the November 1904 ballot; as a result, the issue did not appear on the ballot until the following spring. In the eyes of the Referendum League and many trade unions, Harrison in fact was an obstacle to direct democracy.[40]

Capitalizing on the dissatisfaction with Harrison and the Democratic Party, reform-minded labor leaders spun their own political network across the city's neighborhoods and class lines. At a mass meeting held during the streetcar strike, ironworker delegate Robert G. Wall admonished his audience of workers to join the trade union ward clubs: "Carter Harrison has taught you more in one minute than we have been able to teach you in fifteen years, that you are [politically] unorganized, blind, ignorant, and deceived."[41] Labor reformers like Wall or the cigar makers' leader George Thompson proposed the creation of clubs set up in each city ward or school district, with meetings to be held in public school buildings. These club meetings were to provide a forum of lectures and discussions of civic and educational matters. Chicago trade unions thereby wished to establish a ward-based setting, equivalent to the citywide Chicago Federation of Labor, in order to discuss urban- and neighborhood-based questions and further transcend their trade-based organizational structure. The stated purpose of the ward clubs included a job-related agenda, namely, to defend against "employer aggression," but they were designed mainly to pursue municipal ownership and the popular election of the school board.[42] Civic groups outside the labor movement united with trade unions in the Municipal Ownership Delegate Convention (MODC), which became the leading public organ of the movement and claimed to represent over 250,000 voters. Trade unionists dominated the convention, but representatives of the German Turners, ward-based civic organizations, the Municipal Ownership League, single-tax leagues, and the Referendum League were also seated.[43]

During 1903 and 1904, the CFL ward clubs and the delegate convention undertook an aggressive political campaign on behalf of immediate municipal ownership of the streetcars. Emulating the MVL endorsement policy, for the 1904 spring elections they backed candidates who were committed to their platform. Public-ownership activists managed to get twelve of the thirty endorsees elected, with most of the successful candidates running in working-class wards of the Near West Side and the industrial river districts. (In contrast, returning aldermen who lacked approval by the MODC but were certified by the MVL came from outlying wards.)[44] During the same election, the MODC also organized a petition drive allowing voters to express in overwhelming numbers their opposition to the proposed streetcar franchise, as well as their approval by a five-to-one majority of the Mueller law. This bill issued by the Illinois state legislature authorized the city to issue bonds for the financing of a municipal purchase of the streetcars. Finally, a large majority of voters requested that the city council "proceed without delay to acquire ownership of the street railways."[45]

In the process of campaigning for public ownership, the referendum became a firmly established practice of political expression. Only two years after the teachers' first petition drives, no political decisions of major significance, whether related to mass transit or other matters, could be made without prior majority approval. In 1905, for example, the city council gave in to the continued vigilance of municipal-ownership activists and passed a resolution that rendered franchise extensions subject to prior popular approval. During the next few years, the CFL and the MODC also raised demands for the popular initiation of legislation and the recall of elected officials. The movement applied the principle of unmediated democracy to its own ranks as well. The CFL ward clubs, for example, were "to proceed along lines of simplicity and comradeship . . . rather than by a system of complex officialdom," a structure that would allow the unleashing of a "free exercise of energy" by its members. Even opponents of the referendum did not dare to openly oppose it; instead they sought to make the process more difficult, for example by raising the number of signatures required for placing a referendum on the ballot.[46]

A public eager to impose direct democratic control required public spaces in which to express its opinions. Municipal-ownership advocates sought to open schools, government buildings, and streets to popular participation. The teachers' demand that schools be made accessible to public gatherings was repeatedly rejected by the board of education. Likewise, trade unionists wanted the public to have access to all city hall proceedings, including closed committee sessions, and especially the transportation committee, which they considered held a moral as well as a legal obligation to open its doors to public scrutiny.[47]

With the 1905 mayoral elections approaching, the question became how to translate the municipal-ownership movement's grassroots energy into partisan politics. Should the MODC back an independent candidate for mayor or should it try to nominate a pro-municipal-ownership man on the Democratic ticket? The poor experiences with an independent strategy during the previous mayoral election in 1903 hardly encouraged a third-party approach. During that campaign several trade union locals had unsuccessfully nominated Clarence Darrow as mayoral candidate on a United Labor ticket.[48] Darrow, serving as legal representative of the United Mine Workers during the anthracite strike, acquired a reputation as a friend of organized labor, and he also championed municipal ownership. Yet, only weeks prior to the election, upon the advice of Henry D. Lloyd and national labor leaders Samuel Gompers and John Mitchell, Darrow suddenly annulled his candidacy and endorsed Harrison. Thereafter headed by a lesser-known candidate, the United Labor Party received a bare 3 percent of the votes.[49]

Despite this precedent, and many earlier ones, it appeared as if the movement in January 1905 would opt again for a third-party ticket. Boosted in confidence by their successes in the 1904 election and referenda, MODC and CFL delegates nominated William B. Prentiss on an independent mayoral ticket. A former schoolteacher from Iowa, Prentiss was serving as circuit court judge in Cook County when he became widely known for his campaign against the undervaluation of public utility companies' holdings. The MODC chairman also enjoyed the backing of Chicago's Hearst press.[50]

Prentiss's campaign came to an abrupt halt, however, when the widely respected Judge Murray F. Tuley, who served as a circuit court judge from 1879 until his death in 1905, instead proposed his colleague Edward F. Dunne for mayor. In a widely publicized letter, Judge Tuley, an Altgeld Democrat known for his favorable attitude toward trade unions, posited Dunne as the only man who could save Chicago's inhabitants from the traction interest, this "great corporate combination, engineered from Wall Street." Moreover, Tuley encouraged Dunne to run on the Democratic ticket and alerted municipal-ownership activists to the futility of an independent candidacy.[51]

With an endorsement by the eminent "Nestor of the Chicago bar," Dunne moved to the forefront of the Democratic nomination. Harrison, sensing his growing unpopularity, as early as November 1904 declined to run again. At a convention in Bricklayers' Hall in mid-February, the MODC, the Turner societies, and single-tax organizations endorsed Dunne, while Prentiss resigned his candidacy and backed the Irishman. At the February Democratic Party Convention, delegates unanimously endorsed Dunne as their mayoral candidate. Dunne's main agenda was the immediate acquisition and operation of the streetcars by the city.[52]

Never before had labor leaders involved themselves so closely with the candidacy of a mayoral candidate running on the ticket of one of the main two parties. After briefly hesitating over abandoning Prentiss, most trade union leaders came out in favor of the Irishman. Many recalled the judge's favorable rulings on behalf of labor, as well as his support of the third-party effort in 1903. CFL leaders including John Fitzpatrick and Margaret Haley joined Dunne's campaign. The head of the Municipal Ownership League, T. P. Quinn, a former anarchist, Knights of Labor member, and boyhood foe of T. R. Roosevelt, also backed Dunne's candidacy.[53] Trades like the teamsters and printers set up an E. F. Dunne Workingmen's Club, which counted over one hundred thousand members, to back the man who had "never issued an injunction against striking workers."[54] Dunne held especially close ties to the CTF. As a judge in the circuit court, Dunne had ruled repeatedly in favor of the teachers' tax and salary suits and their efforts to allocate educational funds for wage increases. Haley, a personal friend of Dunne, was particularly impressed by "his kindly humanitarianism, . . . finely balanced judicial sense, and twinkling love of a joke."[55] Although running on the Democrat ticket, Dunne was a virtual labor candidate.

Dunne also received strong support from Chicago's female reform community. In response to the advice of "the venerable and much-loved Judge Murray F. Tuley," members of the Chicago Women's Club formed the Women's Municipal Ownership League specifically designed to work on behalf of Dunne. The league comprised lawyers, doctors, and civic reformers, including Cornelia De Bey, a medical doctor and educational reformer who had acquired prominence in settling the 1904 stockyards strike, the lawyer Nellie Carlin, and Mrs. Louis F. Post, the wife of the single-taxer and Chicago-based publisher. One thousand members strong, the Women's Municipal Ownership League helped make Dunne, who also was a personal friend of Jane Addams, more palatable to Chicago's middle class. For example, its meetings were frequented by Joseph Medill Patterson, then editor and later publisher of the *Chicago Tribune,* real estate lawyer George Wm. Warvelle, and economist John Z. White.[56]

Dunne was backed by Chicago's ethnic communities and by key political ward bosses also. As an Irishman, an observant Roman Catholic, a graduate of Trinity College in Dublin, and the father of thirteen children, he represented the values of Chicago's Irish community.[57] Still, the Irish press employed political rather than ethnic arguments in backing the Democrat. *The Citizen,* Chicago's leading Irish paper, praised Dunne's uncompromising opposition to the "inefficient and disagreeable traction system" and his firm commitment to municipal ownership. On the Northwest Side, an area dominated by German and Irish American families, fifteen local "improvement clubs" unanimously endorsed Dunne. Other ethnic groups, like the Bohemians and the Germans, combined arguments of class and ethnicity. The Bohemian Municipal Ownership League and the Bohemian paper *Denni Hlasatel* regarded Dunne as a defender of "the weak and oppressed against the powerful privileged class," as well as a guarantor of its ethnic interests. The German Turners, actively involved in the municipal-ownership campaign for years, also backed him.[58] Dunne could not have been nominated without support from Democratic regulars. Largely out of hostility to Harrison, two of the notorious ward bosses still in city hall, "Bathhouse" John Coughlin and Michael "Hinky Dink" Kenna, pledged to aid their fellow Irishman. In return Dunne, much to the chagrin of good-government reformers and of some of his own followers, endorsed Kenna for alderman in the first ward. Dunne's ties to long-standing Democratic ward bosses remained tenuous, however, a fact that was to haunt him during his tenure as mayor.[59]

On the brink of political success, the municipal-ownership candidate moderated his rhetoric in order to avoid association with radicalism. For the idea of a labor-backed mayor wishing to place one of the main investments in the city's service industry under government ownership generated considerable anxiety among Chicago's business community. "Eugene V. Debs himself," the *Chronicle* stated, "could not be more enthusiastic in his opposition to the capitalistic classes." Dunne thus set out to stress practical, service-oriented aspects and moved away from what might be perceived as an anti-business stand. He focused on the financial feasibility of a municipal takeover of the streetcar companies and promoted the municipal bonds, authorized by the Mueller law, which would pay for the acquisition. Like many U.S. progressives, Dunne found inspiration in European municipal reform and frequently cited its successes. He was especially impressed by the municipal railway system in Glasgow, Scotland, whose general manager, on the advice of Cleveland reform mayor Tom Johnson, he would eventually invite to Chicago. To Dunne, the European experience demonstrated that municipally operated streetcars resulted in a series of immediate benefits: reduced fares, improved service, less corruption, and fewer strikes. Labor leaders also emphasized service-oriented points. While arguing that a municipal streetcar system would increase wages and reduce employees' hours, they echoed Dunne's call for needed service improvements and the elimination of graft.[60]

Dunne's moderate language reflected a growing acceptance of the possibility of municipal ownership. Dunne's opponent in the mayoral race, Republican John Maynard Harlan, paid lip service to public ownership. Harlan also entered the race as a party outsider. During the last decade, he had made himself a name as a moderate anti-Yerkes traction reformer. He ran for mayor on an independent ticket in 1897 and became widely known for leading Chicago's first governmental investigation of its public utility corporations, the so-called Harlan Report of 1898. Unlike Dunne, Harlan preferred to retain utility corporations in private hands and wanted to use the threat of a public purchase as a mere bargaining tool in negotiations with the companies.[61] Yet during the course of the campaign, he moved toward an outright endorsement of a municipal takeover and differentiated himself from his opponent merely by claiming that Dunne's plan was too hasty and unrealistic. On this ground, Dunne held the advantage as the more principled fighter. Even Chicago's leading business journal, *The Economist*, considered it "refreshing to have a man with a purpose in the lead. For many years past, there has been no leadership." His opponent, the journal lamented, changed his position too many times.[62]

On April 2, 1905, Dunne's grassroots-turned-partisan movement for municipal ownership prevailed over the Republican Harlan, even though the latter was backed by most newspapers, employer organizations, and the traditional civic reform organizations. The Irishman was elected mayor of Chicago by a majority of 24,000 votes, from a total of 322,000 voters. By an even greater margin, voters disapproved of franchise extensions to the streetcar companies. In the so-called slum wards close to downtown and the industrial districts immediately west of the Chicago River, the voting was exceptionally high for the Democratic candidate, though in every single ward of the city an overwhelming majority voted against the franchises.[63] Dunne's election signaled the success of a popular insurgency against the traction companies with origins that began during the previous decade. By the early 1900s, largely through the initiatives of Chicago trade unions, the once marginal call for a public takeover became the winning campaign issue of a mayor. The stage appeared to be set for a municipal takeover in the nation's Second City.

THE DEMOCRATIC IDEALS OF THE MOVEMENT

The municipal-ownership movement in Chicago reflected a variety of developments, both old and new. It certainly was rooted in a nineteenth-century republican anti-monopoly tradition and, in that sense, grew out of an urban variant of 1890s populism. Like the Chicago People's Party's attacks on Yerkes, municipal-ownership advocates characterized the streetcar companies as parasitical, eastern-based monopolies trying to strangle Chicago and its people. This rhetoric did good service in uniting a broad constituency behind the cause, as trolley workers, streetcar riders, and local businesses suffered from the "money sharks of Wall Street." The CFL defined the problem in geographic black-and-white terms: either "we protect *home industry* and preserve the rights and privileges of our citizens or . . . [we] grant the control of our highways and the privilege of placing our citizens in bondage to *outside extortionists.*"[64]

Yet the public-ownership campaign formed part of an urban-centered twentieth-century vision of reform. It encompassed an enlarged understanding of the public interest, included a broader social basis of those seeking to defend it, and insisted on direct forms of democratic representation. By the time of Dunne's election as mayor, most Chicagoans agreed that the city's transportation network constituted a common good, which, whether private or publicly operated, required governmental surveillance. A broad cross section of city residents, including trade unionists, left-wing political groups, middle-class social reformers, intellectuals, and professional experts also coincided in thinking that private corporations left to themselves would not work to uphold the common good and that, therefore, certain regulatory mechanisms were required.

This new concern over the need to uphold the public interest resulted directly from the political mobilization of new social agents: especially the city's trade unionists. Throughout the nineteenth century, organized labor had attempted, albeit sporadically and usually not for long, to form political parties, but it had not entered into general public discussions going beyond its job-related concerns. The story of the municipal-ownership movement is, above all, the account of a newly politicized trade unionism. At the same time, women from both working-class and middle-class backgrounds spoke out on public affairs to an unprecedented extent. Chicagoans spoke increasingly from the standpoint of the consumer, in this case the streetcar rider. The public sphere expanded in a physical sense also, given that Chicago's streets became battlegrounds, hosting fights not only over private interests (as, for example, workers and employers) but also over the public interest in industrial peace and in decent transportation. Municipal-ownership advocates insisted that more public places—whether school buildings, downtown streets, or the galleries of city hall—be rendered accessible to the expression of citizens' political concerns.

Some groups were left on the sidelines. For one, the municipal-ownership campaign was almost exclusively a white affair. There are only two glimpses of black participation in the movement. A Negro Democratic Club took part in the 1898 protests against Yerkes, and in 1907, ninety members of Chicago's black community endorsed Democrat Dunne for mayor, but less out of a strong desire for municipal ownership than to send a message of protest to the Republicans, who they felt had taken the African American vote for granted. At the same time, it seems, recent immigrants of southern or eastern European origin played an equally small role, although Polish and Bohemian constituencies did join in with old-stock British, German, and Irish groups.[65] To what extent the municipal-ownership movement reflected a racially based orientation is hard to ascertain. Even though crowds during streetcar strikes may have learned to associate the "traction magnates" with "black scabs," advocates of municipal ownership rarely used racially based argumentation. To be sure, George Hooker did consider the growing sentiment for municipal ownership to be a sign of "racial virility," and he pointed out that the growing tide of public ownership across the Atlantic was "characteristic, not of southern, but of western Europe."[66] Suspicious more for its utter silence on the race question, however, than for outright assertions of white superiority, the public-ownership movement in Chicago was primarily one of white Americans from northern European descent.

The broadly based constituency that did and could engage in the question of public transportation insisted on direct democracy as the key form of political representation. The electoral process by itself was insufficient to assure the enactment of the people's will: "Democracy succeeds, where, and only where, the people never allow their hired men . . . to suppose themselves to be the government," Henry D. Lloyd declared. Likewise, the CFL, echoing the revolutionary pamphleteer Thomas Payne, asserted: "It is only because it is impracticable for the voters to meet together at a given time and place that agents are selected to represent them."[67] Teachers and other trade unionists were the first to introduce the referendum to Chicago politics and, thereby, stressed the need for majority rule even in such complex and vital questions as urban transportation.

At least judging from contemporary observers, Chicago's public sphere constituted a space where ideas over civic matters could be expressed and interchanged freely and in a relatively egalitarian fashion. If not on a socioeconomic level, at least on a cultural level, Chicago reflected a kind of egalitarianism not found in eastern U.S. cities. Here millionaires like Henry D. Lloyd, the public-ownership campaign's most prominent leader, took their "place with the poor and lowly" and became a "prince condescending to be a democrat."[68] Here intellectuals inserted themselves effectively into a democratic revival. Whereas a city like Boston was said to incite intellectuals to such elitist activities as studying "history and literature," in Chicago, intellectuals, whether in the university set, in the social settlements, or in business and professional life, engaged with the kind of radical ideas usually found only in labor circles or in socialistic and anarchistic groups. According to journalist Hutchins Hapgood: "the word 'radical' is a much more respectable word in the Middle West, or at any rate in Chicago, than in the East."[69] Perhaps most astonishing is the role attributed to workers themselves as the originators of civic proposals. Lloyd insisted that ordinary people "have intuitively comprehended what is being pointed out by the latest authorities." Yet, as theologian and settlement reformer Graham Taylor suggests, the workers' contribution went beyond mere intuition: "Workmen voters, far from being ignorantly inconsiderate[,] . . . are practically the only organized bodies of citizens who made any consecutive effort to understand and publicly discuss the [transportation-related] issues involved." Taylor was astonished by the way "They have been threshing out . . . the points of general public policy . . . in every labor union and in open public meetings."[70] In more general terms, Hapgood was impressed "with the way the workingman . . . had imposed his point of view . . . upon the entire community. . . . It is the only big city I know where . . . he has communicated his needs and his ideals to the general community. . . . Take any Chicago personage of importance whatever his profession or his position, and somehow or other he has been influenced by the spirit of the intellectual proletariat."[71] The surge of the municipal-ownership campaign was thus the product of a cultural climate in which a broadly based polity could engage in new ideas over the public interest.

For the time being, members of the middle class like Lloyd, Hapgood, and Taylor celebrated a city where "the elementary virtues and passions of men stand out most prominently."[72] Yet with trade unions at political center stage, the fate of the municipal-ownership campaign would hinge on the perceived legitimacy of organized labor. A massive offensive by employers against one of the key sectors of the urban trade unionism, the teamsters, right after Dunne's election would interrupt labor's honeymoon with the progressive public.

THE 1905 TEAMSTERS STRIKE

The conflict between the property idea of labor and the citizenship idea of labor

presents the supreme issue of this generation.

—John Fitzpatrick

With the headlines of Chicago's press dominated by the news of Dunne's victory for mayor, the outbreak of a strike almost escaped notice.[1] Right after the election, the strongest trade union in the city once again made use of its powerful organizing tool, the sympathy strike: teamsters called on their members to cease all deliveries to Montgomery Ward, one of the largest department stores in the city. The drivers called the boycott in sympathy with the store's garment workers who for months had sought to unionize. Montgomery Ward and other major downtown employers used this incident to provoke a major standoff between management and labor. Through their new organization, the Employers Association (EA), Chicago merchants and some major manufacturers recruited thousands of strikebreakers, incorporated a non-union teaming company, filed injunctions, called for federal troops, and attacked the teamsters union in the press. When organized labor backed the teamsters with equal dedication, Chicago witnessed over the next several months "one of the worst industrial conflicts in . . . its history," a dispute that not only defined the city's labor relations for years to come but also shaped the prospects of radical progressivism in Chicago.[2]

In leading a frontal attack on the teamsters union, employers sought to end a solidaristic, broad-based trade unionism that also formed the backbone for labor's political campaigns in Chicago. Recognizing the strike as a battle of words as much as of pickets and strikebreakers, employers led a direct assault on the public legitimacy of trade unionism. Denouncing the teamsters as corrupt and violent, employers worked to undermine the newly acquired role of trade unions as representatives of the public interest and as forces of reform. This assault on the public image of organized labor would affect not only the outcome of the strike but also the fate of the municipal-ownership movement.

EMPLOYERS PREPARE THEIR ASSAULT ON THE TEAMSTERS

Since the establishment of the teamsters unions and other new locals in 1902, Chicago employers had chafed under the unions' power. With the aid of the teamsters and of CFL president Fitzpatrick, even weak locals, especially those of female workers, could adopt a militant stand. When in May 1903 a laundry employees' local went on strike, backed by the team drivers, it could go so far as to refuse to negotiate with its employer.[3] And public opinion? Employers charged the press with undue bias in favor of labor. Only "one paper," a leading employer lamented, "has the moral courage to come out and state the true facts." Meanwhile, the *Typographical Journal* noted, "the bosses are beginning to wonder whether they hadn't better stay off their high horses instead of mounting and afterward landing with a hard bump." Given a widespread backing for conciliatory solutions to labor disputes, the best an employer could hope for was to enter into arbitration. Indeed, from 1902 to 1904, team owners joined the teamsters unions in setting up arbitration procedures within their industry and thereby came to recognize the workmen as legitimate bargaining agents. Ralph Easley of the NCF, which actively promoted industrial conciliation, was much impressed with the teaming industry's arbitration machinery.[4]

Yet Chicago's major employers considered trade unions' control over wages and hiring practices intolerable. Describing the labor situation as "more pregnant with danger than any this country has known since 1861," Chicago's leading merchants and manufacturers united in 1902 in the Employers Association.[5] Dominant among its founders were employers in the goods and services sector, department store owners, streetcar managers, and meat-packers, those who were particularly dependent on the urban infrastructure and most affected by the new labor militancy. Their main goal was to defeat the use of sympathetic strikes and to retain their right to hire non-union workers in so-called open-shop establishments. The association provided its members with "strike insurance," assisted them in hiring strikebreakers, provided legal aid, and established employment agencies in order to assure the continual provision of non-union labor. That the president of the new association was the former head of the Illinois Arbitration Board, F. W. Job, only affirmed the more confrontational turn taken by employers.[6]

The Employers Association's determination to combat the teamsters proved emblematic of a nationwide offensive against solidaristic trade union practices. The Chicago EA was inspired by an employer association in Dayton, Ohio. In 1902 there emerged the national Citizens' Industrial Association, designed to spread the Dayton and Chicago model across the country. Other open-shop associations formed around given trades, such as the National Erectors' Association and the National Association of Manufacturers. Employers also, in the courts, fought practices of intertrade solidarity such as the boycott and the sympathy strike. The American Anti-Boycott Association, composed mainly by small-scale manufacturers, gained several spectacular victories over organized labor, including the cases of *Loewe vs. Lawler* and *Buck's Stove vs. Gompers*.[7]

The Chicago EA kept a low profile during its first years of existence but then moved to the fore in 1904. By July it had provoked ninety-two strikes and lockouts in the city, most of which proved successful to the association. Its first major confrontation was with Chicago's packinghouse workers, who during the previous years managed to engage in an unprecedented unionization drive in Chicago's notoriously anti-labor meat-packing industry. Defeated by the packer employers, the butcher workmen would not attempt to organize again until 1919 and managed to finally unionize only in the 1930s.[8]

Yet the employers' main target was the organization at the root of the labor trouble: the teamsters. The EA's first move was a clandestine attempt to undermine the teamsters' control over street traffic by secretly constructing an underground freight tunnel system. Publicly claiming to lay telephone cables, the Illinois Telegraph and Telephone Company, in fact, constructed railway tunnels accommodating three thousand steel cars and one hundred electric locomotives. The secret nature of the operation (only later revealed, to public uproar) demonstrated its main purpose: the freight system assured the delivery of coal or general merchandise to downtown buildings even during possible teamster blockades aboveground. "No blockading of streets during a teamsters' strike . . . [and] no promiscuous destruction of merchandise will be possible in the tunnels," employers assured, and "the strike evils with which Chicago is so thoroughly menaced" would be eliminated.[9] Recognizing the politicized nature of the use of Chicago's public thoroughfares, as manifested by the teamsters and by the municipal-ownership movement, employers initially worked from below.

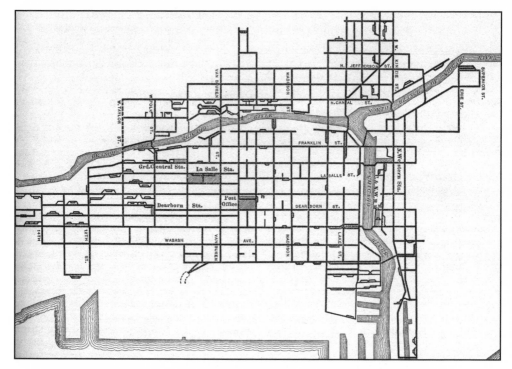

The sixty-two-mile-long tunnel system extended through the Chicago downtown area. Ostensibly designed to lay telephone wires, the tunnels were soon operating railway freight carts that delivered goods such as coal to downtown office buildings.

Electric Railway Journal, October 5, 1912

THE TEAMSTERS STRIKE

Yet in the spring of 1905, employers directed their attention above-ground. Their pretext was the teamsters' sympathy strike with the Montgomery Ward garment workers. This strike had been provoked by the department store's open-shop drive during the previous year, when Ward hired non-union employees in order to weaken the recently unionized women cutters and seamstresses. Responding to calls for aid by the United Garment Workers union, the teamsters' joint council prohibited teamsters from picking up or delivering goods consigned to Montgomery Ward. By April 8, 1905, eight hundred teamsters had followed that call. The EA challenged the teamsters' right to engage in this and any other sympathy strike. A union might have the right to strike in pursuit of its own grievances, the EA argued, but it certainly lacked the right to do so for the bene-

Operated by non-union workers, the freight tunnels were in part designed to literally undermine the power of the on-the-ground teamsters. *Electric Railway Journal,* October 5, 1912

fit of another group of workers. Trade unionists, in turn, defended the sympathy strike as the ultimate expression of labor solidarity: "What brazen effrontery for the Employers Association to tell the teamsters that they cannot go on strike in sympathy with a sister union."[10]

Now firmly organized, employers took unprecedented steps to break the teamsters' stranglehold on the department store. Shortly after the teamsters' declaration of the boycott, Montgomery Ward and the EA resumed deliveries with strikebreakers, who, protected by up to three policemen per car, steered Ward's trolleys through crowds of angry strikers and sympathizers. Professional strikebreaker Levy Meyer was hired by the association to coordinate the recruitment of replacement workers and to arm them with guns. Within a couple of weeks, employers founded an expressly non-union delivery company, capitalized at five hundred thousand dollars, and later at one million dollars. By the end of the month, the firm was operating two thousand teams and employing fifteen hundred drivers.[11] Behind that operation stood most of Chicago's downtown merchants and major manufacturers, all of them EA members.

The conflict soon spread across the city's entire teaming industry. Employers, eager to turn the dispute into a general test case, made the first attempt. Yet, when the EA asked Chicago's teaming companies to require their drivers to deliver goods to the boycotted firm, these refused and continued to do so, even when employers threatened them with a court injunction. Unlike the department stores, the small teaming companies approved of trade unionism as a stabilizing force in a highly competitive industry. At the price of recognizing their drivers' trade unions (and the concomitant increase in labor costs), the teaming enterprises benefited from the teamsters' assurance that they would work only for companies affiliated with their central association, the Allied Teaming Companies. In contrast, large department stores like Montgomery Ward, whose employment of teamsters made up only a small part of their business, lacked interest in such an agreement; all they wished to do was to lower their labor costs.[12]

Finally, it was the teamsters, unable to halt scab-run deliveries to the department store, who escalated the dispute. Any company that continued to ship or receive goods from the downtown Montgomery Ward store, the teamsters joint council boldly declared, would itself face a boycott by the teamsters. Soon, companies daring to engage in business with the department store felt the teamsters' wrath. The E. M. Daniels Coal Company, for example, was forced to hire non-union drivers to continue to deliver fuel to Montgomery Ward. By late April, virtually every business connected with the downtown department store found itself involved in the strike. The conflict spread in other ways as well. Baggage carriers, hotels, and cafes refused to provide their services to strikebreakers arriving from out of town, for example, and the city's cab drivers declined to pick up customers of the department store. By May 1905, five thousand teamsters alone were on strike, not counting the numerous other workers who engaged in these acts of solidarity.[13]

Union labor in Chicago and all across the country understood the high stakes of the strike and solidly backed the teamsters. The CFL alone raised seventy-five hundred dollars a week for the strike fund. During the course of the dispute, it would contribute almost fifty thousand dollars in legal support and strike benefits to the strikers. Over seven hundred different organizations contributed, with carpenters, streetcar conductors, and printers among the most generous donors. Locals from other cities also sent funds; New York City locals, for example, donated almost two thousand dollars a day.[14] Fitzpatrick's CFL published a daily strike bulletin designed to "counteract the capitalist press," organized mass meetings and fundraising picnics, and coordinated sympathetic strike actions. The trade union central even directed a boycott of Chicago's banks; its newly set up special bank committee asked workers to withdraw their savings from those banks that were donating large sums to the EA. How strongly the sting of workers' withdrawals was felt by the banks is unclear, but the Hibernian Bank, one of the few banks not placed on labor's Unfair List, could report three hundred thousand dollars in additional deposits from working-class Chicagoans. Labor leaders held at hand alternative savings options for workers; typographer George Harding encouraged them to purchase city bonds, which, he hoped, would soon be issued in order to finance a municipally operated streetcar system.[15] Labor certainly did not lack creativity in mobilizing against the EA.

The teamsters strike engulfed practically all of the city's territory. Unlike the trolley strike of two years ago, which centered in Chicago's working-class South Side, this strike converged in the city's downtown where up to ten thousand people might gather in front of the Montgomery Ward department store. Chicago's streets, downtown and elsewhere, were the scenes of intense violence. Practically every day, thousands of labor sympathizers engaged in armed battles with strikebreakers and the police over control of the city's thoroughfares. For the first time in an industrial dispute, the employers equipped strikebreakers with firearms, to shoot at blockading crowds. In specially headed daily columns, Chicago's newspapers reported on the number of dead and wounded resulting from beatings, stabbings, and shootings; all in all, the strike claimed twenty-one deaths and over four hundred injuries. With passions at high pitch, even a distinguished journal like *The Chicago Economist* turned belligerent: "Strikebreakers and private detectives," it assured, "can break a head with as much facility as one of the union men if occasion requires." The teamsters, in turn, were reported to hire "labor sluggers" at two dollars a day for beating up strikebreakers. By late April, public disturbances became so severe that the mayor advised the public to stay off the streets as much as possible.[16]

The strike affected unexpected corners of public life. On May 10, at Hendricks School, located in South Side Chicago, eight hundred pupils walked out of their classrooms when they saw strikebreakers delivering scab coal to their building. The following day, despite threats by the principal, only 342, less than half of the student population, returned to school. Within days, the "strike" had spread to eight other schools, most of them in Chicago's South Side. Some boy strikers were arrested for picketing a school. Although leaders of the CTF denied having incited these actions, they still "most heartily endorse[d] and commend[ed] the boldness, spirit and humanity of the striking children" and threatened to extend the walk-out to other schools.[17]

The teamsters strike also rendered visible a new social reality: the violence of racial conflicts. Following a pattern first set by strikes in 1903 and 1904, employers hired African Americans as strikebreakers. By the end of the dispute, the EA had recruited as many as one thousand black workers from the Mississippi Delta. Unlike previous strikes, this one exhibited racial conflict in the community at large, where even African American residents with no connection to the walkout might face deadly beatings by white crowds. On May 16, a virtual race riot erupted in one neighborhood after two black strikebreakers fired into a crowd of jeering children and killed an eleven-year-old boy. During the following days, whites attacked every black person they encountered, even dragging black passengers off the streetcars.[18]

Racial hostility thus acquired a dynamic all its own, with striking whites generalizing their hatred of strikebreaking blacks to the black race as a whole. The teamsters strike constituted a critical step toward a racially fragmented working class and a racially divided city. When black strikebreakers took the place of white teamsters and rode carts through the streets of Chicago, they ruptured an implicit consensus among white Chicagoans of all classes as to the "whiteness" of their city, especially with regard to its public spaces. Most commentators took racial prejudice for granted, blaming the ensuing violence not on the white workers' racism but on the mere presence of blacks. They criticized the EA for having offered this kind of provocation. This proved true even of newspapers that sided firmly with the employers, such as the *Chicago Tribune.* Responding to such public indignation, which included a city hall inquiry "as to whether the importation of hundreds of Negro workers is not a menace to the community and should not be restricted," the EA began to replace black strikebreakers with white ones.[19]

Although some trade union leaders, most notably John Fitzpatrick, advocated interracial cooperation among workers, organized labor in general adhered to Chicago's white consensus. Labor unions also refused to blame racism for the violence and attributed it instead to the presence of "irresponsible Negroes." The way to restore peace on the streets, then, was to get rid of black strikebreakers as soon as possible.[20] Even some blacks themselves blamed the colored strikebreakers for having inflamed racial tensions, as did the *Voice of the Negro,* a journal of middle-class African Americans.[21] At no point did trade unionists address the underlying problems of racial conflict, especially the exclusion of black workers from most industrial jobs, a fact that rendered the latter more likely to become strikebreakers. The *Labor Advocate* considered the "question of the negro's equal right to work . . . foreign to the point" and, instead, joined in the general denunciation of employers importing blacks "with the criminal purpose of inflaming prejudicial minds to the point of violence." White trade union leaders also denied black strikebreakers any agency, pitying them as "little black fellows" who knew no better than to serve as pawns of the capitalist.[22]

Yet accounts of racial tensions in early-twentieth-century labor disputes must be treated with caution. Clearly racial antagonisms were at work during the teamsters strike, but whether motivated by sympathy for employers or sheer sensationalism, the press proved likely to exaggerate racially motivated occurrences. By highlighting the racial passions of street crowds, the press infused strikers' actions with irrationality and thereby managed to obscure the strikers' economic rationale. Moreover, their exaggeration of strike-related violence played into the hands of the employers, who could thereby justify the intervention of state and federal troops. Newspaper accounts lead one to believe that all strikebreakers were black; in fact, a third of them were Caucasian. "Riots," settlement reformer Graham Taylor commented, "have been reserved for the scare-heads of the sensational press."[23] The press also employed gender and ethnic stereotypes as a means to discredit pro-union crowds. Newspapers conveyed an image of streets full of crazed amazons, of "big and strong Eastern European women," who, though quick to charge scabs with rolling pins, "knew little if anything about any conflict between the unions and employers."[24]

Certainly, the teamsters strike left an important legacy for Chicago's race relations. The presence of black workers on Chicago's streets meant violence, an equation that was understood and legitimated by white Chicagoans, trade unionists and non–trade unionists alike. The teamsters strike defined blacks as the "scab race," a white perception that in turn caused African American workers to distrust trade unionism. If these nascent divisions held relatively little consequence for Chicago's labor movement in 1905, by World War I large numbers of southern blacks had moved to Chicago and racial antipathies effectively threatened unionization efforts. "We venture the assertion that from now on racial relations will be somewhat acute in Chicago," the *Voice of the Negro* prophesied cautiously in 1905.[25]

The EA used an array of strategies to combat, and ultimately defeat, the teamsters union. Its ability to continue deliveries with strikebreakers depended on the city's provision of police protection. Setting aside the worries expressed in the conservative press that, as a "socialist," he would side with the strikers, Mayor Dunne declared he would do everything in his power to maintain peace and protect property in Chicago. By early May, at the peak of the strike's violence, the mayor assigned three-quarters of Chicago's police force to strike-related operations and recruited one thousand additional volunteers. At one point he even threatened to close saloons that functioned as strikers' headquarters. *The Economist* was satisfied with Dunne's performance and declared: "The police have done fairly well considering the great extent of territory they have to cover. There will be no need of help from the federal government."[26]

Facing his labor constituency, Dunne excused the vigor of his policy as a means of preventing just this: the intervention of federal troops. Yet trade unionists were not convinced and expressed bitter disappointment with the mayor. "What a shame," the *Advocate* continued, "to find the Mayor of a great city like Chicago dividing the duties of administration with [the head of the Employers Association] Frederick W. Job . . . to debase the conditions of the workingmen who gave the Mayor his majority. . . . Had the mayor been strong," the *Advocate* concluded, "the strike would have ended in ten days." Dunne's use of police force in 1905 has been cited as evidence of the refusal of middle-class progressives to back organized labor's closed-shop tactics. In my view, Dunne acted more in response to political exigencies than out of a personal distaste for the teamsters' strategies. Yet certainly, the mayor's actions undermined his relations with union labor, which bode ill for his reform agenda.[27]

Employers did take advantage of the federal courts to fight the teamsters. They rightly sensed that the local courts were affected by Chicago's general pro-union climate. Of the strikers and sympathizers arrested during the dispute, only 25 percent were fined by Chicago judges; in contrast, about 60 percent of all confined strikebreakers found themselves sentenced. And the latter also faced stiffer fines than the former.[28] The EA thus sought to involve out-of-state courts as much as possible. By incorporating its strike-breaking teaming company in West Virginia, it placed jurisdiction in the hands of the federal courts.[29] The strategy paid off: within a month, employers obtained two federal injunctions, which prohibited teamsters from picketing and from advocating so-called secondary boycotts, meaning that they could not request firms not directly involved in the dispute to cease deliveries to the struck department store. Those businesses continuing to observe the boycott—including several local express companies and the Team Owners Association, which was attempting to steer a neutral course—thus faced threats of federal court orders.

Accounts of the effectiveness of these rulings varied greatly. Whereas one labor journalist reported that "violence at once subsided," trade union leaders asserted they were not intimidated by injunctions. Indeed, a month-long federal injunction resulted in the indictment of only sixty teamsters, all but two cases of which had been dismissed by August 1905.[30] Historians have accorded great importance to the wave of injunction laws at the turn of the century; the federal courts, they argue, acted as one of the main repressive agents of the state and thereby helped induce the "exceptionalist turn" of U.S. labor away from a radical or socialist agenda as was pursued by western European trade unions.[31] Yet trade union leaders on the local level were less impressed by injunctions than Samuel Gompers and the national AFL leaders and subsequent historians. When asked about his reaction to the injunctions during the teamsters strike, CFL president Charles Dold replied: "Injunctions? I am not afraid of them. They don't hurt a hair of my head. Indictments? They are always accompaniments of strikes."[32] Certainly, in the long run, the thousands of injunctions levied against militant workers all across the country left an imprint, yet, as the case of the teamsters strike suggests, it remains necessary to study the precise local impact of these rulings before declaring the final word on the effect of labor law on the behavior and ideology of U.S. trade unions.

PUBLIC PERCEPTIONS

Employers' determination and use of federal courts only partly explains the defeat of Chicago's most powerful trade union in 1905. One of the most telling differences between the teamsters strike and the streetcar strike two years earlier lay in a gradual shift of that most powerful weapon of progressive-era politics: public opinion. In 1903, the major newspapers and civic reformers backed the strikers and opposed the open-shop campaign. In part, this reflected the nature of the business involved; certainly streetcar companies were far less popular in turn-of-the-century Chicago than were department stores (though these were not immune from political conflict).[33] The intense violence of the 1905 strike, rendered visible throughout the city, and severe doubts over the integrity of the teamsters union caused middle-class reformers, generally sympathetic to organized labor, to change their assessment. Events surrounding the teamsters strike belied reformers' faith in a disinterested public interest that could transcend fault lines of society, such as class. Rather, it revived their old fear of an anarchic society, a fear rooted in the labor disputes and the great waves of immigration of the late nineteenth century. Once again, social fragmentation became directly associated with organized labor. The shift in public opinion of trade unionism not only contributed to the teamsters' defeat but would also account for a decline of the city's reform climate.

Most basically, the teamsters failed to convince the public of the legitimacy of their cause: the right to engage in sympathy strikes. Historians have long noted that the toleration of trade unionism by a progressive middle class hinged on the definition of certain legitimate trade union practices, which excluded secondary strike actions and boycotts.[34] In this sense, the EA's arguments against the sympathy strike echoed those of the NCF, which, composed of leading industrialists, AFL representatives, and civic reformers, promoted industrial arbitration and union recognition in exchange for a limited view of what trade unionists could ask for and do. Yet reference to the NCF cannot explain shifts in Chicago's public opinion. Turn-of-the-century Chicago was noteworthy for the widespread toleration that middle-class reformers had granted to militant trade union actions. Many middle-class reformers in Chicago did not reject the sympathy strike as such. Prominent settlement workers such as Jane Addams and Graham Taylor and other reformers, in fact, recognized the beneficial effects of trade union solidarity, which had resulted in the unionization of workwomen, among other things. Addams, for example, pointed out that sympathy strikes had provided "scrub women with the first opportunity to participate in the fellowship of a union."[35]

Yet by the time of the 1905 dispute, this trade union practice had become associated with corruption and conspiracy. When garment workers first struck the department store, critics pointed out, the teamsters repeatedly refused the striking women's appeals for assistance. In reality, the argument went, the strike was nothing but a demonstration of union bosses' thirst for power. Far from being an act of sympathy, the teamsters simply abused their power by striking against those employers who had refused to pay off their leaders.[36] Conspiracy theories permeated public discussion. Municipal-ownership advocates accused the teamsters' boss, Cornelius P. Shea, of pocketing money from the streetcar interests in return for provoking a strike that would discredit Dunne's administration and ruin his streetcar agenda. In a later autobiography, Dunne himself claimed that the strike "was brought about by a conspiracy between the foes of municipal ownership and Con Shea, a disreputable labor leader."[37]

Dunne and many reformers' perceptions of Shea and the teamsters union in general reflected a widely publicized campaign to discredit that organization and associate it, for generations to come, with corruption. In April 1904, EA representatives demanded a hearing by Chicago's grand jury—a body set up to rule on the validity and proceeding of charges put forth by the state's attorney—on the alleged bribing of teamster leaders. For the next several months, these grand jury hearings provided ground for numerous scandalous reports on Shea's alleged misdoings. The teamsters' leader was accused of hiring sluggers to beat up strikebreakers, misappropriating union funds, and accepting bribes from employers. In the daily press, Shea emerged as the personification of evil. He and his cohorts were said to throw orgies in the "notoriously disreputable" Kentucky Home, where they entertained "women of vilest character."[38]

As historian David Witwer demonstrates, these grand jury proceedings resulted from a close personal collaboration between the EA and the state attorney's office. The hearings, for example, admitted only corruption charges levied against union representatives and not those directed against employers. Moreover, with the publisher of the *Chicago Evening Post,* A. A. McCormick, as foreman of the grand jury, employers could rest assured of effective denunciatory coverage in the press. What perhaps most clearly illustrates the political nature of the grand jury hearings is the contents of the indictments themselves. In the end, the jurors did not indict labor leaders for morally questionable behavior, for extortion, or for bribery, but rather for inciting sympathetic strikes. The grand jury thus pinned down and criminalized the practice of central concern to the EA. It is in this sense that one employer considered the grand jury proceedings "of more wide-spread and greater importance than the trial of the Hay Market riots." That Shea and other leaders eventually ended up acquitted of the charges hardly serves to limit the damage done to the public image of the teamsters.[39]

The CFL and various trade unions denounced the trials as efforts by employers to discredit the union. They also jumped to the defense of the teamsters' sympathy strike. By aiding a group of Russian Jewish garment workers, the union engaged in a "Christian-like, democratic, and American act," which would "do more to eradicate religious and racial prejudices . . . than all the 'goody-goody' reform organizations."[40] Yet the "goody-goody" reformers failed to be convinced. Progressives like Taylor and Addams joined employers in dismissing the sympathy strike and condemning "the tyranny and injustice . . . [of] 'closed shop' tactics." The teamsters were "sympathetic in name only, . . . remorselessly without sympathy for the cause of organized labor," Taylor stated. During the anthracite miners strike of 1902, he argued, organized labor "stood higher than ever," but by late 1905, "it has never been dragged lower in Chicago than by the long drawn-out conspiracy of teamsters' union officials with the agent of a few employers." Taylor also severely criticized the otherwise "reputable" leader of the CFL for having allowed the federation to be used by the teamsters' "buccaneers." Some trade union locals, such as the generally conservative typographers union also denounced the sympathy strike as a "prostitution of unionism," although the printers (as did Taylor) resented the hypocrisy in decrying graft among trade union leaders without acknowledging the employers' role in the process.[41] Even so, many reformers became thoroughly skeptical about labor's practices, and especially of the "criminally degenerate" teamsters.[42] As promoted by the grand jury hearings, reformers equated the sympathy strike with corruption. In doing so, they left Chicago labor in the cold amidst the employers' full-fledged open-shop drive.

The intensity and violence of the event evoked reformers' worst fears concerning a fragmented society and a "class-ridden city."[43] Taking an object lesson in the nature of working-class solidarity, Taylor described the actions taken by non-union residents of the seventeenth ward, the site of his settlement:

> [they] became as class-conscious, almost overnight, as were the striking teamsters. When the strike breakers drove the police-protected coal carts down our avenue, men from the sidewalks, women from the tenement-house windows, and even the little children in the playground cried with one voice, "Down with the scabs," some of them hurling missiles at hand at the frightened drivers. Then we learned, what most employers fail to discover, that the "solidarity of labor" extends beyond the membership of unions, and that on occasion the class-conscious spirit emerges from the whole working class.

Yet far from celebrating that "class-conscious spirit," Taylor lamented it as a sign of imminent societal failure. His discovery of working-class action proved "as surprising as it was disappointing and discouraging."[44] It was

In solidarity with coal teamsters on strike in Chicago, pupils of the South Side Tilden School walked out of their classrooms in 1902. "School strikes" such as this one reveal the community backing that union workers enjoyed in blue-collar regions of the city. Unionized schoolteachers were harshly criticized in the press for these walkouts, especially for similar walkouts occurring during the 1905 teamsters strike. Chicago Historical Society DN-471

when children began hurling missiles that, in reformers' eyes, working-class solidarity exceeded all legitimate bounds. It was in this sense that reformers attacked the already mentioned school strikes, for which they held Haley's teachers union responsible. With support from leading reform organizations, the Chicago Board of Education voted to condemn the CTF, which was a crucial link in Chicago's progressive cross-class alliance, and which found itself in the cross fire.[45] The teamsters strike profoundly altered the possibilities of a progressive reform project based on a new social consensus.

In the wake of the teamsters strike, reformers rethought the relationship between leaders and the people, and the nature of democracy more generally. On the one hand, reformers attributed the problem to despotic and immoral leaders like teamster leader Shea. Worse than these men's personal failings was their power of seduction of the rank and file. To contemporary University of Chicago professor John Cummings this signified a "modern instance of the failure of . . . democracy," which can only survive if it develops "an unerring instinct for selecting able leaders." Likewise, the *Typographical Journal* hoped for the day when "leaders would be selected for their high character and sound judgment instead of craftiness and coxcombry." The reelection of Shea as president of the International Brotherhood of Teamsters shortly after the strike confirmed reformers' worst fears over the indifference or weakness of the teamsters' rank and file.[46]

On the other hand, some critics blamed an excessively democratic structure for the teamsters' fall. The problem lay not in the inability of the rank and file to control its leaders but, rather, in the latter's failure to contain rank-and-file sentiment. According to this view, in calling the strike, the teamsters' leaders responded too readily to rank-and-file impulses. Jane Addams noted that the teamsters were "still in the enthusiastic stage" and lacked the organizational discipline of older, more established trade unions. Recently formed unions, she felt, were like impulsive children who required the heavy hand of experienced and rational leaders.[47] Whoever was to blame, corrupt trade union leaders or an impulsive rank-and-file mob, the teamsters strike signaled a crisis within the workings of industrial democracy.

Such attacks implied trade unions' inability to further democracy in Chicago municipal politics as well. Depicted as corrupt organizations dominated by vile and autocratic leaders, trade unions surely could not be entrusted with a larger public role. Taylor drew this conclusion quite explicitly: "As long as that terrorism [of the teamsters] holds the Chicago Federation of Labor in such abject subjection, it can command the respect of neither the community nor its own constituency."[48] Reformers also began to question one of the maxims of radical progressivism: the ideal of direct democracy. Whether applied to the teamsters' rank and file or Chicago's population in general, the critiques of Addams and others suggested in effect that the people could not be trusted to pursue their own good and should be guided instead by strong leaders. Reformers' skepticism about the role of labor in a democracy boded badly for Dunne's municipal-ownership agenda.

By May 1905, the EA's aggressive strategy paid off. The teamsters abandoned their defense of the sympathy strike and pleaded merely for the reinstatement of its members. The EA, however, determined to lead the fight to its conclusion, refused even this demand and rejected the calls for arbitration put forth by the mayor, the popular Judge Tuley, and independent citizen groups.[49] With the support dwindling from other trade unions, one teamster local after another surrendered, the last local of the coal teamsters yielding on August 20, 1905; the teamsters were "utterly defeated and crushed."[50]

THE LEGACY OF THE STRIKE

The strike signaled a full-fledged victory to employers in the sense that the teamsters henceforth abandoned sympathy strike actions; it did not cease with teamster unionism as such. Teamster leaders now openly repudiated the use of sympathy strikes. Running against Shea for president of the International Brotherhood of Teamsters in 1906, Alfred Young was determined to prohibit these acts of solidarity, given that they "ruined the teamsters' organization in Chicago," and he called for the adoption of "conservative tactics."[51] Strict organization, obedience to the law, and responsibility toward the employer were the attributes teamster leaders demanded of their fellow workers. The only community-oriented strategy remaining was the union label campaign, which promoted the purchase of union-made products. The teamsters' retreat from militancy in 1905 thus proved similar to that of the building trades unions in the wake of the 1900 lockout. Occasional rumors of strike action were quickly dispelled. Twice during the following year, the truck drivers threatened a walkout but, within days, agreed to settle on the old terms. The trauma of the strike lived on at least until 1912, when the teamsters denied the freight handlers' request for a sympathy strike by referring to "the lesson we learned in 1905 when our organization was practically ruined."[52] Pointing to the lack of teamsters strikes, one merchant in late 1906 exclaimed: "I never have felt more satisfied with the result of four or five months' work than I did at that time."[53]

Notwithstanding the teamsters' efforts to improve their public image, they continued to be associated with violence and corruption. In August 1906, in opposition to Shea, Young's conservative faction, composed of about half of Chicago's locals, seceded from the International Brotherhood of Teamsters and formed the United Teamsters of America. For months, teamster locals in Chicago engaged in a virtual civil war over jurisdictional rights, with union meetings sometimes ending in fights and shootings. These brawls only confirmed the widespread public perception of the teamsters as a criminal organization. Moreover, the grand jury hearings continued well into 1906 and kept afresh in the public's mind the scandals surrounding the union. Under such circumstances, the unions' efforts at moral improvement, as shown in their banning saloonkeepers from membership, proved of little effect.[54]

The teamsters crisis had a great impact on Chicago's entire labor movement. Many recently organized wage earners who attributed their unions to the truck drivers' sympathy strikes now were left on their own. For example, hospital workers, who formed one of the many new unions that had mushroomed since 1902, now found themselves scattered and decimated.[55] Women's trade unionism in Chicago experienced a decline in this period as well. By 1909 sixteen of the formerly twenty-five female locals had disappeared. The number of organized women workers dropped from thirty thousand to a mere seven or eight thousand. This trend certainly reflected other factors as well, such as the fragility of the new unions in the face of the economic downturn of 1907, but the teamsters' inability or unwillingness to engage in solidaristic actions certainly played a key part. This held true for the special order women garment workers union; having been the supposed cause of the 1905 dispute, their organization ceased to exist once the teamsters found themselves defeated.[56]

The CFL found itself weakened and confronted with numerous factional disputes. Using the fights among the teamsters to his advantage, building trades organizer Skinny Madden reared his head again. On January 8, 1906, the day the CFL's biannual election was to be held, his men "charged the platform, knocked down the chairman, drove the opposition from the hall, and by sheer force of arms captured and ruled the meeting."[57] The CFL's "purification crowd," led by Fitzpatrick, managed to retain control of the federation and to expel Madden's junior steamfitters, yet similar brawls continued to plague the labor central.[58] The 1906 Labor Day parade reflected this weakness. When the CFL, ostensibly for financial reasons, canceled the parade, only Madden's adherents marched. It was one of the smallest Labor Day parades in Chicago's history, and the *Tribune* joyfully noted the lack of "belligerent spirit manifested by the marchers."[59]

Chicago continued a union town, of course. Wishing to counteract the employers' open-shop drive, in May 1906 the CFL launched a major organizing crusade, for which it asked each affiliated international union to send one organizer to the Chicago region.[60] In keeping with national trends, overall trade union membership declined, but Fitzpatrick could still report on the organization of twenty new locals in 1906. Many locals of female workers continued to maintain their organizations, including the waitress locals, janitresses, elevated railroad ticket clerks, and telegraph and telephone operators. Sympathy strikes did not completely disappear from the scene either. For example, janitresses of twenty skyscrapers struck in solidarity with window washers, many of whom also happened to be their husbands. Yet compared to the 1902–1905 period, organized labor tended to recede from militant workplace-related action and, like the teamsters, embraced consumer-oriented strategies instead. Headed by Anna Nicholes, the CFL's label committee coordinated several union label ward clubs, which set up street stands where passersby could observe the great variety of union-made products through the lens of the new stereopticon. The committee also held major product exhibits, which included gymnastic performances by the Turnverein.[61] The CFL's most ambitious venture into the sphere of consumption concerned the founding of a union bank. Alienated by Chicago's financial institutions' backing of the EA, the CFL founded a deposit bank for and by Chicago working people. Opened in May 1906, the Union Labor Bank held a capital stock of $250,000, its directors were union men, and the CFL reserved the right to own at least one thousand shares. By late 1907, however, the bank had consolidated with a regular institution. If Chicago unions engaged in an active consumption-oriented strategy and continued to foster a solid and creative labor culture, its overall strength still paled in comparison with the wave of unionization prior to the teamsters strike. "Never since the 1905 strike, has union labor in Chicago been as strong as it was in the first five years of the century," one historian noted.[62]

During the teamsters strike of 1905, organized labor and capital clashed over competing definitions of trade unions' economic rights and their public standing in Chicago. Employers, through an unprecedented level of organization and through the long arm of the state, succeeded in eliminating the sympathy strike and thereby imposed severe restrictions on a class-based and citywide trade unionism. One need not ascribe to conspiracy theories to note that the timing of the employers' offensive was also designed to weaken Chicago labor's political standing and thus the municipal-ownership movement. The violence surrounding the teamsters strike, along with highly publicized charges of union corruption, certainly damaged the unions' image and led many Chicagoans, including reformers favorably inclined toward trade unionism, to question the legitimacy of a broader civic role on behalf of the unions. If, during a brief period, labor's class-based strength proved compatible with its prominent engagement in Chicago reform politics, the teamsters strike revealed the fragile nature of that moment. For it demonstrated to Chicagoans that class continued a divisive force. However the urban reform agenda would be affected, one thing was clear: with the 1905 teamsters strike the honeymoon of labor progressivism came to an end.

CHAPTER FIVE

THE POLITICS OF STREETCAR REGULATION

In our mighty industrial and social struggle, only the

very elect can escape their demarcation.

—Margaret Dreier Robins

Despite the industrial turmoil surrounding the teamsters strike, the regulation of the city's streetcars remained at the top of the political agenda. Placed in the mayor's chair with a platform calling for "immediate municipal ownership" and backed by several plebiscites in its favor, Edward Dunne was prepared to focus on his main political goal, and he appeared to have the support necessary to accomplish it. With all eyes on the nation's "municipal laboratory," it seemed that Chicago would become the first U.S. city with a publicly owned streetcar system.[1]

Yet the teamsters strike proved a poor beginning for this radical political agenda. The eruption of outright warfare between the classes during this dispute caused many middle-class observers to question one of the main tenets behind the municipal-ownership demand, namely, that complex issues surrounding public services such as mass transportation could and ought to be managed by "the public" itself. This body, the teamsters strike revealed with full force, was divided by class divisions and appeared poorly equipped to formulate reasonable policies. Reformer Margaret Dreier Robins had this worry in mind when she noted that streetcar politics "is distinctly a class struggle."[2]

Adding to this tension a series of systemic legal, financial, and political factors, the task of introducing municipal ownership to Chicago's transportation facilities became exceedingly difficult, one the new mayor ultimately proved unable to handle. By the time Dunne left office in 1907, he had changed his strategy as well as his political allies so many times that his own posture on public ownership was rendered increasingly vague. The debate over the implementation of the municipal ownership of streetcars during Dunne's mayoral tenure ultimately brought to the fore two conflicting notions of the nature of citizens' participation in a democracy. On one hand, the city's labor movement and the advocates of an immediate municipal takeover of the streetcar companies—Dunne's main constituency in 1905—postulated a vision of democracy that accorded citizens a direct participatory role in urban politics. On the other hand and in opposition, there emerged a newly coherent and increasingly powerful counter-ideology of functionalism. According to this opposing view, Dunne's plans for a swift takeover of the trolleys constituted mere "pipedreams," unsuited to the realities and needs of an American city.[3] Public policy with regard to urban transportation and other services ought to be based on objective assessments and "practical" solutions, to be devised by professional experts supposedly removed from the political maelstrom. The leading political figure behind this functionalist currency was Walter Fisher, who also figured prominently in the Municipal Voters League (MVL).

MAYOR DUNNE'S POLICY ON MUNICIPAL OWNERSHIP

During the two years of Dunne's administration, a number of serious practical obstacles surfaced, especially with regard to the question of how to pay for a public takeover. As in all large urban centers in the United States, the expenditures of Chicago's city government were confined by tight debt limits, in this case specified in the 1870 state constitution. Until the late nineteenth century, this posed few problems as public services had largely been financed by private property owners. The campaign for greater public control over urban services, however, placed growing political pressures on this system and led to calls to raise the ceiling of the debt limit and strengthen the city's political autonomy ("home rule"). In the case of transportation, the state of Illinois passed the Mueller law in 1903, which appeared to offer Chicago and other cities a means to purchase their streetcars by authorizing city governments to raise funds for public takeovers through the sale of financial certificates to the public. Radical reformers hailed the bill as a big step toward a municipal takeover. Henry D. Lloyd exclaimed: "No other great city in the world possesses such powers as Chicago now has . . . under the Mueller law."[4]

In fact, the Mueller law turned out to create more problems than it solved, beginning with the challenge to its constitutionality, which effectively delayed its implementation during the entire period of Dunne's administration. The problems were multiple. By allowing for a high valuation of company property, the law permitted the streetcar companies to charge unaffordable amounts for a public purchase. Following the arguments of the companies' lobbyists, the law specified that valuations would be based not on the actual market value of the companies' equipment but on the profit this equipment generated; thus, Mueller certificates would never suffice to raise the money needed for a public purchase. Furthermore, the requirement of public approbation for policies through the referendum, heretofore demanded by advocates of a municipal takeover, could now be used against such radical plans, for the Mueller law required the approval of two-thirds of voters in order for the city to issue bonds for a public purchase. Not without basis, some municipal-ownership advocates considered the Mueller law to result from a conspiracy led by their opponents.[5]

It was a slow and powerful legal system that contributed considerably to dampening the hopes for municipal ownership. Obviously no one would invest in Mueller certificates as long as the Illinois Supreme Court's decision on their constitutionality remained outstanding. In fact, shortly after Dunne's defeat as mayor in 1907, the Supreme Court struck the law from the books. In enacting radical or even moderate changes, reformers in the United States, unlike their European counterparts, had to act on a double front, the legislative and the judicial. The attempt to municipalize Chicago's streetcars was no exception.[6]

Adjusting to these difficulties, Dunne proposed a scheme whereby streetcar lines no longer covered by valid franchises could be owned by private investors but under strict regulation by the city. This so-called contract plan entailed a municipal purchase of the lines as soon as legal authorization, which in fact never materialized, was certain. In the meantime, strict public regulation of transportation could be assured by the presence of publicly appointed men and women on the companies' board of directors.[7] Dunne advocated his plan, issued within a few months after assuming office, as the best option available under the circumstances. Although the mayor attributed his move to the legal obstacles against financing a municipal streetcar system, in fact his new proposal resembled the "regulatory solution" that had been advocated for years by the opponents of immediate municipal ownership: an operation of streetcars in private hands, under improved public regulation, and retaining the possibility of a future governmental takeover.

One of the principal intellectual authors of the regulatory approach to the transit question was Walter L. Fisher whose career spanned diverse activities within the progressive movement. Born in West Virginia in 1862, he practiced law in Chicago from 1888 until 1935. He also served a one-year term as president of the Conservation League of America in 1908 and served as secretary of the interior under President Taft from 1911 to 1913. In Chicago, he acquired prominence as secretary (1901–1906) of the Municipal Voters League, which over the past six years had worked to "purify" the council of corrupt aldermen. Serving off and on as transportation counsel from 1906 until 1932, Fisher imbued the city's transit policy with a functionalist view, which proved a powerful opposite to the participatory and statist view of politics advocated by the municipal-ownership movement.[8] Like his radical opponents, Fisher insisted that business corrupts politics and that, if left unregulated, business failed to serve the interests of the public. Through the MVL, Fisher worked at clearing the city council of the influence of the traction-magnate Charles T. Yerkes. Moreover, Fisher considered it necessary to create the possibility for a municipal operation of public utilities. In fact, he himself had drafted the Mueller Enabling Act. Yet unlike the proponents of immediate municipal ownership, the long-time lawyer regarded public ownership as a mere bargaining tool in negotiations with the streetcar companies. The threat of a public takeover alone, he felt, sufficed to appeal to public utility companies' enlightened self-interest and to induce them to furnish adequate service upon fair terms.[9]

Behind such confidence in the possibility of redirecting the workings of the private sector toward public ends lay a strong distaste for radical and statist solutions. Although he was aware that the companies might well exhibit a selfish attitude, Fisher worried foremost about a public sentiment that was likely to exceed reasonable bounds. Moderate reformers like Fisher continued the long tradition of Jeffersonian liberalism that trusted in the enlightened self-interest of businesses, though they came to accept the need for some state-based pressure. Only the companies' abject refusal to be subject to governmental regulation, Fisher argued, would necessitate more drastic measures, which, he was quick to add, were abhorred by "all disinterested and sincere friends of good government."[10] To this reformer, the best guarantee for a moderate and rational traction policy lay in putting in charge thoroughly trained and practical-minded experts. These were best equipped to discipline the corporations while putting a stop to the radical and irrational "disposition to injure capital."[11]

The main person Fisher had in mind here was Bion J. Arnold, the city's chief traction engineer since 1902. As consulting engineer of the city's committee on local transportation, Arnold acquired nationwide fame for his report on the Chicago traction question in 1902 and served as transportation consultant not only in the midwest metropolis but also in cities such as New York City, Providence, Pittsburgh, San Francisco, Seattle, and Toronto. Filled with detailed statistics and maps on questions of traffic congestion and services, Arnold's report seemed to offer the kind of disinterested technical solution to the traction question that was needed. Like Fisher, Arnold believed that, with some kind of governmental guidance and mild coercion, the companies could be made to cooperate in providing a coherent and integrated citywide streetcar service. All that was needed was to have experts (like him) conduct the traction policies of the city.[12]

An advocacy of practical thought lay at the heart of these moderate reformers' attack on radical solutions to the traction problem. As they argued, the main problem with radicals was not their political demands as such—in this case the advocacy of public ownership—but their deviation from practicality. Unlike the radicals, who liked to see things "as they might be or as we would like them to be," Fisher not only was endowed with the "best set of brains" (to cite Dreier Robins) but also studied the traction question "without any preconceived notions."[13] In the long run, the anti-intellectual strain implicit in such celebrations of practicality would come to haunt any kind of reformer wishing to assert the role of the state, albeit a weak one, in assuring public ends. Fisher himself, while always quick to denounce idealist intellectuals, was frequently abhorred for his pedantic and lengthy speeches and in the press was mockingly referred to as "Dr. Fisher."

Mayor Dunne's political skills proved no match to an ideological and legal environment hostile to plans for immediate municipal ownership. A political newcomer, he lacked negotiation skills, a shortcoming that affected his relationship with the city council especially. For several years now, Fisher's MVL had worked to fill the city's legislative branch with "honest" aldermen. While ostensibly a good-government measure, in fact the league's selection criteria favored candidates with a moderate, if not hostile, attitude toward immediate municipal ownership. Upon the election of Dunne, the council body in charge of traction matters, the committee on local transportation, continued to negotiate directly with the companies concerning a renewal of their franchises, and it rejected several attempts by the mayor to cease these negotiations.[14] Even when Dunne turned toward the more moderate regulatory-oriented contract plan, he failed to improve matters. In fact, Dunne offended many committee members by refusing to consult with them when he was drafting his contract plan. Under the previous mayor, Carter Harrison II, who had displayed a lackluster interest in this matter, the committee on local transportation had executed virtually every policy initiative and report on public transportation. Now Dunne chose to consult outsiders instead, including his friend Mayor Tom Johnson of Cleveland and also James Dalrymple, a traction expert from Glasgow, Scotland. Dunne even assumed a confrontational stand by publicly denouncing aldermen for surrendering to the commercial interests of the traction companies. His accusations provoked a virtual riot on the city council floor and a formal resolution, albeit unpassed, that the mayor "refrain from presiding over the deliberations of this body." To make matters worse, Dunne's request for advice from the Glasgow expert backfired when the Scotsman publicly affirmed that Chicago was still unfit to successfully undertake municipal ownership.[15]

Dunne's weak ties to Democratic Party regulars further contributed to his political problems. Several powerful ward bosses had backed him in the 1905 election, but out of short-term political calculations not a firm commitment to Dunne or municipal ownership. As a political outsider and a novice, Dunne lacked sufficient finesse to consolidate their support and obtain the backing of a fragmented and ward-based party while at the same time maintaining his ties to an essentially non-partisan grassroots movement. Perhaps because of Dunne's weak steering of the political rudder, public backing of municipal ownership diminished significantly. In the spring of 1906, a referendum on the question for the first time yielded mixed results. Although voters did approve the issuance of city bonds (whose constitutionality, to be sure, remained doubtful), no two-thirds approval materialized that would have authorized the city to actually operate the streetcars.[16] The direct-democracy clause of the referendum, which had always aided the cause of municipal ownership, now worked against it.

Prospects for municipal ownership stalled, but so did the streetcar companies' hopes for a swift franchise renewal. In their negotiations with the committee on local transportation, the companies insisted that a state law passed in 1865 endowed them with rights to the city's streets for ninety-nine years. Yet in March 1906, the Illinois Supreme Court denied such claims. Both the proponents of immediate municipal ownership and the moderate reformers such as Fisher considered such extensive franchises unacceptable and applauded the court's decision.[17]

Seeing the companies weakened by the Supreme Court decision, Mayor Dunne moved to implement his regulatory proposal. A change in the position of chief traction counsel confirmed his turn toward a moderate regulatory solution. The labor lawyer and municipal-ownership activist Clarence Darrow occupied this post from the time of Dunne's election until November 1905, when he resigned, largely out of frustration over the slow progress of municipalization. In April the following year, Dunne surprisingly announced the appointment of Walter L. Fisher as the new traction counsel.[18] Fisher immediately drafted a traction plan, according to which the city would issue a revocable license to the streetcar companies, gain the right to purchase the lines on six months' notice, and receive greater control over the companies' service and managerial decisions. The companies, fearing worse and shaken by the court's ninety-nine-year decision, agreed to the proposal. By the end of 1906, they also entered into an agreement with the council's committee on local transportation whereby the city would yield greater regulatory control and receive 55 percent of the companies' net profits. The purchase price for an eventual public takeover was set at fifty million dollars, a value set by a governmental estimation. As a solution to the traction crisis appeared imminent, Dunne declared confidently: "nothing short of an earthquake can prevent a settlement of this long drawn-out traction controversy."[19]

With only three months remaining in Dunne's term, the politics of traction had changed drastically. Dunne had entered office with the determination of an immediate municipal takeover, but faced with a variety of legal, financial, and political obstacles, he himself came to embrace the regulatory approach. Although he continued to express his hope for a future city purchase and his opposition to the theory of public regulation, in fact he allied himself with the foremost spokesman of precisely that approach, Walter L. Fisher.[20]

Yet such a shift would prove unacceptable to the mayor's original, main constituencies—organized labor and the municipal-ownership movement. To these, Dunne's appointment of Fisher represented the final blow in a series of overly cautious and vacillating actions by the mayor. As early as 1905 they attacked Dunne's proposal for regulatory control of the streetcar companies as "a franchise under a different name." Even the mayor's main backer during the 1905 campaign, the Municipal Ownership League, only narrowly approved the plan.[21] Trade unionists joined the mayor's right-wing critics in attacking his shifting stance. "Five months after the election," the *Advocate* stated, "the situation is more clouded than when the mayor took [office]. . . . How disgusted the people are with the mayor's traction tactics." Another observer recalled: "Consternation [over Dunne's appointment of Fisher] reigned supreme in the radical camp. . . . The opposition is wild—they are howling."[22]

Dunne's collaboration with Fisher was symptomatic of the widening gap between trade unionists and the mayor. To organized labor, Fisher stood not only for the regulatory approach to mass transit but also for the city's anti-unionist, open-shop campaign. Labor leaders considered Fisher responsible for having printed the Mueller law certificates in non-union shops.[23] Worse, they attacked Fisher's organization, the MVL, for repeatedly endorsing political candidates hostile toward trade unionism. The main cause for the rift, of course, was the 1905 teamsters strike. Although Dunne managed to prevent the call for federal troops, the active intervention of his police force left the CFL embittered for some time to come. Two years later, driver locals still expressed their resentment toward the mayor, a sentiment echoed by the leader of the Municipal Ownership League, T. P. Quinn, who charged Dunne with having "struck at every labor union where he has had a chance."[24] There were exceptions to this attitude, especially among public employees who benefited from the mayor's tolerant attitude toward their organizing efforts. Indeed, Dunne acknowledged the right of firemen, policemen, and other public servants to unionize; thus, in late 1906, the firemen established their first union and affiliated with the CFL.[25] The teachers union enjoyed a particularly close relationship with Dunne. Upon assuming office, the mayor appointed CFL sympathizers to the board of education. Although this move would assure that a majority of the board stood favorable to the teachers' cause, it also resulted in widespread public hostility toward the Irishman's administration.[26]

There was no doubt, however, that organized labor and Dunne were moving toward a collision course, especially over transportation politics. While Dunne took on a more moderate position, the CFL adopted a more aggressive one when it extended its demand for municipal ownership to virtually all public utilities, including telephone, gas, and electricity.[27] The CFL targeted the Illinois Telegraph and Telephone Company, which had participated in underground warfare against the teamsters through the construction of the freight tunnels. With regard to the streetcars, organized labor for years had fought the efforts of the city council and the committee on local transportation to extend franchises to the streetcar companies. To the CFL, the "revocable license" proposed by Dunne and Fisher was yet another name for a system allowing the renewal of franchises by private companies. Some trade unionists, like teacher union leader Margaret Haley, continued to endorse the mayor's traction policy; most steered away from the Irishman.[28]

Sensing a betrayal of their cause on behalf of the municipal executive, trade unionists set up new political organizations designed to promote measures of direct democracy. In the council elections of spring 1906, the CFL endorsed all aldermanic candidates who pledged themselves to work for the municipalization of public utilities. Aldermen acting against the will of their ward's constituency would be removed from office through a procedure known as the recall.[29] The upcoming election prompted a flurry of political activity. On April 8, three hundred delegates representing fifty-two labor organizations and eight civic societies gathered at Brand's Hall. Declaring war on "A merciless band of pirates, more absolute and cruel than the Russian autocracy," the convention—led by T. P. Quinn and soon to be known as the Chicago Protective Alliance—demanded public ownership of utilities as well as the initiative, referendum, and recall. It also called for the suspension of business on primary days, tax reform, anti-injunction measures, and a charter that would guarantee home rule. The delegates finally moved to request assistance from San Francisco's labor party mayor Eugene Schmitz.[30]

The intensification of labor's political activities reflected changes on the national level. Alienated by a series of anti-labor decisions by the U.S. Supreme Court, Gompers and the AFL leadership became convinced of the necessity of a more active political engagement. While never abandoning their official non-partisan stand, AFL leaders encouraged their affiliates to formalize efforts to "reward friends and punish enemies." Yet labor politics were far from being initiated or directed by the national trade unions. In the case of Chicago, San Francisco, and elsewhere, the AFL's call for political action was more a response to already existing political activity on the local level than an initiation of the same.[31] Moreover, the political priorities of the national leadership could be quite distinct from those of local trade unions: whereas Gompers focused on work- and industry-related matters, labor in Chicago stressed municipal reform measures.

Such political enthusiasm among trade unions did not result in a united front, however. On the contrary, without a unifying leader, the political campaign led only to further fragmentation of the cause. During 1906, several new organizations emerged that shared similar platforms with the Chicago Protective Alliance but differed in strategy; these included the Cook County Democracy, the Independence League, and the Workingmen's Municipal Ownership Union of Illinois. Whereas Quinn's Protective Alliance sought to "oust Dunne and all other regulars," and Fitzpatrick's CFL recommended that organized labor repudiate both the Republican and the Democratic tickets, the County Democracy backed the mayor.[32] Attempts to agree on the same slate of candidates for the November 1906 elections met with failure. Whereas the CFL's political action committee nominated one set of candidates, the Workingmen's Municipal Ownership Union together with the County Democracy nominated a different one. CFL secretary Ed Nockels lamented the fragmentation and resulting weakness of labor's political agenda. Indeed, of the twenty-seven candidates endorsed by the CFL for the state senate and legislature, only six were elected.[33]

Hearst-ism would further diffuse labor's political power. The newspapers of William Randolph Hearst constituted a powerful force in support of municipal ownership but proved unpredictable in their political stand, both with regard to Mayor Dunne and organized labor. Following his success in the newspaper publishing business in New York City, Hearst opened two papers in Chicago in 1902: the *Chicago American* and the *Chicago Examiner,* both led by A. M. Lawrence. Like Hearst's papers in New York, the Chicago-based papers offered a left-wing version of progressive-era muckraking, publishing the alleged abuses of various "trusts" in sensationalist style, and proclaiming to support organized labor. The call for the municipal ownership of utilities as well as the active backing of petition drives and referenda stood at the core of Hearst's political engagement. In the spring of 1905, while running, unsuccessfully as it turned out, for mayor of New York City, he backed Dunne's mayoral campaign.[34]

Yet Hearst's support for Dunne proved a mixed blessing. Just as trade unionists and municipal-ownership advocates attacked the utility companies' ties to Wall Street, now the opposition to public ownership portrayed Dunne as a puppet of the New York–based leader.[35] Furthermore, it soon became clear that Hearst was entering the cause mainly because of his own political interests. Eyeing a run for the U.S. presidency in 1908, he formed local political clubs, called independence leagues, in cities all over the country. Although the Chicago local, formed in July 1906, ostensibly backed Dunne, by the mere fact of its existence it served to further dilute and fragment the municipal-ownership constituency. Dunne's backers feared the worst from Hearst. As Dreier Robins noted: "The Hearst newspapers have been doing their best to play a trick on Mayor Dunne and Raymond [Robins]; Margaret Haley and Mr. Post . . . have realized that however great the Hearst newspapers are in destructive work, they are utterly unable to construct."[36] Likewise, trade unionists grew increasingly weary of Hearst-ism, especially as the newspaper man's pro-labor attitude became doubtful. By 1910, the CFL and Hearst were to engage in open war, when the publisher sought to operate his papers on a non-union basis.

Sensing the loss of support from his original constituency on the eve of the municipal election of 1907, Dunne switched his traction policy yet another time. In a last-minute desperate move to gather the municipal-ownership forces behind him, he denounced the license agreement set forth by his own traction counsel, just when the committee on local transportation was about to come to terms with the companies. Although the mayor attributed his turnaround to last-minute additions to the agreement, which altered it in such a way as to render a future city purchase impossible, most observers considered Dunne's decision a sign that he lacked constancy.

THE 1907 DEBATE OVER THE SETTLEMENT FRANCHISE

Dunne's refusal of the streetcar compromise, which would be promoted as the "settlement ordinance," assured that the 1907 mayoral race would center again on the traction question. The election campaign pitted the once-again "radical" Mayor Dunne against Republican challenger Fred A. Busse who fully backed the settlement ordinance. To further ignite traction-related sentiments, the ordinance, which stipulated the continued private operation of the streetcars with greater regulatory powers and a right to purchase the lines granted to the city government, would be subject to a referendum in the same elections. Busse and "settlement" became the rallying cries of traction interests, business leaders, and reformers in favor of a regulatory solution, all of whom united in an amply financed and solidly organized campaign. "For the next six weeks," journalist Tarbell recalled, "Chicago was filled with such a traction din as she had not heard since the campaign against the Allan bill [in 1897]. The newspapers, the clubs, the barrooms, the streets rang from morning until night with arguments." Even "ordinary shopgirls," Tarbell noted, debated the meaning of things like the "55 percent provision."[37]

With a weak mayor, a divided municipal-ownership movement, and a specific compromise proposal at hand, Chicago's business community smelled victory for the first time. Describing the matter as "a crisis in our history," the *Economist* called on its readership to use all means available to work on getting the referendum passed.[38] In February, the Chicago Commercial Association and the Chicago Real Estate Board organized the Citizens Non-Partisan Traction Settlement Committee, which soon boasted of representing 150,000 businessmen and members of neighborhood associations. Its executive members consisted of realtors, merchants, and manufacturers, all of whom belonged to Chicago's Union League Club.[39] Moreover, the committee enjoyed the backing of the Republican Party, conservative reform organizations such as the MVL, and all major newspapers except the Hearst press. Business and regulatory reform groups now adopted the same direct-democracy strategies pioneered by municipal-ownership advocates. This time it was the *Economist,* not the *Labor Advocate,* that urged people to "organize in every ward, to hold meetings there, [and] to hold a general meeting in some big hall downtown." During the weeks prior to the referendum, the committee flooded Chicago households with pamphlets, canvassed neighborhoods, and held public meetings. One mailing alone consisted of four hundred thousand postcards. The costs of the campaign were heavily subsidized by the streetcar companies, which were said to have spent about $350,000. The stakes were high, the *Economist* noted: "It is Dunne, municipal fads and chaos, or Busse, traction settlement, and prosperity."[40]

The central pillar of the campaign in favor of a new franchise was to present the issue as a practical, service-oriented one. What really counted, and what Chicagoans really cared about, was whether they were receiving decent streetcar service, and pro-franchise representatives asserted that only a swift approval of the ordinance would give them what they wanted. Showing a picture of modern, roomy streetcars, one of the committee's flyers proclaimed: "Here's the *real* Street Car Question right before your eyes. Which do you want—A *seat* in big, fast cars or, A *strap* in tumble-down cars? Your vote April 2nd will get you what you want."[41] Chicago's mainstream newspapers highlighted the gravity of the service question by featuring large pictures of deadly trolley accidents and overcrowded streetcars captioned by titles such as "DUNNE MUST END CAR HORRORS." Given that annually about 140 people died in streetcar-related accidents, such calls reverberated in the minds of Chicagoans.[42] Yet advocates of a franchise renewal managed to reverse the logic of the service question.

Whereas in the past, expositions of high accidents and poor service served to condemn the streetcar industry and to argue for greater public control, now the grievance was exploited to support a new franchise agreement with the companies.

In highlighting the urgency of service improvements and the legal and financial limitations of a public purchase, advocates of a regulatory franchise agreement between the city and the streetcar companies insisted on the "practical impossibility of acquiring municipal ownership at the present time." Even if the Illinois court approved the Mueller certificates, Fisher argued, the city would have difficulty selling an amount sufficient to cover the companies' respective purchase price. Given that the proposed ordinance included a provision for a future city takeover, Fisher felt that it offered "an infinitely better, safer, and quicker plan, either for improved service or municipal ownership."[43]

The functionalist interpretation of Chicago's transportation politics put forth by pro-franchise representatives at once acknowledged the existence of a broadened public sphere and at the same time narrowed the scope of civic engagement. Unlike a previous generation of Mugwump reformers, this generation acknowledged the citizenry as an important force in urban politics but immediately reduced its role to that of discerning consumers. "The people of Chicago are primarily concerned, not with a theoretical treatment of public utilities," the *Tribune* asserted, "but with the immediate question . . . as to the best available solution to the street railway problem."[44] Past popular votes in favor of municipal ownership, pro-franchise advocates argued, were really plebiscites for service improvements.

Political scientist Arthur F. Bentley, one of the fathers of pluralist theory, promoted the same interpretation of municipal-ownership referenda. In a study of the Chicago traction debate, he correlated referenda votes on the streetcar question with residential location and found that people in districts with poor streetcar service, that is, inner-city working-class districts, were more prone to vote for municipalization. From such data Bentley jumped to the conclusion that these voters were concerned solely with service improvements. According to Bentley, ideas and principles simply masqueraded the "real stuff" of practical concerns.[45] The political scientist thus neutralized the civic engagement of Chicago's most vociferous political actors at the turn of the century, organized labor and its working-class constituency, by interpreting their concerns in functional ways. Here lay the seeds of a pluralist understanding of politics; Bentley characterized this conflict, and politics in general, as a negotiation of different social and residential groups each with a clearly identifiable material interest, which, thus stripped of all ideological content, could be determined empirically. Functionalism and pluralism stood so strong precisely because they managed to deny their own political and ideological nature in the name of practicality and objectivity. As philosopher Karl Mannheim noted, the "denial that dominant thoughtways were ideological, that they were [none] other than the plainest common sense, was . . . the key move in the subordination of intellect to power."[46] In the case of Chicago, Bentley's apparently scientific objective study really formed part of the elite's project to wrench control of urban service policy from the masses, and especially from organized labor. What began as a political project ended with a winning ideology: pluralism. This political philosophy assumed a certain (capitalist-liberal) consensus as a given and would express no interest in such drastic shifts in the political universe, as proved the case with organized labor's marginalization from Chicago's public affairs.[47]

Functionalist politics went hand in hand with an attack on those who were considered responsible for the far-flung ideas produced by radical reformers: the intellectuals. Whereas the people were basically practical, the argument went, their leaders, deluded intellectuals from places like the University of Chicago, filled their minds with useless theories and ideas. This critique reached satirical proportions, associating all kinds of inventions with the municipal-ownership mayor. According to the Business Men's Busse Club, Dunne's "latest 'Hot-Air and Bull-Con'" was a moving sidewalk instead of streetcars. He was also said to be promoting trolley cars for individuals, a sort of head wire–driven, individualized, machine on roller-skates. Along with this, he offered an appropriate ideology: "let us individually and independently stand on our own wheels and glide with our own trolleys; let us be free agents, untrammeled by capital."[48] It is ironic that these fantastical ideas, attributed to Dunne in order to highlight his lack of practicality and distance from reality, in fact came close to predicting the main means of transportation in the decades to come: the private automobile.

The backlash against Dunne and municipal ownership was tied to an outright assault on the presence of women in Chicago politics. Amidst a group of municipal-ownership advocates in attendance at a city council session, the *Tribune* detected a group of women "from the University of Chicago, members of a class in sociology . . . wearing eye glasses." This observation not only mocked intellectuals but questioned the political activism of women. Women who played a prominent role in Dunne's administration came under scathing attack. Teacher leader Margaret Haley was given the title "Deputy Assistant Mayor" and charged with secretly controlling her personal friend Dunne.[49] According to these views, when women engaged in Chicago political affairs, they not only transgressed into the male sphere but also, in doing so, invariably sought to dominate those men cooperating with them. Just as Dunne supposedly depended on Haley, civic reformer Raymond Robins was accused of not being able to control the anarchistic excesses of his wife, Margaret Dreier Robins. Men

Key leaders of the municipal-ownership movement arriving at city hall to file petition ledgers opposing the extension of streetcar franchises in the spring of 1907. First row, from left to right: settlement house residents George E. Hooker and Raymond Robins; activist and entrepreneur David Rosenheim; and president of the Chicago Teachers Federation, Margaret Haley. *Chicago Tribune,* February 1, 1900

associated with the municipal-ownership movement and Dunne were repeatedly derided as "long-hairs," a term that served to question their manliness. The backlash against Dunne and municipal ownership thus signified a severe setback to a newly acquired presence of women in Chicago's public affairs.[50]

In the face of intellectuals' fancies and women's intrusion into male affairs, experts were heralded for their detached wisdom and their ability to apply knowledge in utilitarian ways. These qualities proved indispensable, given the inability of the general populace to comprehend the kind of intricate propositions required in public administration. According to elite civic reformers, the workings of government equaled those of a business enterprise and therefore required experts' knowledge: "The more and weightier the business undertaken, the greater the requirement for centralized authority and specialized skill; and consequently the less can be permitted of popular dictation," the secretary of the Civic Federation of Chicago stated. And he added that direct democracy only worked with simple forms of government, but these were no longer suitable to the present-day needs of a modern city.[51] Notwithstanding their elitist notions, reformers opposed to municipal ownership assured that the popular will was actually being yielded to, given that all the people wanted were immediate service improvements. Petition drives and postcard polls, organized by Chicago newspapers, were designed to document these popular needs—in this case for immediate service improvements that would be met by the 1907 settlement ordinance. They were no longer used to sustain direct popular input in decision making.[52] Functionalism and the rise of expert rule thus constituted an elite response to the widening of the public sphere in the turn-of-the-century city; the force with which new social groups, such as organized labor and women reformers, entered urban political discussions could be absorbed into the system only by ideologically delimiting that popular expression to consumer- and need-related issues.[53]

Yet trade unionists and advocates of municipal ownership resisted this effort by asserting a vision of democracy that accorded citizens a greater participatory role in urban politics. During the debate over the 1907 settlement ordinance, they reminded Chicagoans of the importance of public vigilance over corporate maneuverings that had "seriously impair[ed] the essential foundations of . . . American democracy." Recalling the popular uprisings against streetcar magnate Yerkes, the *Advocate* highlighted the crucial role played by organized labor, then and now, in "rall[ying] to the defense of our city against a gang of New York grafters before whom so many prominent business men of Chicago have supinely struck their colors." Moreover, these working-class Minute Men were described as perfectly able to "grasp the inner meaning and true perspective of public questions" and thus could be trusted to help shape public policy. Municipal-ownership advocates thus upheld a notion of the citizen as a participating democrat, not as a mere consumer.[54]

This is not to say that organized labor rejected the need for expert guidance in the administration of public services. Rather, it worried about the lack of democratic accountability of expert administration. The CFL criticized the 1907 streetcar franchise for granting the board of supervising engineers exclusive authority to assess the value of the streetcar companies' property without the need to consult the city council. Trade unionists felt that thereby the board acquired "almost unlimited power." Municipal-ownership advocates also objected to the lack of checks and balances within the administration of mass transit: "They give Bion J. Arnold two jobs at $15,000 each, or $30,000, per year. In one job he O.K.'s the work which he does in the other job."[55]

Beneath the controversy over the streetcar franchise of 1907 lay a deep awareness of class-based divisions. Trade unionists were the first to point to Chicago employers' united front against Dunne and municipal ownership: "The Employers' Association, The Union League Club, The Merchants' Club, The Commercial Club, and every other CLUB and organization opposed to organized labor, backed by the trust press, are supporting these franchise ordinances." Trade unionists thus considered the streetcar-related campaign as part of a generalized assault directed against themselves.[56] When addressing the streetcar service, labor representatives stressed class-based injustices suffered by trolley employees and riders. The bad faith of the companies toward their workers was made evident by the companies' unwillingness to include stipulations on wages, arbitration mechanisms, or a maximum workday in the new franchise. Workers were also cheated in their role as consumers of streetcar service. Referring to the high number of streetcar accidents, the CFL charged the companies for "slaying, maiming, and browbeating our citizens" and made clear that this occurred especially "in those parts of the city occupied mainly by the people who actually work."[57] Poor streetcar service, in the eyes of trade unionists, reflected class-based iniquities and hostilities; it was not a merely functionalist matter.

Employer organizations also confronted the municipal-ownership question in class terms. Along with most newspapers, they attacked the Dunne administration for granting too much political power to organized labor. Under Dunne, the city's fire department and school board, they charged, had fallen under complete labor control.[58] In the eyes of employers, public ownership of the streetcars would only make things worse, as this meant the inclusion of an additional fourteen thousand employees in the city payroll, which would thereby double in its size.[59] This would lead to an unacceptable degree of political influence by organized labor, employers feared. Already unionized policemen, firemen, and schoolteachers were engaging in municipal-ownership propaganda on their jobs, by circulating referendum petitions, for example.[60] In this sense, from the employers' perspective, the campaign for a franchise settlement constituted the political equivalent of the open-shop drive; both the EA's move against the teamsters in 1905 and now the drive for the continued private operation of the streetcar companies targeted the public influence of Chicago trade unions.

Next to the streetcar question, it was educational policy that provoked the ire of Dunne's opponents. Having, as judge, ruled favorably toward the teachers, Dunne as mayor continued to act on behalf of the schoolteachers union. In 1905 and in 1906, he staffed the Chicago Board of Education with thirteen new members, most of them sympathetic to the CTF. Among those appointed were educational reformer Cornelia De Bey, secretary of the garment workers union John P. Sonsteby, single-taxer and publisher of the *Public,* Louis Post, and social reformers Jane Addams and Raymond Robins. The new board not only opposed the teachers' longtime antagonist, superintendent of schools Edwin Cooley, but also criticized head-on two of Chicago's most influential newspapers, the *Daily News* and the *Tribune*. For many years these two publishers had been leasing and occupying municipal lots reserved for financing public education. The teachers, and now the board of education, claimed that the rent paid by these papers was far below the land's property value and demanded greater compensation to the city. Here then was an obvious basis for hostility on behalf of these two newspapers against the teachers, the board of education, and Dunne's administration in general. Mixing functionalist and anti-intellectual arguments with class-based ones, the *Tribune* and other papers charged: "When Dunne packs the board of education with freaks, cranks, monomaniacs, and boodlers, he is doing much to bring Chicago into disrepute . . . [and he] invites strikes."[61] Thus behind "public opinion," that ubiquitous and much-hailed force of the Progressive Era, stood at least two Chicago newspapers not only generally ill-disposed toward organized labor but now directly affected by its newly gained political influence.

As the conflict over traction policy intensified in the 1907 campaign and revolved along class lines, middle-class reformers sympathetic toward trade unionism and a left-wing progressive agenda struggled to maintain their ground. On the one hand, reformers affirmed their support of organized labor and its political agenda: "It is fashionable to be contemptuous of labor movements," Louis Post affirmed, "but the classes that hold such movements in contempt have yet to lay before the public a fairer and more American platform of political principle" than that presented by the CFL.[62] Reformers also realized that Chicago's political culture was suffused with class conflict. Margaret Dreier Robins regarded the opposition to Dunne and municipal ownership as an "effort to stamp out trades unionism absolutely and entirely in Chicago. . . . To my mind, it is distinctly a class struggle." Yet Dreier Robins, like many middle-class progressives, still adhered to the ideal of transcending this struggle; she realized that "only the very elect can escape [its] . . . demarcation."[63] For her and for other like-minded reformers, this meant loyalty to Dunne, a posture that placed them at the city's political front line. Whereas trade unionists denounced the mayor's traction policy, Dreier Robins—along with her husband, Robins, and Post—applauded Dunne's pragmatic course of action and praised the integrity of his new traction counsel, Fisher. She even adopted the rhetoric of franchise advocates when she denounced the "long-hairs" who "never can understand why things are not done all at once."[64] This criticism was implicitly directed against Chicago's labor movement, which continued to back immediate municipal ownership. In the context of a confrontational political climate, reformers like Dreier Robins thus found themselves in contradictory positions. At one point she even denounced the new members of the board of education as "Creators of Anarchy, discontent, and class strife," notwithstanding the fact that her own husband counted among them![65]

On April 2, 1907, the traction controversy in Chicago came to an end. Edward Dunne lost to Fred Busse by a slight margin of 12,923 ballots, or 4 percent of the total vote. Perhaps President Theodore Roosevelt's surprise intervention on behalf of the Republican helped him squeeze in the final decisive votes. At the same time, a more substantial majority of over thirty-three thousand voters (12 percent) approved the settlement ordinance and thereby repudiated immediate municipal ownership. Class divisions help explain the election outcome. Voters in several outlying middle-class wards who had backed Dunne two years earlier, now, apparently motivated by the hope for immediate service improvements, opted for Busse. Working-class Chicagoans still backed Dunne but with far less enthusiasm than before. Although he again carried the city's Irish and working-class districts, he mobilized far less of their inhabitants; up to 30 percent less of them bothered to vote than in 1905.[66] The day after the election was met with a sigh of relief by the city's press and business circles. According to the *Economist:* "Everything in Chicago was worth more on Wednesday morning than on Tuesday morning." Chicago, it seemed, had rid itself of "the champions of fads and fancies . . . [and] the city can now go forward with courage to the realization of its destiny." The *Tribune,* in celebrating Dunne's defeat, reasserted government as the realm of male practicality: Chicago, it declared, rejected "petticoat government and pipe dream government. It has rejected Hearst . . . Dunne, . . . Haley, De Bey and the whole crew of female politicians and other long-haired freaks."[67]

Later historians have interpreted the 1907 Chicago election as being in keeping with the functionalist ideology that took shape at the time. Chicagoans opted for the franchise settlement out of practical, pragmatic reasons and rejected the more idealistic, theoretical options. Voters simply wanted good streetcar service.[68] Besides leaving the question unanswered as to whether a continuation of private operation of the trolley system indeed meant better service, this argument obscures the political and class-related dynamics that underlay the traction controversy. When Dunne assumed office in 1905, open class conflict reared its head in the form of the teamsters strike. Two years later, workers and employers confronted each other again, this time at the ballot box. Right beneath the arguments for better streetcar service stood efforts on behalf of Chicago's elite to reduce the political influence of organized labor and of the citizenry in general. Major employer groups, the streetcar and real estate interests, as well as conservative civic reformers thereby helped reorient the city's political culture. While acknowledging a newly expanded public sphere and the importance of working for the public interest, they reduced the same to questions of practical needs.

THE ECLIPSE OF REFORM IN A FRAGMENTED CITY

The defeat of Mayor Edward Dunne and the acceptance of the settlement franchise in the 1907 elections proved a decisive moment in Chicago politics, both with regard to the city's mass transit policy and the future of reform politics. The decision against public ownership of the streetcars in 1907 set the stage for weakened public control over this urban service, notwithstanding the hopes of moderate reformers. With a government takeover becoming an ever more remote possibility and with the removal of public regulatory powers from the municipal to the state level, efforts to publicly influence streetcar service proved difficult. New mass transit initiatives—such as plans for the construction of a subway—proved untenable. The limited nature of regulatory reform gave way to the rise of a far less controversial, but certainly revolutionary, means of urban mobility: the automobile.

The failure of a more ambitious public policy on mass transit and the rise of privatized transportation took place in the context of a general shift in the city's political culture. The years following 1907 witnessed the consolidation of a functionalist ideology, which stipulated that any policy proposals must adhere to immediate needs and practical solutions and ascribed to the average citizen the role of a passive consumer of urban services rather than that of an active agent in the political process. Under the mantle of practicality, more ambitious plans for a restructuring of the urban environment, of both moderate and radical types, were easily denounced as the product of intellectual hotheads. Politically this meant the failure of even moderate reform platforms, as evidenced in Charles Merriam's mayoral campaign in 1911, and the rise of Chicago's famed political machine, first evidenced in the government of William Hale Thompson (1915–1923, 1927–1931).

Under these circumstances, organized labor remained on the sidelines of public debate. While the CFL continued to address municipal questions such as transportation policy and urban planning, it no longer assumed the central position it had enjoyed during the earlier part of the Progressive Era. During the World War I period, the CFL politically expressed its revived strength and militancy in the form of a labor party ticket. The possibility for a broader reform coalition inserted into mainstream politics dwindled.

The 1911 campaign for mayor by University of Chicago political scientist Charles E. Merriam appeared to revive reform politics. Dissatisfied with Dunne's successor, Fred Busse, who exhibited regular Republican ward politics without a broader agenda, reformers placed their hopes in Merriam, who was known for his efforts to run the city administration along business principles. Elected an alderman in 1909, he soon proposed and directed the Bureau of Public Efficiency, an agency designed to serve as a watchdog for the city's financial activities. Merriam's reform platform of efficient city government was in tune with the philosophy of Chicago's moderate reform community, which included figures such as Fisher and Arnold as well as organizations such as the MVL, the City Club, and the Civic Federation. Even the CFL backed Merriam's candidacy, though this reflected more labor's long-standing hostility to Merriam's opponent in the 1911 election, Carter Harrison II, than its commitment to the reformer.[1]

Despite relatively strong civic support, Merriam failed, which gave way to yet another mayoral term by longtime Democratic Party regular Carter Harrison II. Chicago's political climate no longer proved conducive to a reform ticket. For one, Merriam could not muster the broad-based and crossclass constituency that had elected Dunne in 1905. Then, Merriam proved vulnerable to the functionalist and anti-intellectual language first utilized by Dunne's opponents in 1907. His academic background proved a great handicap. He was mocked as a high-headed intellectual unable to deal with Chicago's practical concerns: "I do not favor anyone from the University of Chicago. They are all Socialists out there. There's too much damn Hull House in it for me." The author of these words, outgoing Mayor Busse, here rhetorically raised two red flags in the city's political universe, radicalism and intellectualism, and associated them with Merriam.[2]

Thus set in the rise of Chicago machine politics, put in place by Republican William Hale Thompson throughout most of the 1920s. Thompson managed the difficult task of centralizing power into the mayor's office and the ruling party, in a city whose governing structure had been fragmented and whose residents' political loyalties had been divided. Whether he accomplished this through corruption—as many critics, including political scientist Merriam, charged—is less to the point than the fact that he successfully employed the ideology of functionalism. Thompson justified his autocratic style of rule with claims of servicing the needs of a diverse array of interest groups. Unlike the reformers, he refused to resort to "fancy" ideas and presented himself as a pragmatic leader. The mythic opposition between boss and reformer, the practical ward chief versus the idealistic but aloof reform candidate, was born. Adopted, somewhat uncritically, by a later generation of urban historians, this distinction grew out of the political and ideological conflicts of the Progressive Era.[3]

These political shifts affected the nature of Chicago's mass transit policy. Hailed for its practicality and reasonableness, the new franchise with the streetcar companies approved by voters in 1907 did entail some improvements in the operation of the streetcars. Assured of their continued right to operate, the companies rehabilitated their rolling stock and expanded their network; from 1907 to 1914, they built or rebuilt 560 miles of track. The city's transportation counsel Walter Fisher, at least, boasted that Chicago enjoyed the "best surface street railway system . . . in the U.S."[4]

Experts also claimed that the 1907 franchise resulted in effective governmental regulation of this public utility. Through its newly created board of supervising engineers, headed by Bion Arnold, the city was said to enter a practical partnership with the companies in the operation of the streetcars. All across the nation, the Chicago case was heralded as a model of a moderate path of utility regulation, where the mere possibility of municipal ownership had sufficed to turn the companies into publicly responsible entities. In fact, the city had acquired the legal right to purchase the streetcar lines upon six months' notice at any time during the twenty-year term of the franchise.[5]

In reality, however, the possibility of a municipal purchase proved quite remote. First, there was the question of finances. Only days after the 1907 election, the Illinois Supreme Court declared the Mueller certificates—the means by which the city was to finance a purchase—unconstitutional. Furthermore, the terms by which the companies' assets were valued and purchase prices set became increasingly unfavorable to a municipal takeover. In 1913, chief traction engineer Arnold proposed and enacted the unification of all traction lines under the mantle of one single company, the Chicago Surface Lines. While this consolidation resolved an ongoing complaint over the lack of citywide coordination of streetcar service by establishing, for instance, a universal fare across the entire city, the agreement set such a high valuation of company property that it rendered a public purchase of the system prohibitive. It was for this reason that George C. Sikes, an investigator of public transportation and backer of the 1907 ordinances, considered the unification plans "more vicious by far . . . than the notorious Allen law of 1892," the attempt by streetcar entrepreneur Charles Yerkes to extend his franchise to fifty years.[6] Reformers like Sikes rejected municipal ownership as a concrete solution, but they appreciated being able to threaten the companies with a public takeover. With the 1913 unification agreement, regulatory reformers found themselves deprived of even this important bargaining tool.

Behind this arrangement stood a figure that henceforth played a key role in the provisioning and politics of Chicago's public utilities: Samuel Insull. In some ways, his history parallels that of Yerkes. Insull emigrated from England, worked for many years as assistant to Thomas Edison, and arrived in Chicago during the early 1890s where he orchestrated that city's "electrical revolution." He effectively consolidated the fragmented industry by combining a sophisticated rate system with technological innovations in the generation and distribution of electricity. By the late 1890s, his Chicago Commonwealth Edison Company enjoyed a virtual monopoly over electrical service. Insull then orchestrated what occurred in many cities: the merger of the electrical and streetcar industries. Throughout the 1890s, Chicago's traction companies had still generated their own electrical power, but they eventually preferred Insull's central-generator-based and more economical service. They soon found themselves indebted to—and soon, one by one, bought up by—Commonwealth Edison. By 1913 they had all merged into the Chicago Surface Lines.[7]

Such maneuvers entailed a calculated political strategy to remove regulatory policy decisions as far as possible from that potential democratic hotbed Chicago. Insull established close ties to Chicago's incipient political machine. He would become a close collaborator of Mayor William Thompson. Insull's lawyer, Samuel Ettleson, for example, served as the mayor's corporation counsel. Yet Insull further depoliticized the operation of his utility businesses by placing public regulatory powers into the hands of the state government. In 1913, the same year Insull consolidated control over Chicago's streetcar lines, the newly established State Public Utility Commission of Illinois assumed jurisdiction. As a result, the city of Chicago found its hands tied; not only could it no longer afford to purchase the streetcar lines, but now it was also prevented by state law from building competing lines. (This had been one of Mayor Dunne's proposed solutions when faced with obstacles to a municipal takeover.) The transfer of regulatory powers to the state level was widespread in other states of the Union, the best-known case being Robert La Follette's Wisconsin commission plans. While these new state bodies exemplified progressive-era recognition of the need for a certain degree of governmental regulation of private utilities, they took away decision-making powers from the immediately affected citizenry and essentially smoothed the way for the private monopoly operation of urban services. Utility expert Delos F. Wilcox recognized these broader political implications: "a great many are coming to fear that the commissions . . . are primarily organs of the public utility interests to protect themselves from the mosquito bites of rampant democracy."[8] In placing governmental jurisdiction over the streetcars on the state level, Insull thus succeeded where Yerkes had failed in the late 1890s. At the price of accepting a certain degree of state regulation, he rested assured that municipal ownership no longer proved a threat.

The paths between Yerkes and Insull diverge most drastically with regard to the two utility barons' public reputations. Whereas the former was forced to flee the city, Insull became a widely respected corporate leader, which illuminates a great deal about the changing nature of Chicago's political culture and Insull's skill at operating within it. The Englishman converted electricity from an exclusive article to a product for the masses and also became one of the first experts in "public relations." Yerkes had alienated streetcar users with phrases such as "straphangers pay the dividends," whereas Insull placed himself at the service of the consumer. Eager to sell electricity to small households as well as to large users such as streetcar companies, Insull devised a graduated rate system that rendered the service affordable to small consumers. With the notion of the common good reduced to functional, need-based concerns and the citizen conceptualized primarily as a recipient of services, Insull found it easy to claim to serve the public interest by delivering ever better and cheaper electricity to the masses. That he enjoyed monopoly power over two utilities, infiltrated local- and state-level politics, and effectively stifled independent government control over these public services apparently proved of little concern to Chicagoans during the 1910s and 1920s. It was only in the 1930s that Insull's and Yerkes's fates would converge, when Insull was placed on trial and charged with being "more responsible than any other man in Chicago's history for the degradation of municipal government to its lowest level of corruption and incompetence."[9]

Notwithstanding Insull's consumer-oriented posturing and his claims of improvements in the provision of urban services, the extent to which these innovations could be used as tools for ambitious planning initiatives remained quite limited. This is illustrated by 1910 plans to construct a fifty-six-mile-long subway system. Transportation experts, most notably the city's longtime traction counsel Bion Arnold, had long considered a subway the panacea to the city's transportation problem. They admitted that the companies, following the 1907 franchise settlement, had made some improvements in scheduling and improvement of cars, but they also realized that the city's main transportation problem—that of downtown traffic congestion—continued unabated. In a city such as Chicago, where transportation flows centered downtown, improvements in streetcar technology or scheduling did little to alleviate the congestion of downtown traffic, where stubborn teamsters, pedestrians, and (new on the scene) automobilists, along with the high number of streetcars themselves prevented the trolleys' free travel. As one traction expert noted: "the new cars, as the old ones, were compelled to creep by inches through the downtown district." For Arnold and the transportation board, the solution was clear: avoid the street by means of a subway line.[10]

Yet other forces in the city rejected this logic and thereby provoked a fundamental debate over the priorities of public transit policy and its effect on city spaces. The most vocal opposition to the project stemmed from small businesses located outside the downtown area. Organized in the North West Side Commercial Association and in the Greater Chicago Federation, backed by the Cook County Real Estate Board, these small businesses argued that subways would reinforce a long-held policy of favoring downtown commercial and real estate development over a more decentralized retail structure. For decades businessmen from outlying districts had been arguing against the centralization of the city's commerce. Back during the 1890s, they mobilized against the dominance of downtown department stores. Yet by the 1910s, 75 percent of the city's business was conducted within the city center. Fearful that a radial subway line would even further accentuate this tendency, retailers on the periphery argued that the design of public transportation should serve to revert such spatial and social imbalances. In the words of the Greater Chicago Federation's vice president, Benjamin Levering: "The problem facing the city administration at the present time is not how to bring people into the loop and take them out again with greater facility, but rather how to divert the business of the city to other sections, in order that we may have a Greater Chicago instead of a Greater Loop." In concrete terms, this meant abandoning the subway project and instead constructing a series of so-called crosstown streetcar lines that would allow passengers to travel from one outlying area of the city to another without having to traverse the Loop. Advocates of the subway rejected such proposals; transportation lines should be built "in the general direction of existing traffic and not . . . to suit particular theories."[11] Yet, in claiming the pursuit of the citizenry's immediate needs, this functionalist logic in fact was underwriting a spatial and social development that favored certain regions and social groups over others.

Even though subway opponents managed to expose the underlying geopolitics of public transportation, they remained precisely that: opponents. Outlying retailers—backed by the streetcar company, which feared competition from a subway system—managed to defeat the construction of the subway, as expressed by two referenda held in 1914 and 1918. Yet they did not gather sufficient political strength to put forth an alternative mass transit plan. In part, this reflected the fact that decisions over public transportation in Chicago were now made in Springfield, Illinois, not in city hall. In part, the look of a more propositive stand was the product of a functionalist ideology that defined needs in such narrow terms that rendered more ambitious mass transit projects, of whatever kind, politically untenable. As a result, in Chicago of the 1910s neither cross-town lines nor subways proved feasible. No subway would run under Big Shoulders until after World War II, and rail-based cross-town lines would never be implemented.[12]

The divisiveness of transportation planning and its limited capacity in altering existing social and geographical realities was revealed in the individual neighborhoods as well, in this case in Kenwood–Hyde Park. In the spring of 1909, the City Railway Company, the company delivering trolley service to the city's southern region, proposed the extension of a streetcar line on Lake Avenue north from Fifty-fifth to Forty-seventh streets. The plan provoked immediate protests by residents of the wealthy Kenwood residential district, which bordered Lake Street from Fifty-first to Forty-seventh streets along the northern portion of the proposed extension (see map 4). Associated in the Kenwood Improvement Association, property owners described the potential streetcar as a missile that would do away with residential property and middle-class civilization altogether. A streetcar "would prostitute one of our best streets to the constant demoralization of a noisy street car service," Theodore K. Long, the alderman of the affected district, explained to a reporter. The noise and danger generated by the trolley would "largely destroy the value of the Kenwood public school, . . . [and] destroy the usefulness of the Blackstone Free Library as a reading and reference room." Moreover, a trolley line through Kenwood was utterly unnecessary, they argued, for residents already could commute downtown far more comfortably (though more expensively) by means of the Illinois Central Railroad.[13]

More than the trolley itself, it was the people who rode it that worried Kenwood residents. As they saw it, the new line would connect their high-class residential street with a district further south on Lake Avenue that was characterized by "cheap stores, laundries, livery stables, saloons, beer gardens," and above all, undesirable residents, who would be traversing their neighborhood on the proposed trolley line. By "undesirable residents," members of the Kenwood Improvement Association clearly meant African Americans. The same year the new streetcar line was being debated, this improvement association was founded in order to keep Kenwood white. It monitored real estate agencies in order to prevent house

4. PLAN FOR EXTENSION OF STREETCAR LINE IN SOUTH CHICAGO, 1915

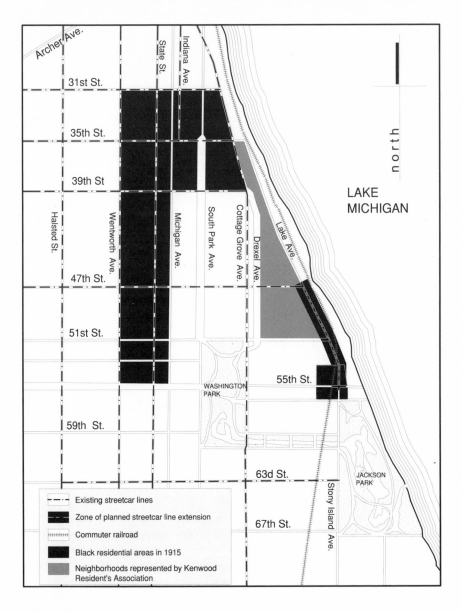

Existing streetcar lines

Zone of planned streetcar line extension

Commuter railroad

Black residential areas in 1915

Neighborhoods represented by Kenwood Resident's Association

sales to blacks on the region's South and West sides.[14] In later years, the association also resorted to physical violence in order to force black residents to leave the neighborhood. For now, Kenwood segregationists, in fighting against the streetcar extension, employed the same strategies as were instituted by the municipal-ownership advocates a few years earlier: the circulation of petitions, the organization of rallies in and around city hall, and the demand for a popular referendum. One day in 1909, for example, several hundred citizens of the Kenwood district packed a city hall committee room, the hallways, and the stairs in order to protest the streetcar extension.[15]

Measures of direct democracy continued to be applied in debates over public transportation, but instead of pursuing the integration of the city, as municipal-ownership advocates did, now the call was to keep racial and class segregation intact. In the following decades, streetcars continued as focal points of racial conflicts. During the 1920s, African Americans who needed to travel on a streetcar within the Kenwood–Hyde Park district dared to do so only during a few hours in the morning and the afternoon. The route was dubbed "nigger line" by whites and "African Central" by the black newspaper the *Chicago Defender*.[16] Until this day, public transportation in Chicago is marked by racial and class divisions. Residents of Hyde Park still shun all public transportation that runs through black ghettos to the north, south, and west and only ride the Jeffrey Lakeside Express bus or the suburban railroad in order to commute downtown. By now this neighborhood, which houses the University of Chicago, has opened its doors to the black middle class (in fact, it is one of Chicago's most racially integrated areas), yet racial fault lines in mass transit remain.

Given the political difficulties of mass transit on both the neighborhood and the city level, the private automobile loomed as a logical solution and could rise to dominance without any clear policy ever having been devised or debated. Thus it was Chicago's park system's boulevards, greatly amplified as part of Daniel H. Burnham's Chicago Plan of 1909, that offered travel possibilities to the new "leisure vehicles," undisturbed by other vehicles not allowed to enter the parks. Linking Chicago's downtown to many exclusive neighborhoods in the city's outskirts, the parkways soon became the new commuting paths of suburban residents. Unlike the monopolistic trolleys, privately owned individual automobiles, at least in the first decades, were politically safe. In general, road construction plans, especially when disguised as parkways, provoked little political controversy. No public referendum had ever to be approved in order to inaugurate the automobile-based city.[17] One of the few dissenting voices stemmed from organized labor. In 1912, for example, the CFL pointed to the high rate of deaths and injury caused by "reckless, careless driving of automobilists" and accused police officers of not arresting them because of their wealth

10

and influence. Yet such critique did not develop into a broader public argument, a fact symptomatic of the marginal position of organized labor within mainstream Chicago politics. The car proved irresistible to even the most spirited advocates of mass transit policy; when Edward Dunne was elected governor of Illinois in 1912, his generous state subsidies for road construction caused the once municipal-ownership mayor to become known as "the first Good Roads Governor of Illinois."[18] The automobile is often considered the cause of the spatial sprawl and social fragmentation of U.S. cities. Yet, at least in the case of Chicago, the rise of the car was as much effect as cause of the fragmented city. For it was an unwillingness to adopt ambitious policy initiatives in mass transit, a functionalist political climate, and segregationist movements on the neighborhood level that literally paved the road for the automobile-dominated metropolis.

So what became of organized labor's role in Chicago politics? With regard to transportation matters, the CFL continued to speak out and mobilize its constituency. It continued to call for public ownership of the transit utility, although it centered its efforts on more immediate demands for improvements in streetcar service and working conditions, and it insisted, as it always did, in linking these two aspects: "polite, patient, and affable service" could only result from alert and well-rested streetcar operators. Trade unionists still offered detailed, empirically based proposals on how to improve the quality of the service especially in working-class regions of the city. The streetcar conductors local, for example, demanded improvements from the city's board of supervising engineers with regard to the number of cars per train, the hours of operation, as well as matters such as heating, ventilation, cleanliness, and safety devices on board the cars. In November 1907 the CFL participated in a "No-Seat-No-Fare" campaign, which called for the refund of fares in the case of excessively overcrowded or delayed cars.[19] The CFL also passed resolutions regarding other municipal questions, such as street cleaning, school meal programs, and park maintenance, and even participated in a "Go-to-Church-Campaign." In 1908, it joined Samuel Gompers and the AFL in their call for an aggressive political campaign on the state level. Like its counterparts in cities across the nation, the CFL formed political action committees designed to influence state policy, by means of nominating, punishing, and rewarding legislators in Springfield. In August 1908, the CFL asked for one hundred thousand volunteers to monitor the primary voting booths and distributed three hundred thousand letters of endorsements; after primary day it reported that 31 of its 105 endorsed candidates had been successful.[20]

Yet such political engagement did not place organized labor back in the center of Chicago politics; municipal political reform, as far as it still existed, and trade union politics took very different paths. This is illustrated by the CFL's stand on the construction of a subway and the Chicago Plan. When the Greater Chicago Federation exposed the downtown-centered bias of the subway plan, it echoed a critique frequently raised by the CFL and other radical reformers. Both federations, in effect, suggested that a transportation system motivated by private and profit-based concerns would operate to the detriment of the public. Fitzpatrick coincided with Tomaz F. Deuther, secretary of the North West Side Commercial Association (an affiliate of the Greater Chicago Federation), in their belief in the need to construct more cross-town streetcar lines. Whereas Deuther wished to improve business for outlying regions, the labor leader sought to avoid lengthy and costly commuting for workers who lived in one outlying zone and worked in another. Yet the political and industrial climate in the 1910s worked against cooperation between these two civic organizations. When Deuther began to address CFL delegates in order to gain support for his anti-subway agenda, a delegate of the waitress union accused him of having led the fight in Springfield against an eight-hour law for women workers. By the end of the meeting, Fitzpatrick informed the invited speaker that until such time as his associates "recognized and dealt with Organized Labor, this Federation did not propose to come to their assistance."[21] In a similar vein, iron molder leader John P. Frey, addressing the Chicago City Club, pointed to the hostility of many reform organizations toward labor legislation as the major obstacle to cooperation. Ever since the municipal-ownership debacle, cross-class urban reform appeared to be halted.

In 1909, Mayor Busse invited CFL president Fitzpatrick to join a committee on the city's Chicago Plan. In a sense, Daniel Burnham's sweeping effort to redesign the city center with wide diagonal boulevards that would converge on a newly built dome-topped city hall might find appeal among trade unionists who for years mobilized to strengthen public-minded initiatives and to overcome urban fragmentation. Yet CFL president Fitzpatrick ringingly declined the mayor's invitation to participate in the plan. To the labor leader, the upholding of a public spirit did not entail a grandiose civic center, nor a superficial beautification of the city, but rather, "a better citizenship and an understanding of the responsibility we have to protect and promote the welfare of the human family." In criticizing the plan, Fitzpatrick invoked Christian ethics; when city planners "ignored the cry of despair among the men, women, and children whose only fault is that they must toil to live, [it] makes one . . . ask if we are in the era before Christ, or in the twentieth century of Christianity." The city urgently needed a "Chicago Plan," but one directed at improving the standard of living of all its inhabitants.[22] In Fitzpatrick's eyes, Chicago's official reform projects no longer proved suitable for the pursuit of such broad-minded goals.

Neither could they be achieved within the city's partisan structure. The CFL continued to keep its distance from Harrisonian Democracy and from the later Thompson machine, whose anti-labor policies only strengthened this posture. During key disputes, such as a streetcar and textile strike in 1915, Thompson refused to arbitrate. Worse, the Chicago Board of Education staffed with his appointees adopted a hostile stand toward one of the main pillars of reform unionism in Chicago, the CTF. In 1915, the education board's Loeb Rule outright forbade the unionization of public-school teachers. For the next two years, Haley's CTF fought the ruling in the courts, only to face a final defeat when in 1917 the Illinois Supreme Court upheld this "yellow-dog" contract and forced the CTF to withdraw from the CFL.[23]

, , ,

Chicago trade unions' clash with the Hearst press, a key opinion maker in the city, further contributed to labor's weakened public presence. During the early 1900s, the *Chicago Examiner* and the *Chicago American* both proved crucial to the organizational drive of the new trade unions and the launching of the municipal-ownership campaign. Yet it soon became evident to labor leaders that Hearst subordinated his pro-union and public-ownership principles to his political ambitions. Labor leaders were already complaining of Hearst's sensationalist and hostile coverage during the 1905 teamsters strike, but it was a conflict in the newspaper industry itself, in 1912, that provoked the final rupture. In April 1912, the two Hearst papers affiliated with the open-shop American Newspaper-Publishers' Association and set out to break their employees' unions altogether. All pressmen, stereotypers, and newspaper deliverers who refused to turn in their union cards were locked out.[24] The CFL responded by forming an Anti-Hearst Trade Union League and led a personal attack on the once "friend of labor": "Resolved, that Mr. Hearst's character and conduct, industrially, politically, and journalistically are so saturated with egotism, ambition, and avarice as to place him outside of the pale of influence with any self-respecting, liberty loving organization of men."[25]

The breakdown of the labor-Hearst alliance held dire consequences for both. While reform-oriented trade unionists lost a central organ of publicity, the Hearst press now lacked a credible social base for its reform-oriented claims. It descended into the kind of empty sensationalism that has marked its fame ever since. This decline in what might be termed a civic function of the yellow press played a key role in Habermas's account of the transformation of the public sphere. According to the German philosopher, the mass media, and especially newspapers, became degraded—from being the means of critical interchange among citizens they became organs of mass manipulation. The case of Chicago's Hearst press somewhat complicates this notion, however. During its founding years, it backed trade union–led reform and helped involve an unprecedented number of Chicagoans in urban civic affairs. It was only later, and in the context of an anti-labor and anti-reform climate, that it conformed to Habermas's model.[26]

Notwithstanding Chicago trade unions' (forced) retreat from the center of public affairs, during the 1910s and especially the years surrounding World War I, the city confirmed its reputation as a storm center of labor activism. Already in 1911, a strike of clothing manufacturer Hart, Schaffner and Marx acquired nationwide fame, as the company and the Amalgamated Clothing Workers Union led by Sidney Hillman hammered out a model agreement of conciliation in a heretofore unregulated, highly competitive industry populated by unskilled and immigrant wage earners. As always, the CFL provided key support to the—mainly female—garment workers on strike. Prominent progressive reformers and organizations aided the call for industrial arbitration. Chicago also continued to be the site of an exceptionally well-organized metropolitan unionism, dominated by the city's teamsters, building trades, and building-service workers. The teamsters occasionally resumed their engagement in sympathy strikes, assisting the unionization of service workers such as dairy employees, coal-yard laborers, bakers, and (new to the scene) oil station attendants.[27]

The World War I period witnessed a full-fledged resurgence of labor militancy. From 1915 to 1919, the city witnessed an unprecedented number of strikes, which peaked in July 1919. In that month alone, 250,000 workers, about a third of those employed in industries, were either on strike or preparing to strike. Although labor disputes proved common in most U.S. cities during this period, Chicago stood out for the major role played by the CFL, which Communist leader William Z. Foster described as "the most progressive labour council in the United States." Foster could count on Fitzpatrick's cooperation in attempting to organize workers in the city's two most solid anti-union bastions: the packing houses (in 1917) and the steel industry (in 1919). While both organizing efforts ultimately failed, they set precedents for the permanent unionization of these industries, dominated by unskilled, immigrant workers, during the 1930s.[28]

On the political front, the CFL opted for independent action. In late 1918 Fitzpatrick helped found the Cook County Labor Party and ran as its mayoral candidate in the following spring municipal elections. Among other demands, the new party called for the immediate municipal ownership of the city's public utilities, but this time with a radical edge added: the call for worker participation in their management. Although the labor ticket represented a serious threat to a number of Democratic ward bosses, its overall turnout (8 percent) proved somewhat disappointing. With its ties to the Democratic Party ruptured since the Dunne mayoralty of 1905–1907, and with a functionalist—and, after World War I, outright anti-radical—climate in place, Chicago trade unions could not regain the political presence they held during the first years of the century.[29]

The defeat of labor radicalism in the post–World War I era reflected a variety of factors: a wave of police- and court-led repression, the "Red Scare" of the early 1920s, as well as long-term tendencies toward ethnic- and especially racial-based divisions within the labor movement. Curiously, however, accounts of labor militancy in Chicago pay little attention to the trade unions' positioning within local and state politics. In the years from 1915 to 1919, had the CFL been able to occupy a more central position in the city's political landscape, its work-place-centered efforts might have proved more effective. By the 1920s, as Chicago political bosses acquired fame for their political machinations and alliances with gangsters and boodlers, organized labor operated on the fringes of a delimited public sphere. Only the crisis of the depression would catapult trade unionists back into the public orbit and would lead Chicago workers to "make a New Deal." This would have been impossible without their vibrant political activism during the Progressive Era, especially during the period's early phase. It was this legacy, as much as the rise of mass culture among workers during the 1920s and 1930s, that shaped worker and trade union demands during the era of Franklin D. Roosevelt.[30]

From about 1902 to 1907, Chicago was indeed a laboratory of progressive reform, and a reassertion of the common good went hand in hand with the democratization of politics, best represented by the public presence of the city's labor movement. Yet during the following decade, political activism from below and calls for a socially responsive government were replaced by the abandonment not only of left-wing progressive reform, but of reform politics altogether. In its stead emerged a functionalist ideology, which regarded politics as a negotiation over a public interest defined in terms of the supposedly objective and immediate needs of essentially passive citizen consumers. In such a climate, neither statist radicals nor regulatory moderates held sufficient breathing space. Chicagoans had to come to terms with living in a city fragmented in political as well as geosocial terms. It was the political machine that proved best suited to manage the fragmented city, and the automobile was the mode of transportation to traverse it.[31] Organized labor, despite its continued militancy on the industrial and political levels, would remain on the sidelines, a fact that proved not coincidental to but reflected the very design of the functionalist city.

CLASS, REFORM, AND DEMOCRACY
IN EARLY TWENTIETH-CENTURY AMERICA

The history of Chicago streetcar politics is indicative of major transformations undergone by the political culture of industrialized nations during the late nineteenth century. A general collectivization of economic and social life resulted in the entrance of new social groups into the political process. Workers of most European countries received the right to vote, and trade unions formed labor-based parties, which, by the early twentieth century, enjoyed an unprecedented degree of political representation. Organized labor used its power to translate a profound sense of economic, social, and urban crisis into a political reform agenda. As a result, most countries of the Northern Atlantic world, as elsewhere, witnessed the rise of more interventionist state governments, which, in one form or another, addressed matters that were now recognized as being of public concern: hygiene, health insurance, pension funds, working conditions, industrial relations, consumer standards, and, in the cities, urban services, public works, and city planning. In other words, labor movements throughout the world proved crucial for the rise of social democracy.

Progressivism in Chicago also rose through a politically assertive labor movement. When in the late 1890s, Chicagoans mobilized against streetcar magnate Charles Tyson Yerkes, they reaffirmed a public interest in safe-guarding their city's transportation system and entered a ten-year-long de-bate over exactly how to accomplish the same. Debates over the common good were, of course, nothing new in Chicago, but—as the extent of popu-lar outrage against Yerkes suggests and as subsequent developments, espe-cially the movement for the municipal ownership of the streetcars, confirms—reform politics now involved a broad section of the city's popu-lation. In demanding the municipalization of Chicago's streetcars, trade unions and their allies pursued a variety of interests, which partly con-cerned work-related matters: teachers fought the streetcar companies in or-der to obtain wage increases; streetcar unions advocated public ownership because they hoped to improve their lot as employees of the municipality; many workers simply wished to get rid of a large company known for its anti-union stance. Municipal-ownership advocates also spoke as con-sumers who depended on intra-urban transportation: many wage earners, especially the more skilled segment that formed the backbone of the CFL, engaged in daily streetcar commutes. Most workers were keenly aware of the need to be mobile in an ever-expanding and -specializing city and knew full well that the less privileged were the first to lose from a trans-portation system operated solely out of profit-oriented motives. Finally, la-bor activists spoke as citizens and as reformers; they held a stake as great as, if not greater than, their middle-class counterparts in safeguarding their government from corruption, in asserting the power of the citizenry to shape public policy, and in promoting far-sighted policies.

Citizens and organizations stemming from the city's middle class shared the same concerns held by organized labor and took this numerous and powerful new political force quite seriously. While some reformers allied directly with trade unionists, as in the municipal-ownership movement, others, more moderate in their political outlook and more skeptical about the enlightened nature of blue-collar workers, purported to shift policy making into the hands of professional experts, although they still granted the people an approbatory role, be it through occasional referenda or at the ballot box. Whatever approach middle-class reformers took, they all furthered their reform agenda on the basis of a newly democratized polity.

The progressive moment was thus contingent upon the political actions of new social agents, especially organized labor, who sought to reaffirm the ideal and scope of a singular public interest even as they claimed their right to politically pursue their own group- or class-based concerns. This posture was inscribed in the basic aims that gave rise to progressivism: to reunite a nation and a society that appeared deeply divided along class, ethnic, and cultural lines and to strengthen the relative weight of the pub-lic and governmental sector. This is not a matter of historiographical nit-picking over the precise nature of the Progressive Era. Rather, my argument asserts a quite basic point, namely, that the political engagement of social groups and of trade unions, in particular, are compatible with—indeed, necessary for—the pursuit of broadly conceived, integral public politics, and that the Progressive Era constituted such a historical moment. If such a view seems exotic today, this is only testament to the serious current crisis of democracy and the public ideal.

Several developments originating from Chicago's industrial and financial elite weakened and ultimately ended the progressive moment. Attempts to enact municipal ownership in Chicago were partly defeated by undermining the movement's social basis. The teamsters strike of 1905 substantially weakened the kind of solidaristic trade practices that underwrote the rise of a metropolitan unionism. Moreover, as open industrial conflict reared its head again, first during the 1904–1905 period, and again by 1917, many of labor's middle-class allies abandoned ship. Convinced by a public discourse that branded trade unions as corrupt and violent, many reformers lost faith in organized labor and in the people, in general, as a force that would be sufficiently reasonable to help promote a progressive agenda.

Such skepticism, which could turn into outright disdain for "mob rule," helped foster a new political culture that worked against a broader reform agenda. Beginning with the 1905–1907 debate over municipal ownership and consolidating during the 1910s, a functionalist-pluralist ideology dominated Chicago's political culture. Its twin design was to marginalize the new social forces behind the democratization of the progressive polity and to drastically reduce the scope of public policy. Functionalism ideologically reduced citizens' concerns to seeming no more than immediate and materially oriented needs. While the "masses" were now accepted as part of the political system, their role was reduced to that of passive spectators, a *Publikum* (or audience), of decisions increasingly made elsewhere. Meanwhile, pluralism declared the reconciliation of competing group interests as an end in itself and abandoned any transcending search for the common good. It thus relegated the political process to a zero-sum game of competing group concerns. Urban government limited its role to that of catering, alongside consolidated and privately managed public utilities, to the practical "needs" of city residents. As a result, attempts to enact farsighted policies on mass transit—as with the radical municipal-ownership campaign, and again, with the more moderate plans for constructing a subway—proved futile.

Yet it is a key contention of this study that the rise of a functionalist and fragmented political culture, in Chicago and elsewhere, occurred only *after* an extended period of intensive democracy that was closely tied to the rise of a politically oriented labor movement. It was not progressives, but pluralists and subsequent historical interpretations that argued for the incompatibility of group-based political engagement and an ambitious, far-sighted political agenda. My argument contrasts with Habermas's model, which asserts that the entrance of group agents into the public sphere ipso facto led to the decline of the liberal public sphere and the rational search for the public interest. Habermas, in keeping with the cultural pessimism of the Frankfurt School, crafted a more skeptical account of the communicative and normative possibilities of mass-based, twentieth-century Western democracies than the one put forward here.[1]

Nothing better confirms the argument that pluralism was an ideological reaction to the progressive moment than the fact that many of its theorists lived through and participated in those struggles and formulated their ideas in response to that experience. The founder of pluralist group theory, political scientist Arthur F. Bentley based his findings on a study of Chicago's public referenda on transportation policy (see chapter 5). Another social theory that can be considered a reaction to Chicago's progressive moment is the theory of urban ecology, which was developed by the Chicago School of Sociology and has greatly influenced models of urban society and development ever since. In brief, urban ecology ascribed one of the central concerns of reform politics—namely, the tendency of a city like Chicago to fragment along functional and class lines—to the natural realm. Ernest W. Burgess's theories on urban development relegated mass transit, the very utility that stood at the heart of Chicago politics for a decade, to a natural, biotic sphere. Echoing the functionalist argumentation of city planners such as Bion Arnold, Burgess argued that transportation simply provided a tool of a natural process of urban physical growth and was therefore out of bounds of political deliberation.[2]

Why then, in comparison with other countries such as England, France, and Germany, did U.S. cities shy away from a more ambitious reform agenda? What role did trade unions and the country's class relations play in that posture? Notwithstanding an enthusiastic willingness on the part of U.S. activists and professionals to learn from and apply the lessons of Continental reform, as recently demonstrated by historian Daniel Rodgers, American municipalities never witnessed the kind of direct state interference in such questions as housing, city planning, or urban transportation as did their European counterparts. For instance, in 1914, 80 percent of British streetcar riders rode on city-owned trains, whereas only a tiny fraction of U.S. passengers did the same.[3]

As this account of Chicago's streetcar struggle reveals, statist reform, in the form of municipal ownership, failed partly because of the way class conflict resurfaced and polarized the city's reform community. As citizens from a broad social spectrum, including trade unionists, claimed a say in public policy, many middle-class and elite reformers shifted gears. Whereas in 1897, civic leaders like Walter Fisher fought the corrupt machinations of streetcar entrepreneur Yerkes, a few years later, and with the labor-led municipal-ownership movement in full swing, they focused on how to insulate policy making from working-class and popular incursions. In the process, however, they threw out the baby with the bathwater; the functionalist ideology they devised in order to oppose municipal ownership left little room for a reform agenda. In contrast, municipal reform in Europe remained for the most part an undertaking of the elite, which did not have to meddle in the messy waters of democracy or face interference from reform-minded trade unionists. For example, the municipalization of the streetcars in Glasgow, a case much heralded by U.S. progressives including Mayor Dunne, constituted a project directed by the city's elite, a sort of "socialism of the business class," with little involvement from the city's trade unions.[4]

Organized labor's positioning in the urban political universe thus provides a key variable for explaining the different reform paths taken in America and Western Europe. The United States was indeed exceptional, but not in the sense normally argued. It is commonly held that, whereas German, British, Australian, and other countries' trade unions formed labor parties and contributed greatly to the rise of the welfare state, their U.S. counterparts remained on the sidelines. These notions of an exceptionally apolitical U.S. working class have been seriously undermined with regard to the nineteenth century, but when it comes to twentieth-century labor politics, U.S. exceptionalism is alive and well.[5] Yet, as the case of Chicago's streetcar struggle illustrates, U.S. trade unions, looking back on at least a fifty-year-long tradition of civic involvement, found themselves right in the middle of reform politics. In contrast, European (at least German and British) labor parties tended to focus on work-related problems and generally left municipal reform to the elite, a posture that perhaps reflected the fact of their more recent enfranchisement.[6] Returning to the case of the early-twentieth-century United States, here the revival of labor's civic engagement, along with the absence of more channeled and predictable forms of political expression by means of a labor party, generated a climate of social turmoil that proved threatening to an American civic elite and ultimately contributed to the eclipse of urban reform. Progressives' attempts to put forth a far-sighted reform agenda through a democratization of the polity proved thoroughly difficult, if not impossible. As Alexis de Tocqueville noted over a century and a half ago, democracy works wondrous ways in America.[7]

NOTES

ABBREVIATIONS

CHS-Mss—Chicago Historical Society, Manuscripts Division.

CLT—Committee on Local Transportation

CFL Minutes—Chicago Federation of Labor Minutes, CHS

CTF Minutes—Chicago Teachers Federation Minutes, box 1, CTF Papers, CHS

CTF Papers—Chicago Teachers Federation Papers, CHS-Mss

Harlan Report—"Report of the Special Committee of the City Council of Chicago on the Street Railway Franchises and Operations." Chicago: City Documents, 1898.

Hooker Collection—George E. Hooker Collection of Pamphlets, Special Collections, University of Chicago.

Journal of Proceedings—City Hall, *Journal of Proceedings,* City Council of Chicago, in Harold Washington Municipal Library, Chicago.

Lloyd Memorial—"In Memoriam. Henry Demarest Lloyd, May first, 1847–September twenty-eighth, 1903. The Auditorium, Chicago, November 29th, 1903." Pamphlet, Newberry Library, Chicago.

Lloyd Papers—Henry Demarest Lloyd Papers. State Historical Society of Wisconsin.

MDR Papers—Margaret Dreier Robins Papers. *Papers of the Women's Trade Union League and Its Principle Leaders.* Woodbridge, CT: Research Publications, 1979.

MER—Margaret E. Robins

Pierce Collection—Bessie L. Pierce Collection. Special Collections, Joseph Regenstein Library, UC.

Proceedings—City Council Proceedings file, box 304, Illinois Regional Archives Depository, housed at the University of Northeastern Illinois

UC—University of Chicago

USIC—U.S. Industrial Commission. *Reports of the United States Industrial Commission.* Washington, DC, 1900–1902

INTRODUCTION—A STREETCAR NAMED DEMOCRACY

1. *Chicago Tribune* (hereafter *Tribune*), December 16, 1901; *Chicago Inter-Ocean* (hereafter *Inter-Ocean*), September 2, 1902; Chicago Federation of Labor Minutes (microfilm), February 7, 1904, Chicago Historical Society (hereafter CFL Minutes); James R. Barrett, *Work and Community in the Jungle: Chicago's Packinghouse Workers, 1894–1922* (Urbana: University of Illinois Press, 1987), 142; Leo Wolman, "The Extent of Labor Organization in the United States in 1910," *Quarterly Journal of Economics* 30 (May 1916), 486–518, cited in Gerald Friedman, "New Estimates of Union Membership: The United States, 1880–1914," *Historical Methods* 32 (Spring 1999): 75–86.

2. Barbara W. Newell, *Chicago and the Labor Movement: Metropolitan Unionism in the 1930s* (Urbana: University of Illinois Press, 1961); J. Barrett, *Work and Community;* David Brody, *Steelworkers in America: The Nonunion Era* (1960; repr., New York: Russell and Russell, 1970). General histories of Chicago tend to focus on these two major industries: steel and meat-packing. See Janet L. Abu-Lughod, *New York, Chicago, Los Angeles: America's Global Cities* (Minneapolis: University of Minnesota Press, 1999), 119–22. This study joins a substantial literature arguing against characterizations of the AFL as the bastion of a skilled male labor aristocracy. See, for example, Dorothy Sue Cobble, *Dishing It Out: Waitresses and Their Unions in the Twentieth Century* (Urbana: University of Illinois Press, 1991); Richard Schneirov, *Labor and Urban Politics: Class Conflict and the Origins of Modern Liberalism in Chicago, 1864–1897* (Urbana: University of Illinois Press, 1998); J. Barrett, *Work and Community;* Michael Kazin, *Barons of Labor: The San Francisco Building Trades and Union Power in the Progressive Era* (Urbana: University of Illinois Press, 1987); Lisa M. Fine, *The Souls of the Skyscraper: Female Clerical Workers in Chicago, 1870–1930* (Philadelphia: Temple University Press, 1990); John B. Jentz, "Labor, the Law, and Economics: The Organization of the Chicago Flat Janitors' Union, 1902–1917," *Labor History* 38 (Fall 1997): 413–31; Marjorie Murphy, *Blackboard Unions: The American Federation of Teachers and the National Education Administration, 1900–1980* (Ithaca: Cornell University Press, 1990); Georg Leidenberger, "'The Public Is the Labor Union': Working-Class Progressivism in Turn-of-the-Century Chicago," *Labor History* 36 (Spring 1995).

3. Clinton Rogers Woodruff, "Practical Municipal Progress," *American Journal of Sociology* 12 (1906–1907): 201.

4. "Frederick Jackson Turner on the Frontier as the Source of American Democracy," in Leon Fink, ed., *Major Problems in the Gilded Age and the Progressive Era* (Lexington: D. C. Heath, 1993), 82–83.

5. Jürgen Habermas, *Historia y crítica de la opinión pública* (Naucalpan, Mexico: Gustavo Gili, 1994), esp. 94–123, translation of *Strukturwandel der Öffentlichkeit: Untersuchungen zu einer Kategorie der bürgerlichen Gesellschaft* (Frankfurt am Mein: Suhrkamp, 1962); Jürgen Habermas, "The Public Sphere," in Steven Seidman, ed., *Jürgen Habermas on Society and Politics: A Reader* (Boston: Beacon Press, 1989); Craig Calhoun, ed., *Habermas and the Public Sphere* (Cambridge, MA: MIT Press, 1992); Philip J. Ethington, *The Public City: The Political Construction of Urban Life in San Francisco, 1850–1900* (New York: Cambridge University Press, 1994), 17–19.

6. This study's attention to spatial aspects as both generators and products of Chicago politics draws on a theoretical and historiographical literature that incorporates geography into historical analysis. Edward W. Soja, *Postmodern Geographies: The Reassertion of Space in Critical Social Theory* (London and New York: Verso Press, 1989); Henri Lefebvre, "Industrialization and Urbanization," in Henri Lefebvre, *Writings on Cities,* ed. and trans. Eleonore Kofman and Elizabeth Lebas (Cambridge, MA: Blackwell, 1996), 65–85; David Harvey, *The Condition of Postmodernity: An En-*

quiry into the Origins of Cultural Change (Cambridge, MA: Blackwell, 1989), 201–39; the issue of *Social Science History* 24, no. 1 (Spring 2000), dedicated to "The Working Classes and Urban Public Space"; Georg Leidenberger, "Proximidad y diferenciación: el manejo del concepto del espacio en la historia urbana," *Historia y Grafía* (Ibero-American University), no. 22, 2004.

7. Daniel T. Rodgers, *Atlantic Crossings: Social Politics in a Progressive Age* (Cambridge: Harvard University Press, 1998), 145; David P. Thelen, *The New Citizenship: Origins of Progressivism in Wisconsin, 1885–1900* (Columbia: University of Missouri Press, 1972), 289; Robert D. Johnston, *The Radical Middle Class: Populist Democracy and the Question of Capitalism in Progressive Era Portland, Oregon* (Princeton, NJ: Princeton University Press, 2003), 101–6.

8. Shelton Stromquist, "The Crucible of Class: Cleveland Politics and the Origins of Municipal Reform in the Progressive Era," *Journal of Urban History* 23 (January 1997): 192–220; Leslie S. Hough, *The Turbulent Spirit: Cleveland, Ohio, and Its Workers, 1877–1899* (New York: Garland, 1991), 175–206; Melvin G. Holli, *Reform in Detroit: Hazen S. Pingree and Urban Politics* (New York: Oxford University Press, 1969), 33–55; Philip S. Foner, *History of the Labor Movement in the United States*, vol. 3, *The Policies and Practices of the American Federation of Labor, 1900–1909* (New York: International, 1964); Thelen, *New Citizenship*, 250–89.

9. Georg Leidenberger, "Labor and Reform Politics in Two Metropolis: Streetcar Unions in San Francisco and Chicago at the Turn of the Century" (conference paper, American Historical Association—Pacific Coast Branch, San Francisco, August 1996). Perhaps this is why, in his study of San Francisco politics, Ethington argues that pluralism dominated political culture by 1900 already. Ethington, *Public City*, 41, 414–16.

10. Abu-Lughod, *New York, Chicago, Los Angeles*, 74–76; Kenneth Finegold, *Experts and Politicians: Reform Challenges to Machine Politics, New York, Cleveland, and Chicago* (Princeton, NJ: Princeton University Press, 1995), 61.

11. William T. Stead, *If Christ Came to Chicago: A Plea for the Union of All Who Love in the Service of All Who Suffer* (Chicago: Laird & Lee, 1894); Hutchins Hapgood, *The Spirit of Labor* (New York: Duffield, 1907).

12. Richard Hofstadter, *The Age of Reform: From Bryan to F.D.R.* (New York: Knopf, 1955); Robert H. Wiebe, *The Search for Order, 1877–1920* (New York: Hill and Wang, 1967), 111–32; Gabriel Kolko, *The Triumph of Conservatism: A Reinterpretation of American History, 1900–1916* (New York: Free Press of Glencoe, 1963); James Weinstein, *The Corporate Ideal in the Liberal State, 1900–1918* (Boston: Beacon Press, 1968); Samuel P. Hays, "Politics of Reform in Municipal Government in the Progressive Era," *Pacific Northwest Quarterly* 55 (1964): 157–69. To be sure, Johnston rightly points to Hofstadter's appreciation of the moral conceptions of character and justice inherent in progressive thought. Johnston, *Radical Middle Class*, 10.

13. Finegold, *Experts and Politicians*, 26, 171; Thomas R. Pegram, *Partisans and Progressives: Private Interest and Public Policy in Illinois, 1870–1922* (Urbana: University of Illinois Press, 1992).

14. George E. Mowry, *The Era of Theodore Roosevelt and the Birth of Modern America, 1900–1912* (New York: Harper and Row, 1958), 102.

15. Bruce M. Stave and Sandra A. Stave, eds., *Urban Bosses, Machines, and Progressive Reformers*, rev. ed. (Malabar: R. E. Krieger, 1984); Amy Bridges, *A City in the Republic: Antebellum New York and the Origins of Machine Politics* (New York: Cambridge University Press, 1984); Ira Katznelson, *City Trenches: Urban Politics and the Patterning of Class in the United States* (New York: Pantheon, 1981), 45–86; J. Joseph Huthmacher, "Urban Liberalism and the Age of Reform," *Mississippi Valley Historical Review* 49 (1962): 231–41.

16. Thelen, *New Citizenship*, 287–89; Holli, *Reform in Detroit*, 74–100. For an important exception to studies that marginalize workers in urban reform politics, see Johnston, *Radical Middle Class*. Thelen's work is among a number of studies that stress progressives'

idealistic concerns and ideals, including their intent of social conciliation. Richard L. McCormick, "Progressivism: A Contemporary Assessment," in *The Party Period and Public Policy: American Politics from the Age of Jackson to the Progressive Era* (New York: Oxford University Press, 1986), 263–88; Daniel T. Rodgers, "In Search of Progressivism," *Reviews in American History*, 1982, 113–32; David P. Thelen, "Social Tensions and the Origins of Progressivism," *Journal of American History* 56 (September 1969): 336–41.

17. For example, historian Ira Katznelson postulated a dual identity for workers in the city: a class-based one at work and an ethnic-based one at home and in the neighborhood. Whereas U.S. workers exhibited remarkable militancy at the job front, he contends, within their neighborhoods they were incorporated into political ward organizations based on ethnic affiliations. Katznelson, *City Trenches*, 45–86.

18. Julie Greene, *Pure and Simple Politics: The American Federation of Labor and Political Activism, 1881–1917* (Cambridge: Cambridge University Press, 1998); Kazin, *Barons of Labor.* Greene and Kazin draw on the pioneering work of Gary M. Fink, "The Rejection of Voluntarism," *Industrial and Labor Relations Review* 26 (1973): 805–19.

19. David Montgomery, *The Fall of the House of Labor: The Workplace, the State, and Labor Activism, 1865–1925* (New York: Cambridge University Press, 1987); James Weinstein, "The National Civic Federation and the Concept of Consensus," a chapter in his *Corporate Ideal.* Studies that tend to fall into this conceptual trap include Stromquist, "Crucible of Class"; Michael Kazin, *The Populist Persuasion: An American History* (New York: Basic Books, 1995), 49–77; Richard Oestreicher, *Solidarity and Fragmentation: Working-People and Class Consciousness in Detroit, 1875–1900* (Urbana: University of Illinois Press, 1986), the chapter "The Legacy of the 1880s: Detroit Workers in the 1890s."

20. Johnston, *Radical Middle Class*, 1–17, esp. 14; Ethington, *Public City*, 15, 33.

1—SERVICE WORKERS AND THE NEW METROPOLITAN UNIONISM

1. "A Chicago Organization of Employers," *Iron Age* 71 (February 19, 1903): 3.

2. "Tunnel Vision," *Chicago History*, December 1992, 26–43; *World To-Day* 6 (1904): 782–83. Quotation from Harold M. Mayer and Richard C. Wade, *Chicago: Growth of a Metropolis* (Chicago: University of Chicago Press, 1969), 216.

3. J. Barrett, *Work and Community*, 142; *Tribune*, December 16, 1901; *Inter-Ocean*, September 2, 1902; *Union Labor Advocate* (hereafter *Labor Advocate*), October 1903. According to the *Chicago Record-Herald* (hereafter *Record-Herald*), 40 percent of the 800,000 workers organized in 525 trade unions. *Record-Herald*, October 5, 1902.

The U.S. Census of 1900 lists 705,382 wage earners for Chicago. Based on conservative estimates of 300,000 CFL-affiliated workers, the CFL represented 42 percent of the city's workforce. If we accept the higher figure of 400,000, the proportion of CFL-affiliated workers would rise to 57 percent. The proportion of unionized workers in Chicago was probably even higher than these estimates, given that several unions (such as the railroad brotherhoods) were not affiliated with the CFL. See Statistics of Population, U.S. Census, 1900; George E. Barnett, "Growth of Labor Organization in the United States, 1897–1914," *Quarterly Journal of Economics* 30 (1916): 780–95, esp. 789; G. Friedman, "New Estimates."

4. Quotation from Royal E. Montgomery, *Industrial Relations in the Chicago Building Trades* (Chicago: University of Chicago Press, 1927), 13; D. Montgomery, *Fall of the House*, 295; S. V. Lindholm, "Analysis of the Building-Trades Conflict in Chicago: From the Trades-Union Standpoint," *Journal of Political Economy* 8 (1900): 327–46, esp. 338–39. For President McKinley, see *Workers' Call*, June 30, 1900; James A. Miller, "Coercive Trade-Unionism as Illustrated by the Chicago Building-Trades Conflict," *Journal of Political Economy* 9 (1901): 321–50.

5. *Chicago Economist*, January 5, 1907, 129; D. Montgomery, *Fall of the House*, 293; Robert A. Christie, *Empire in Wood: A History of the Carpenters' Union* (Ithaca: Cornell University Press, 1956), 156.

6. Richard Schneirov and Thomas J. Suhrbur, *Union Brotherhood, Union Town: The History of the Carpenters' Union of Chicago, 1863–1987* (Carbondale: Southern Illinois University Press, 1988), 76. See also R. Montgomery, *Industrial Relations,* 13–33; William Haber, *Industrial Relations in the Building Industry* (Cambridge and New York: Cambridge University Press, 1930), 23–38; Howard Barton Myers, "The Policing of Labor Disputes in Chicago" (Ph.D. diss., University of Chicago, 1927), 302; Christie, *Empire in Wood,* 121; Kazin, *Barons of Labor,* 82–112. For a fictional account of corruption in the building trades, see Scott Leroy, *Walking Delegate* (1905; repr., Upper Saddle River, NJ: Literature House, 1969); D. Montgomery, *Fall of the House,* 295–96.

7. Quotations from Miller, "Coercive Trade-Unionism," 321, and Lindholm, "Building-Trades Conflict," 332. See also R. Montgomery, *Industrial Relations,* 17; Andrew Dawson, "The Parameters of Craft Consciousness: The Social Outlook of the Skilled Worker," in *American Labor and Immigration History, 1877–1920s: Recent European Research,* ed. Dirk Hoerder (Urbana: University of Illinois Press, 1983); Schneirov and Suhrbur, *Union Brotherhood,* 86–87.

8. Schneirov and Suhrbur, *Union Brotherhood,* 35, 57; D. Montgomery, *Fall of the House,* 298; Richard S. Schneirov, "The Knights of Labor in the Chicago Labor Movement and in Municipal Politics, 1877–1887" (Ph.D. diss., Northern Illinois University, 1984), 562. In his study of San Francisco's BTC, Michael Kazin arrives at similar conclusions. In the Bay City, the building trades unions established an even stronger position than in Chicago. Kazin, *Barons of Labor,* 91.

9. Schneirov, "Knights of Labor," 311–32, and *Labor and Urban Politics,* 139–61; D. Montgomery, *Fall of the House,* 293.

10. Schneirov, "Knights of Labor," 376.

11. Ibid., 273. See also ibid., 375–83, 497–532; Edward B. Mittelman, "Chicago Labor in Politics, 1877–1896," *Journal of Political Economy* 28 (1920): 407–27, esp. 419.

12. Memoirs of Edward Marshall Craig, 1922, box 5, folder 7, Gerhardt F. Meyne Papers, typescript (hereafter Craig memoirs), Manuscript Division, Chicago Historical Society (hereafter CHS-Mss).

13. Myers, "Labor Disputes," 208; *Skandinaven,* May 5, October 7, 1900, Foreign Language Press Survey (Norwegian), reels 1–2. Quotation from R. Montgomery, *Industrial Relations,* 43. Testimonies of employers James L. Board and W. J. Chalmers at the U.S. Industrial Commission, *Reports of the United States Industrial Commission* (Washington, DC, 1900–1902), 40, 423 (hereafter *USIC*); D. Montgomery, *Fall of the House,* 271; Eugene Staley, *History of the Illinois State Federation of Labor* (Chicago: Chicago University Press, 1930), 285.

14. Quotation from Miller, "Coercive Trade-Unionism," 332. See also Christie, *Empire in Wood,* 159–69; R. Montgomery, *Industrial Relations,* 24–32; Lindholm, "Building-Trades Conflict," 342.

15. Myers, "Labor Disputes," 308–13, 324; *Tribune,* May 17, 26, 1900, May 18, 1901; *Arbeiterzeitung,* May 15, 1900; Miller, "Coercive Trade-Unionism," 334. Testimonies of Abraham Bliss, Board, and Chalmers, *USIC.*

16. Quotation from James A. Miller, *USIC,* 516; R. Montgomery, *Industrial Relations,* 29; *Arbeiterzeitung,* April 30, May 15, 1900; Myers, "Labor Disputes," 316–22; *Workers' Call,* May 5, 1900, July 7, 1901.

17. *Tribune,* October 29, 1901; Craig memoirs, 21.

18. Leidenberger, "'The Public'"; David Witwer, *Corruption and Reform in the Teamsters Union* (Urbana: University of Illinois Press, 2003), 7–19.

19. Quotations from Myers, "Labor Disputes," 898; "On Sharkey," in Howard L. Willett Papers, CHS-Mss. Robert D. Leiter, *The Teamsters Union: A Study of Its Economic Impact* (New York: Bookman, 1957), 18; John R. Commons, "Types of American Labor

Organizations: The Teamsters of Chicago," *Quarterly Journal of Economics* 19 (1904): 419. For a personal account of a teamster's workday, see "The Chicago Strike—By a Teamster," *Independent* 59 (1905): 15–20.

20. *Record-Herald,* February 25, 1901; Donald Garnel, *Rise of Teamster Power in the West* (Berkeley and Los Angeles: University of California Press, 1972), 47. Motorized trucks did not appear until 1909. Quotation from Leiter, *Teamsters Union,* 22. Garnel, *Teamster Power,* 1–10; Luke Grant, "True Story of the Chicago Strike," *The Public,* June 17, 1905, 173, found in Philip Taft Papers, CHS-Mss; Witwer, *Corruption and Reform,* 14–15.

21. Leiter, *Teamsters Union,* 20–24; Commons, "Teamsters," 419, 426. Quotation from "Chicago Strike—By a Teamster," 15–20. For a discussion of the social construction of skill, see Susan Porter Benson, "'The Customers Ain't God': The Work Culture of Department Store Saleswomen, 1890–1940," in *Working-Class America: Essays on Labor, Community, and Society,* ed. Michael H. Frisch and Daniel J. Walkowitz (Urbana: University of Illinois Press, 1983).

22. Garnel, *Teamster Power,* 1–10; Commons, "Teamsters," 405; Ernest Poole, "How a Labor Machine Held Up Chicago and How the Teamsters' Union Smashed the Machine," *World To-Day* 7 (July 1904): 896–905, esp. 897–98; Grant, "True Story," 173.

23. Quotation from *Inter-Ocean,* May 26, 1902. *Arbeiterzeitung,* March 9, *Inter-Ocean,* May 26–June 6, *Record-Herald,* June 4, 5, 1902; Myers, "Labor Disputes," 348.

24. Myers, "Labor Disputes," 23, 353.

25. Quotation from *Tribune,* June 5, 1902. "Chicago Strike—By a Teamster," 18; *Inter-Ocean,* May 30, August 31, *Arbeiterzeitung,* June 3, *Record-Herald,* June 5, 1902; Poole, "Labor Machine," 898; Myers, "Labor Disputes," 353.

26. Quotations from Myers, "Labor Disputes," 350, 357, and Poole, "Labor Machine," 904. See also *Inter-Ocean,* May 31, *Arbeiterzeitung,* June 6, 1902; Leiter, *Teamsters Union,* 22–23, 33; Commons, "Teamsters," 57.

27. *Arbeiterzeitung,* February 9, *Record-Herald,* February 7, 1903; *The Public* 5 (February 14, 1903); *Labor Advocate,* January 1903; Poole, "Labor Machine," 897.

28. *Inter-Ocean,* May 18, 1902.

29. *Tribune,* December 16, 1901, September 1, 1902.

30. *Inter-Ocean,* September 2, *Arbeiterzeitung,* September 2, 1902; *Typographical Journal* (official paper of the International Typographical Union of North America) 21 (September 15, 1902): 258.

31. Quotation from Murphy, *Blackboard Unions,* 10.

32. David Swing Ricker, "Unionizing the Schoolteachers," *World To-Day* 8 (1905): 394–402; Chicago Teachers Federation Minutes (hereafter CTF Minutes), May 10, 1902, box 1, Chicago Teachers Federation, CHS-Mss (hereafter CTF Papers); Murphy, *Blackboard Unions,* 83; Marjorie Murphy, "From Artisans to Semi-Professionals: White-Collar Unionism among Chicago Public School Teachers, 1870–1930" (Ph.D. diss., University of California at Davis, 1981), 33; Catherine Goggin, "Brief History of Chicago Teachers Federation," typescript, November 3, 1906, box 1, CTF Papers.

33. Murphy, *Blackboard Unions,* 11–45, 125. Murphy defines reformers as middle-class (ibid., 25).

34. Margaret Haley, letter to [unknown], July 26, 1906, folder 1, box 39, CTF Papers.

35. Report submitted by Cornelia De Bey, Chairman, J. J. Sonsteby, and Louis F. Post, "Proceedings of the Board of Education," January 16, 1907, folder 4, box 39, CTF Papers.

36. Quotation from Catherine Goggin, "Brief History of Chicago Teachers Federation," typescript, November 3, 1906, box 1; affidavit of Mary P. Squier, September 15, 1906, folder 1, box 39; letter by CTF Committee to E. G. Cooley, Superintendent of Schools, Chicago, December 8, 1903, box 37; CTF Minutes, November 14, 1903; all in CTF Papers.

37. Murphy, *Blackboard Unions,* 29; John C. Harding, chair of CFL's special committee on schools, *CTF Bulletin,* April 8, 1904; Ricker, "Unionizing," 396, 399–400.

38. Ricker, "Unionizing," 398.

39. A.M.M. [?], "The Moral Significance of the Tax Fight," *CTF Bulletin*, February 7, 1902; Haley to Jane Addams, May 4, 1906, Anita McCormick Blaine Papers, copy in box 39, CTF Papers; Ricker, "Unionizing," 398.

40. CTF Minutes, November 8, 1902. The meeting elected Goggin and Haley as delegates to the CFL. CTF Minutes, October 12, November 8, 1902. Murphy, *Blackboard Unions*, 45; W. M. Persons to Haley, July 23, 1905, box 38, folder 2, CTF Papers; *New World*, November 15, 1902.

41. CTF Minutes, September 13, 1902.

42. Goggin to Carter Alexander, May 27, 1901, box 40, CTF Papers.

43. *Labor Advocate*, April 1902; Murphy, *Blackboard Unions*, 40; *The Public* 5 (November 15, 1902).

44. CTF Minutes, October 18, 1902.

45. Quotation from Adolph Grethen (?), violinist at Wisconsin House, Headquarters for Traveling Men and Tourists, in Baraboo, Wis., to CTF, February 1903, box 37, CTF Papers.

46. Goggin to Alexander, May 27, 1901, box 40, CTF Papers.

47. Quotation from CTF Minutes, November 10, 1902. *CTF Bulletin*, November 14, 1902. Rowe later resigned her office in protest over the CTF's affiliation with the CFL.

48. Speeches in favor of affiliation by Haley, Fitzpatrick, and Addams, CTF Minutes, November 8, 1902; *CTF Bulletin*, November 14, 21, 1902, CTF Papers.

49. Murphy, "Artisans," 15; Maureen Flanagan, *Seeing with Their Hearts: Chicago Women and the Vision of the Good City, 1871–1933* (Princeton, NJ: Princeton University Press, 2002), 61; CTF Minutes, October 18, November 2, 1902; Ricker, "Unionizing," 396. Quotation from Murphy, *Blackboard Unions*, 29.

50. Murphy, *Blackboard Unions*, 11, 25, 29, 125; Haley to Franklin S. Edmonds, June 2, 1903, box 37, CTF Papers.

51. Flanagan, *Seeing with Their Hearts*, 60–70.

52. Julia Wrigley, *Class Politics and Public Schools: Chicago, 1900–1950* (New Brunswick, NJ: Rutgers University Press, 1982), 23; CFL Minutes, February 7, 1904; *Tribune*, December 16, 1901.

53. The *Inter-Ocean* and the Hearst press provided the most detailed coverage, but even anti-union papers, such as the *Tribune* and the *Daily News*, could not afford to ignore the CFL's resolutions.

54. Chester McArthur Destler, *American Radicalism, 1865–1901* (1946; repr., Chicago: Quadrangle Books, 1966), 232–41; H. W. (probably Harold Woodman), "Organization of Labor in Chicago, 1893–1914," in folder 10, box 228 (Labor), Bessie L. Pierce Collection, Special Collections, Joseph Regenstein Library, UC (hereafter Pierce Collection, UC); Staley, *History*, 88; *Arbeiterzeitung*, August 18, 1902.

55. *Tribune*, August 11, 1902. Quotation from *Tribune*, November 5, 1902.

56. Murphy, "Artisans," 3–15.

57. *Arbeiterzeitung*, June 4, *Chicago Socialist*, July 26, 1902; Allen Friedman, *Power and Greed: Inside the Teamster Empire of Corruption* (New York: F. Watts, 1989), 8.

58. Robert L. Reid, ed., *Battleground: The Autobiography of Margaret A. Haley* (Urbana: University of Illinois Press, 1982), 91–93.

59. CFL Minutes, September 20, 1903.

60. Ibid., September 6, 1903; *Labor Advocate*, August 1905; CFL resolution, April 17, 1904, box 38, CTF Papers; Truman C. Bigham, "The Chicago Federation of Labor" (M.A. thesis, University of Chicago, 1924), 22.

61. CFL Minutes, September 20, November 1, 1903.

62. *Labor Advocate*, August 1904; *Tribune*, January 25, 1904; J. Barrett, *Work and Community*, 131–37; William M. Tuttle Jr., *Race Riot: Chicago in the Red Summer of 1919* (New York: Atheneum Press, 1985), 116–20.

63. D. Montgomery, *Fall of the House,* 259–60.

64. CFL Minutes, August 2, December 6, 1903; John Keiser, "John Fitzpatrick and Progressive Unionism, 1915–1925" (Ph.D. diss., Northwestern University, 1965), 5.

65. D. Montgomery, *Fall of the House,* 269–75; Weinstein, *Corporate Ideal,* chapter entitled "The National Civic Federation and the Concept of Consensus."

66. Quotation from *Record-Herald,* November 20, 1903. D. Montgomery, *Fall of the House,* 269–75; Witwer, *Corruption and Reform,* 26–27.

67. CFL Minutes, December 6, 1903. Quotation from *Labor Advocate,* May 1903. *Chicago Socialist,* April 25, 1903.

68. Jane Addams, *Newer Ideals of Peace* (New York: Macmillan, 1907), 128; *Arbeiterzeitung,* August 19, 21, *Inter-Ocean,* August 12, 1902; *Tribune,* July 20, *Labor Advocate,* January 1903. McGee quoted from *Record-Herald,* July 12, 1902.

69. Thompson cited in Bigham, "Chicago Federation of Labor," 22; CFL Minutes, November 1, 1903.

70. CFL Minutes, December 20, 1903; *Tribune,* December 21, 1903. Another study that points to the flexible nature of AFL voluntarism is Cobble, *Dishing It Out.*

71. Keiser, "John Fitzpatrick," 10–20, 74. Quotation from CFL Minutes, September 6, 1903.

72. AFL headquarters nominated carpenter Albert C. Cattermull, a close associate of national leader Peter McGuire. However, Gompers finally yielded to the CFL's protests and accepted Fitzpatrick. *Inter-Ocean,* May 8, 19, 1902; CFL Minutes, August 17, 1903.

73. CFL Minutes, November 1, 1903; *Labor Advocate,* March 1904; Leon Fink and Brian Greenberg, *Upheaval in the Quiet Zone: A History of Hospital Workers' Union, Local 1199* (Urbana: University of Illinois Press, 1989), 1–27; *Chicago American* (hereafter *American*), December 15, 1902; *Tribune,* January 2, 1904; CFL Minutes, December 20, 1903.

74. Petition by Streetcar Union to Committee on Local Transportation, received September 12, 1906, filed April 4, 1907, box 304, City Council Proceedings file, Illinois Regional Archives Depository, housed at Northeastern Illinois University (hereafter Council Proceedings); H. W., "Labor in Chicago," in folder 10, box 228, Pierce Collection, UC; Myers, "Labor Disputes," 389; *Record-Herald,* June 12, May 5, 1902.

75. Anna Nicholes, "Women and Trade Unions," *The Commons* 9 (June 1904): 268–73; John B. Andrews and W. D. P. Bliss, *History of Women in Trade Unions,* vol. 10 of *Report on Conditions of Women and Child Wage-Earners in the United States,* U.S. Senate Document No. 645, 61st Cong., 2nd sess. (Washington, DC: GPO, 1911), 148.

76. Andrews and Bliss, *History of Women,* 138, 140–48; H. W., "Labor in Chicago"; Nicholes, "Women and Trade Unions," 268–73; *Tribune,* September 1, 1902; J. Barrett, *Work and Community,* 291, 293.

77. Agnes Nestor Papers, CHS; Keiser, "John Fitzpatrick," 16; *American,* January 7, 1903; *Labor Advocate,* June 1903.

78. *Labor Advocate,* January 1904; CFL Minutes, December 6, 1903.

79. Quotation from Paul Barrett, *The Automobile and Urban Transit: The Formation of Public Policy in Chicago, 1900–1930* (Philadelphia: Temple University Press, 1983), 39; Cobble, *Dishing It Out,* 8.

80. *Inter-Ocean,* August 31, 1902; *The Public* 6 (May 30, 1903): 120; Cobble, *Dishing It Out,* 66.

81. *Chicago Socialist,* June 17, 1905.

82. CTF Minutes, February 11, 1905; letter of October 30, 1903, box 37; *CTF Bulletin,* October 23, 1903, all in CTF Papers.

83. Maureen A. Flanagan, "Gender and Urban Political Reform: The City Club and the Women's City Club of Chicago in the Progressive Era," *American Historical Review* 95 (October 1990): 1032–50, esp. 1041–44.

84. Cobble, *Dishing It Out,* 75.

85. Richard R. Wright Jr., "Industrial Conditions of Negroes in Chicago" (typescript, 1901, CHS), 30.

86. *Inter-Ocean,* August 18, 1902; Wright, "Industrial Conditions," 31–33.

87. All quotations from *Labor Advocate,* July 1903.

88. James R. Grossman, *Land of Hope: Chicago, Black Southerners, and the Great Migration* (Chicago: University of Chicago Press, 1989), 217. The waiters union had deep roots in Chicago's African American community. Pastors of black congregations were reported to actively back the union during mass meetings. *American,* December 13, 29, 1902; Myers, "Labor Disputes," 420; Howard Kimeldorf and Robert Penney, "'Excluded by Choice': Dynamics of Interracial Unionism on the Philadelphia Waterfront, 1910–1930," *International Labor and Working-Class History,* no. 51 (Spring 1997): 50–71.

89. James R. Barrett, "Ethnic and Racial Fragmentation: Toward a Reinterpretation of a Local Labor Movement," in *African American Urban Experience: Perspectives from the Colonial Period to the Present,* ed. Joe W. Trotter, with Earl Lewis and Tera W. Hunter (New York: Palgrave Macmillan, 2004), 298.

90. Poole, "Labor Machine," 905.

91. Schneirov, *Labor and Urban Politics,* 307–16.

2—PRIVATE STREETCARS, PUBLIC UTOPIAS, AND THE CONSTRUCTION OF THE MODERN CITY

1. CFL, "Organized Labor against the Humphrey Bills," pamphlet, April 4, 1897 (Chicago: Eight Hour Herald Print, 1897; in Newberry Library, Chicago); *Scientific American,* cited in Charles W. Cheape, *Moving the Masses: Urban Public Transit in New York, Boston, and Philadelphia, 1880–1912* (Cambridge, MA: Harvard University Press, 1980), 406.

2. Alan Trachtenberg, "Leyendo la ciudad de la edad dorada: del misterio al realismo," in *Nuevas perspectivas en los estudios sobre historia urbana latinoamericana,* ed. Jorge E. Hardoy and Richard P. Morse (Buenos Aires: Grupo Editor Latinoamericano, 1989), 183–93, esp. 190–91; Theodore Dreiser, *Sister Carrie* (1907; repr., Philadelphia: University of Pennsylvania Press, 1981); Marshall Berman, "Baudelaire: Modernism in the Street," chapter in *All That Is Solid Melts into Air: The Experience of Modernity* (New York: Simon and Schuster, 1982).

3. William Cronon, *Nature's Metropolis: Chicago and the Great West* (New York: Norton, 1991), 1–10; Bessie Louise Pierce, *A History of Chicago,* vol. 3, *1871–1893* (New York: A. A. Knopf, 1937); Mayer and Wade, *Chicago;* Maureen A. Flanagan, *Charter Reform in Chicago* (Carbondale: Southern Illinois University Press, 1987), 11–16.

4. Abu-Lughod, *New York, Chicago, Los Angeles,* 115–17; Mayer and Wade, *Chicago,* 140–54; Howard P. Chudacoff and Judith E. Smith, eds., *The Evolution of American Urban Society,* 4th ed. (Englewood Cliffs, NJ: Prentice Hall, 1994), 102–7.

5. Homer Hoyt, *One Hundred Years of Land Values in Chicago* (Chicago: University of Chicago Press, 1933), 280–81, 284; Carl Sandburg, "Chicago," *Chicago Poems* (New York: Dover, 1994).

6. Sandburg, "Clark Street Bridge," *Chicago Poems;* Michael P. McCarthy, "New Metropolis," in *Age of Urban Reform: New Perspectives on the Progressive Era,* ed. Michael Ebner and Eugene M. Tobin (Port Washington, NY: Kennikat Press, 1977), 43–44; P. Barrett, *Automobile,* 15; Harry P. Weber, *An Outline History of Chicago Traction* ([Chicago]: s.n., [1936]), 14–38.

7. Frederick C. Howe, *The City: The Hope of Democracy* (1905; repr., Seattle: University of Washington Press, 1967), 18; Delos F. Wilcox, *The American City: A Problem in Democracy* (New York: Macmillan, 1904), 14–15.

8. *Chicago Economist,* May 28, 1904; Joel A. Tarr, "From City to Suburb: The 'Moral' Influence of Transportation Technology," in Alexander B. Callow Jr., ed., *American Urban History: An Interpretive Reader with Commentaries,* 2nd ed. (New York: Oxford University Press, 1973), 207; John Ericson (chairman of the Harbor and Subway Commission of Chicago), "Synopsis of an Address to the Irish Fellowship Club, March 2, 1912," in George E. Hooker Collection of Pamphlets, Special Collections, University of Chicago (hereafter Hooker Collection, UC); P. Barrett, *Automobile,* 15.

9. P. Barrett, *Automobile,* 14–15; Mark S. Foster, *From Streetcar to Superhighway: American City Planners and Urban Transportation, 1900–1940* (Philadelphia: Temple University Press, 1981), 9–15; Joel A. Tarr and Josef W. Konvitz, "Patterns in the Development of the Urban Infrastructure," in *American Urbanism: A Historiographical Review,* ed. Howard Gillette Jr. and Zane L. Miller (New York: Greenwood Press, 1987), 204–7; Joel A. Tarr, *Transportation Innovation and Changing Spatial Patterns in Pittsburgh, 1850–1934* (Chicago: Public Works Historical Society, 1978), 1–24; Glen E. Holt, "The Changing Perception of Urban Pathology: An Essay on the Development of Mass Transit in the United States," in *Cities in American History,* ed. Kenneth T. Jackson and Stanley K. Schultz (New York: Knopf, 1972), 324–43; Howard P. Chudacoff, "Industrialization and the Transformation of Urban Space," in Chudacoff and Smith, *American Urban Society,* 85–89.

10. Ernest W. Burgess, "The Growth of the City: An Introduction to a Research Project," in *The City,* ed. Ernest W. Burgess and Roderick McKenzie (1925; repr., Chicago: University of Chicago Press, 1967), esp. 52; Chudacoff, "Industrialization," 87–107, esp. 99.

11. Burgess, "Growth of the City," 52; Homer Hoyt, *The Structure and Growth of Residential Neighborhoods of American Cities* (Washington, DC: U.S. Federal Housing Administration, 1939); Sam Bass Warner Jr., *The Urban Wilderness: A History of the American City* (New York: Harper and Row, 1972), 101–12.

12. Hartmut Keil and John B. Jentz, eds., *German Workers in Chicago: A Documentary History from 1850 to World War I* (Urbana: University of Illinois Press, 1988); Warner, *Urban Wilderness,* 109.

13. Hoyt, *Structure and Growth,* 144; Harry R. Stevens, "Some Aspects of the Standards of Living in Chicago, 1893–1914," in Pierce Collection, UC; Foster, *Streetcar to Superhighway,* 15, 17–18; Holt, "Urban Pathology," 92–93.

14. David R. Goldfield and Blaine A. Brownell, *Urban America: A History,* 2nd ed. (New York: Houghton Mifflin, 1990), 263–66; Tarr, *Transportation Innovation,* 1–12. Quotation from Warner, *Urban Wilderness,* 107. Hoyt, *Structure and Growth,* 201, 210. Friedrich Engels, *The Condition of the Working Class in England* (New York: Macmillan, 1958), compares the social geography of Manchester and Chicago.

15. Quotation from Warner, *Urban Wilderness,* 102–8 (108). J. Barrett, *Work and Community,* 73–81; Eric H. Monkkonen, *America Becomes Urban: The Development of U.S. Cities and Towns, 1780–1980* (Berkeley and Los Angeles: University of California Press, 1988), 177; Allan H. Spear, *Black Chicago: The Making of a Negro Ghetto, 1890–1920* (Chicago: University of Chicago Press, 1967), 11–28.

16. Richard C. Wade, "Urbanization," in C. Vann Woodward, ed., *The Comparative Approach to American History* (New York: Basic Books, 1968), 191–94; Monkkonen, *America Becomes Urban,* 158–62; Tarr, *Transportation Innovation,* 1–15.

17. Burgess, "Growth of the City," 52 (my emphasis). See also Robert Ezra Park, "The City: Suggestions for the Investigation of Human Behavior in the Urban Environment," in Burgess and McKenzie, *The City,* 1–46.

18. Wade, "Urbanization," 193–94. For a critique of such determinism, see Glenn Yago, *The Decline of Transit: Urban Transportation in German and U.S. Cities, 1900–1970* (New York: Cambridge University Press, 1984), 131; Terrence J. McDonald, "Comment," review essay in *Journal of Urban History* 8 (August 1984): 454–62.

19. Monkkonen, *America Becomes Urban,* 164.

20. Goldfield and Brownell, *Urban America,* 274–75, 200–207; Foster, *Streetcar to Superhighway,* 9–10.

21. Stead, *If Christ Came to Chicago,* 34; Paul Boyer, *Urban Masses and Moral Order in America, 1820–1920* (Cambridge, MA: Harvard University Press, 1978), 184–87.

22. Theodore Dreiser, *The Titan* (New York, John Lane Company, 1914); William W. Demastes, *Beyond Naturalism: A New Realism in American Theatre* (New York: Greenwood Press, 1988); Upton Sinclair, *The Jungle* (1905; repr., New York: Signet Classics, 1960); Karen Sawislak, *Smoldering City: Chicagoans and the Great Fire, 1871–1874* (Chicago: University of Chicago Press, 1995), 61–63; John K. Winkler, *William Randolph Hearst: A New Appraisal* (New York: Hastings House, 1955), 2–6; Ferdinand Lundberg, *Imperial Hearst: A Social Biography* (New York: Equinox Cooperative, 1936).

23. Rudyard Kipling, cited in L. Fink, *Major Problems,* 140; *New Republic,* cited in Steven J. Diner, *A City and Its Universities: Public Policy in Chicago, 1892–1919* (Chicago: University of Chicago Press, 1980), 73; Max Weber, "In Chikago," in *Max Weber: Ein Lebensbild,* ed. Marianne Weber (Tübingen, Germany: J. C. B. Mohr, 1926), 298–99 (my translation).

24. Max Weber, "In Chikago," 300.

25. David John Hogan, *Class and Reform: School and Society in Chicago, 1880–1930* (Philadelphia: University of Pennsylvania Press, 1985), 25–28; Allen F. Davis, *Spearheads for Reform: The Social Settlements and the Progressive Movement, 1890–1914* (New York: Oxford University Press, 1967), 18–19; Boyer, *Urban Masses,* 220–32; Flanagan, *Charter Reform* 22.

26. Addams quoted from Hogan, *Class and Reform,* 26.

27. Quotations from Howe, *The City,* 22–23. Howe, *The Confessions of a Reformer* (Kent, OH: Kent State University Press, 1988); Wilcox, *American City,* 14–15.

28. Howe, *The City,* 23, 45–48; Dorothy Ross, "Toward a Sociology of Social Control," in *The Origins of American Social Science* (Cambridge: Cambridge University Press, 1991).

29. Bemis cited in Holli, *Reform in Detroit,* 36. Tarr, "From City to Suburb," 205–7; Frank Parsons, "Lessons in Municipal Ownership," *American,* December 1, 1905; L. S. Rowe, "Municipal Ownership and Operation: The Value of Foreign Experience," *American Journal of Sociology* 12 (1906–1907): 241–53.

30. John R. Commons, "Municipal Monopolies," in *Social Reform and the Church* (1894; repr., New York: Cromwell, 1967), 134.

31. Cooley cited in Boyer, *Urban Masses,* 227; Carroll D. Wright, "The Ethical Influence of Invention," *Social Economist* 1 (September 1891): 341–42.

32. Wright, "Ethical Influence of Invention," 341–42.

33. Howe, *The City,* 22–23; George Hooker to Patterson, January 5, 1902, Hooker Collection, UC.

34. Tarr, "From City to Suburb," 209. Realtor quoted from Olivier Zunz, *The Changing Face of Inequality: Urbanization, Industrial Development, and Immigrants in Detroit, 1880–1920* (Chicago: University of Chicago Press, 1982), 125. Boyer, *Urban Masses,* 254–55.

35. "Report of the Special Committee of the City Council of Chicago on the Street Railway Franchises and Operations" (Chicago: City Documents, 1898; hereafter Harlan Report), 11; George T. Bryant, personal recollections on Chicago city transport, Bryant Papers, CHS-Mss.

36. Bion J. Arnold, "Report on the Engineering and Operating Features of the Chicago Transportation Problem" (Chicago: City Documents, 1902), 49. Quotation from P. Barrett, *Automobile,* 14.

37. Edward F. Dunne, "Municipal Ownership: How the People May Get Back Their Own," an address before the Men's Club of the Stewart Avenue Universalist Church of Englewood, January 12, 1904, in Municipal Ownership Central Committee pamphlet,

Hooker Collection, UC; Petition by residents of Stock Yards district to the City Council of Chicago, January 15, 1904, filed March 23, 1904, box 271, Council Proceedings; Chicago City Directory, CHS; "Jetzt oder nie!" (Now or never; my translation), pamphlet, 1905, in Hooker Collection, UC; Report of the Department of Transportation, May 1st, 1906 to December 31st, 1906, filed February 18, 1907, box 304, Council Proceedings.

38. Victor S. Yarros, "Chicago's Significant Election and Referendum," *American Monthly Review of Reviews* (1904): 584–87, 586. Quotation from "Jetzt oder nie!" pamphlet.

39. *Daily News Almanac and Year-Book,* 1905, 406, and 1907, 437; P. Barrett, *Automobile,* 18.

40. Robin L. Einhorn, *Property Rules: Political Economy in Chicago, 1833–1872* (Chicago: University of Chicago Press, 1991), 1–32; Karen Sawislak, "Processes of Urban Construction," *Journal of Urban History* 21 (November 1994): 130–36, esp. 133.

41. Petition to Mayor Carter H. Harrison, May 12, 1902, filed March 23, 1903, box 260; Petition by Wentworth Avenue residents to Mayor Harrison and City Council, June 12, 1902, filed March 23, 1903, box 260; complaint dated May 14, 1904, filed April 4, 1907, box 304; all in Council Proceedings.

42. A cursory examination of the signers of the Wentworth Avenue petition and of the 1900 manuscript census reveal, however, that some signers of the petition did not actually reside there. Most likely, these were building owners renting out multiple-apartment buildings. Petition by Wentworth Avenue residents to Mayor Harrison and City Council, June 12, 1902, filed March 23, 1903, box 260, Council Proceedings.

43. Sam Bass Warner Jr., *Streetcar Suburbs: The Process of Growth in Boston, 1870–1900* (Cambridge, MA: Harvard University Press, 1962), 3–17; Foster, *Streetcar to Superhighway,* 16–18; P. Barrett, *Automobile,* 12; Goldfield and Brownell, *Urban America,* 265; Edward R. Kantowicz, *Polish-American Politics in Chicago, 1888–1940* (Chicago: University of Chicago Press, 1975), 28.

44. Quotation from Chicago City Council, *Journal of Proceedings* (Harold Washington Municipal Library; hereafter *Journal of Proceedings*), December 8, 1902; Sinclair, *The Jungle,* 78.

45. Tarr, *Transportation Innovation,* 12, 19, 20–23; Illinois Bureau of Labor Statistics, *Fifteenth Biannual Report, 1908,* 449–51; Joanne J. Meyerowitz, *Women Adrift: Independent Wage Earners in Chicago, 1880–1930* (Chicago: University of Chicago Press, 1988), 46–48.

46. These figures are based on average census information of a random sample of eleven families residing in Chicago's Packingtown. The families' occupations ranged from laborer to skilled machinist and meatcutter. Although we can assume that the heads of families worked near their residence (within one or two miles) in the slaughterhouses or stockyards, many of their older sons and daughters worked downtown and had to rely on streetcars. Ethelbert Stewart Census, CHS-Mss.

47. Stephen H. Norwood, *Labor's Flaming Youth: Telephone Operators and Worker Militancy, 1878–1923* (Urbana: University of Illinois Press, 1990), 44–45; Illinois Bureau of Labor Statistics, *Fifteenth Biannual Report, 1908,* 449–51.

48. Quotation from *Journal of Proceedings,* December 8, 1902. Fine, *Souls of the Skyscraper,* 43.

49. *Journal of Proceedings,* December 8, 1902.

50. Hooker, "Paper read by . . . at Dinner of Merchants' Club of Chicago," typescript, December 8, 1900, 14, in Hooker Collection, UC; Sinclair, *The Jungle,* 78, 199 (quote).

51. Quotation from United Brotherhood of Carpenters and Joiners of America, Local Union No. 181 to Hon. City Council, December 20, 1902, filed March 23, 1903, box 260, Council Proceedings. Hooker, "Crowding on Halsted Street Cars," *Record-Herald,* June 11, 1904; Hooker to Mayor Edward F. Dunne, October 17, 1905, Hooker Collection, UC.

52. Sinclair, *The Jungle,* 199, 78–79.

53. George Hooker to Patterson, January 5, 1902, Hooker Collection, UC; Harlan Report, 11; Hooker, "Crowding on Halsted Street Cars," *Record-Herald,* June 11, 1904.

54. Flanagan, *Charter Reform,* 20–21.

55. Jerome E. Edwards, "Government of Chicago, 1893–1915," manuscript in Pierce Collection, UC.

56. Ida M. Tarbell, "How Chicago Is Finding Herself," *American Magazine,* November–December 1908, 29–41, 124–38, esp. 31–32.

57. Quotation from George S. Schilling, *Ninth Biennial Report of the Bureau of Labor Statistics, 1896* (Springfield, 1897), 69.

58. Tarbell, "Chicago," 30–31. Dooley quoted from Ray Ginger, *Altgeld's America: The Lincoln Ideal versus Changing Realities* (New York: Funk and Wagnalls, 1958), 109; Theodore Dreiser, *Trilogy of Desire: Three Novels* (New York: World, 1972).

59. Richard L. McCormick, "The Discovery that Business Corrupts Politics: A Reappraisal of the Origins of Progressivism," *American Historical Review* 86 (1981): 247–74; Stead, *If Christ Came to Chicago.* Tarbell quoted from P. Barrett, *Automobile,* 21.

60. Destler, *American Radicalism,* 242.

61. Christopher L. Tomlins, *The State and the Unions: Labor Relations, Law, and the Organized Labor Movement in America, 1880–1960* (Cambridge: Cambridge University Press, 1985), 61–69; Destler, *American Radicalism,* 169–76, 232.

62. Howe, *The City,* 72, 90; Hooker, speech dated June 30, 1897, typescript, in Hooker Collection, UC.

63. Lloyd quoted from Destler, *American Radicalism,* 242.

64. Ibid., 199, 249 (quote).

65. Hooker, speech dated June 30, 1897, typescript, in Hooker Collection, UC; Destler, *American Radicalism,* 239.

66. Destler, *American Radicalism,* 198–99 (Lloyd quoted, 217, 198–99).

67. Ibid., 249.

68. Waldo R. Browne, *Altgeld of Illinois: A Record of His Life and Work* (New York: B. W. Huebsch, 1924), 48–49.

69. Ginger, *Altgeld's America,* 68.

70. Ibid., 72; Harvey Wish, "Altgeld and the Progressive Tradition," *American Historical Review* 46 (July 1941): 813–31.

71. Browne, *Altgeld of Illinois,* 114; Ginger, *Altgeld's America,* 68, 71 (quotes).

72. Charles Darrow, *Story of My Life* (New York: Scribner's, 1932), 105–7; Browne, *Altgeld of Illinois,* 50.

73. Tarbell, "Chicago," 34; Newton A. Partridge, "Suggestions on the Chicago Street Railway Problem: Address delivered before the Civic Federation of Chicago, June 9, 1898" (Chicago: R. R. Donnelley and Sons, 1898), Hooker Collection, UC; "Acts of February 14, 1859, and other Legislative Acts Involved in the Chicago Street Railway Litigation," Hooker Collection, UC.

74. Tarbell, "Chicago," 33.

75. Quotation from Independent Anti-Boodle League, "Listen to the Voice of the People, 'Lest We Forget,'" pamphlet (1898, Hooker Collection, UC), 5–6; Robert E. Beret, "Municipal Ownership of Street Railways in Chicago," [1898?] in Hooker Collection, UC.

76. Independent Anti-Boodle League, "Listen to the Voice of the People," esp. 29; Alexis de Tocqueville, *Democracy in America* (New York: Vintage Classics, 1990), 2:106.

77. All quotes from Independent Anti-Boodle League, "Listen to the Voice of the People," 7–17, and CFL, "Organized Labor against the Humphrey Bills," pamphlet, April 4, 1897, Newberry Library.

NOTES TO PAGES 74–81

78. Quotation from "Pamphlet in opposition to Humphrey Bills, resolution of 'Mass Meeting of the Citizens, Property Owners and Business Men of the 17th Senatorial District,' May 7, 1897." "Articles and By-laws of The Seventeenth Ward Municipal Club" (undated, ca. 1900). Both in Graham Taylor Papers, Newberry Library.

79. Tarbell, "Chicago," 34.

80. Davis, *Spearheads for Reform*, 189; Hogan, *Class and Reform*, 38–39; Edwin Burritt Smith, "Council Reform in Chicago: Work of the Municipal Voters' League," *Municipal Affairs* 4 (June 1900): 347–62, esp. 347–48; Michael McCarthy, "Businessmen and Professionals in Municipal Reform: The Chicago Experience, 1887–1920" (Ph.D. diss., Northwestern University, 1971); McCarthy, "New Metropolis"; Homer Harlan, "Politics, 1897–1905: Project Report," in Pierce Collection, UC; Destler, *American Radicalism*, 247.

81. Flanagan, *Charter Reform*, 38.

82. Quotation from Tarbell, "Chicago," 33. See also Hogan, *Class and Reform*, 39; Burritt Smith, "Council Reform," 356–61; Edwards, "Comments on Chicago Politics, 1893–1915," in box 237, Pierce Collection, UC; P. Barrett, *Automobile*, 16.

83. McCarthy, "New Metropolis," 48–51.

84. Hogan, *Class and Reform*, 47; Burritt Smith, "Council Reform," 351.

85. Ginger, *Altgeld's America*, 181; *Abendpost*, January 13, 1899; Ralph Tingley, "1899 Election," chapter draft in box 237, Pierce Collection, UC.

86. Edgar B. Tolman, "Chicago's Traction Question," *World To-Day* 10 (1905–1906): 641–42; George C. Sikes, "Chicago's Struggle for Freedom from Traction Rule," *Outlook* 82 (March 1906): 750; Edward R. Kantowicz, "Carter H. Harrison II: The Politics of Balance," chapter 2 in Paul M. Green and Melvin G. Holli, *The Mayors: The Chicago Political Tradition* (rev. ed.; Carbondale: Southern Illinois University Press, 1995), 16–32, esp. 25–28; Ralph R. Tingley, "From Carter Harrison II to Fred Busse: A Study of Chicago Political Parties and Personages from 1896 to 1907" (Ph.D. diss., University of Chicago, 1950), 35; Edwards, "Comments on Chicago Politics, 1893–1915," chapter draft in box 237, Pierce Collection, UC.

87. Darrow, *Story of My Life*, 108–9. Ginger, *Altgeld's America*, 183; Flanagan, *Charter Reform*, 43.

3—THE MOVEMENT FOR MUNICIPAL OWNERSHIP

1. Carl Sandburg, "Halsted Street Car," *Chicago Poems*.

2. *Labor Advocate*, February 1905.

3. *The Public* 5 (February 7, 1903): 689.

4. "Suggestions to Teachers," flyer in folder "1902 Tax Petitions," box 37, CTF Papers, CHS-Mss. Quotation from Haley to Franklin S. Edmonds, June 2, 1903, box 37, CTF Papers.

5. Quotation from *American*, April 2, 1902. See also Leopold Saltiel to CTF, January 24, 1902, box 37; CTF Minutes, January 25, 1902; Petition dated March 18, 1902, folder 1, box 37; W. M. Persons to Haley, July 23, 1905, box 38; all in CTF Papers.

6. *American*, November 21, 1902.

7. CTF Minutes, September 21, 1901, box 1, CTF Papers.

8. Margaret Haley, "The Tax Situation," *CTF Bulletin*, November 22, 1901; Ricker, "Unionizing," esp. 399.

9. Letter of CTF to City Council, referred June 18, 1900, filed March 23, 1903, box 260, Council Proceedings; Catherine Goggin, "Brief History of Chicago Teachers Federation," typescript, November 3, 1906, box 1, CTF Papers.

10. A.M.M. [?], "The Moral Significance of the Tax Fight," *CTF Bulletin* 1 (February 7, 1902).

11. Letter of CTF to City Council, referred June 18, 1900, filed March 23, 1903, box 260, Council Proceedings. Quotation from A.M.M. [?], "The Moral Significance of the Tax Fight." On Dewey, see Andrew Feffer, *The Chicago Pragmatists and American Progressivism* (Ithaca: Cornell University Press, 1993).

12. Maureen Flanagan, "Charter Reform in Chicago: Political Culture and Urban Progressive Reform," *Journal of Urban History* 12 (1986): 121. Quotation from *CTF Bulletin,* January 16, 1903.

13. Received February 11, 1901, filed March 23, 1903, box 260, Council Proceedings. "Age of Consent Bill," folder 2, box 38; CTF Minutes, January 14, 1905, both in CTF Papers.

14. Murphy, *Blackboard Unions,* 45; Flanagan, *Seeing with Their Hearts,* 61–62. Quotation from CTF Minutes, October 30, 1903. See my discussion of Flanagan's argument in chapter 1.

15. *CTF Bulletin* 1 (November 15, 1901): 1.

16. Foner, *History of the Labor Movement,* 45–58; D. Montgomery, *Fall of the House,* 273–81.

17. United Brotherhood of Carpenters and Joiners of America, district council minutes, August 16, 1902, folder 12, box 2, CHS-Mss; CTF Minutes, April 12, 1903; *American,* January 12, 1903; *CTF Bulletin* 2 (January 9, 1903): 4; *Typographical Journal* 21 (September 15, 1902): 258.

18. For the Bohemians, see *Denni Hlasatel,* October 14, 1902, in Foreign Language Press Survey (Bohemian), reels 1–2, CHS. For the German Turners, see the Chicago Single Tax Club, Minutes, August 1, 1902. For the religious organizations, see *New World* (The Official Organ of the Archdiocese of Chicago and Province of Illinois), September 13, 1902, January 24, 1903; *The Commons* October 1902.

19. Addams's speech at memorial meeting for H. D. Lloyd; "In Memoriam. Henry Demarest Lloyd, May first, 1847–September twenty-eighth, 1903. The Auditorium, Chicago, November 29th, 1903," pamphlet, Newberry Library (hereafter Lloyd Memorial); *Abendpost,* October 6, 1902. Quotation from *The Commons,* October 1902.

20. Quotation from Margaret Haley, "Why the Federation Voted to Aid the Striking Miners," *CTF Bulletin,* October 3, 1902; Hayes Robbins, "Public Ownership versus Public Control," *American Journal of Sociology* 10 (1904–1905): 787–813, esp. 788; *New World,* September 13, 1902, January 24, 1903.

21. "Biographical Information," reel 1, Henry Demarest Lloyd Papers, State Historical Society of Wisconsin (henceforth, Lloyd Papers); *American,* January 12, 1903.

22. Foner, *History of the Labor Movement,* 45–58; D. Montgomery, *Fall of the House,* 273–81.

23. Myers, "Labor Disputes," 393–95; George C. Sikes, "Observations on the Street Car Strike," *The Voter,* December 1903, 30, in Hooker Collection, UC.

24. Stockholder Record of Chicago City Railway Co., September 15, 1900, Chicago Surface Lines Papers, folder 20, box 4, CHS-Mss; *Record-Herald,* November 6, 9, 25, 1903; *Tribune,* November 20, 1903; *World To-Day* 6 (1903): 24–25; Sikes, "Observations," 32.

25. Myers, "Labor Disputes," 398–400; *Record-Herald,* November 14, 1903.

26. Myers, "Labor Disputes," 415; *Tribune,* November 18, *Arbeiterzeitung,* November 18, 13, 1903. Quotation from *Record-Herald,* November 16, 1903.

27. Myers, "Labor Disputes," 402; *Tribune,* November 14, 1903; *World To-Day* 6 (1903): 24–27.

28. *Tribune,* November 20, 1903; *Svenska Nyheter,* November 17, 1903, in Foreign Language Press Survey (Swedish), CHS.

29. Quotations from CFL Minutes, November 1, 1903, December 8, 1902. Letter of Cook County's German Democrats to city council, May 21, 1902, filed March 23, 1903, box 260, Council Proceedings.

30. *Journal of Proceedings,* 1903–1904, esp. 1577–78; *The Commons,* October 1903; Sikes, "Observations," 31–32.

31. Petition by the Bridge and Structural Iron Workers Local No. 1, November 19, 1903, filed November 23, 1903, box 267, Council Proceedings; CFL Minutes, November 1, 1903; *Tribune*, November 23, 1903.

32. *Arbeiterzeitung*, November 24, 1903; *Svenska Nyheter*, November 24, 1903, in Foreign Language Press Survey (Swedish), CHS; Report by the Special Committee on Municipal Ownership, *Journal of Proceedings*, 1903–1904, 1577–78.

33. *Tribune*, November 14, 1903.

34. *Journal of Proceedings*, 1903–1904, 1524; "Resolution," November 16, 1903, filed March 23, 1904, box 271, Council Proceedings.

35. *Record-Herald*, November 16, 18, 1903; Myers, "Labor Disputes," 400; *Tribune*, November 16, 23, *Arbeiterzeitung*, November 23, 1903.

36. *Tribune*, November 25, 1903; Myers, "Labor Disputes," 411.

37. *Tribune*, November 13, 1903.

38. Resolutions by the Building Material Trades Council, November 19, 22, 1903, filed November 23, 1903, box 267, Council Proceedings; *Record-Herald*, November 16, 1903.

39. *Arbeiterzeitung*, November 25, 1903; *Labor Advocate*, April 1904.

40. *Tribune*, August 14, 1904.

41. Ibid., November 23, 1903.

42. *Arbeiterzeitung*, November 2, 1903; Flyer by the CFL Committee on Ward Clubs, November 11, 1903, box 37, CTF Papers; CFL Minutes, December 20, 1903.

43. *The Public* 6 (July 4, 1903): 196; Henry Demarest Lloyd, "The Chicago Traction Question," [1903], 39, at Newberry Library, Chicago; Municipal Ownership Delegate Convention (MODC) to the Mayor and City Council of Chicago, November 7, 1903, filed March 23, 1904, box 271, Council Proceedings.

44. "List of Municipal Officers," *Journal of Proceedings*, 1907–1908, lxii–lxxx; "Report of the Municipal Ownership Central Committee on Candidates and Address to Voters," [April 1904], Hooker Collection, UC; Ralph Tingley, "Politics 1904," 14, box 237, Pierce Collection, UC.

45. First Annual Report of the Board of Supervising Engineers, "Chicago Traction" (Chicago: Board of Supervising Engineers, 1908), in Walter L. Fisher Papers, Library of Congress, Washington, DC (hereafter Fisher Papers, LC); A. B. Adair, "Argument against Traction Grants, Addressed to Transportation Committee of Chicago City Council," December 1903, Hooker Collection, UC.

46. "Report of the [CFL] Legislative Committee," January 5, 1907, folder 5, box 39, CTF Papers; "Report of [CFL] Special Charter Committee," July 21, 1907, "Chicago City Wide Collection," folder 8, box 68, Special Collections, Chicago Public Library; Flyer by the CFL's committee on ward clubs, November 11, 1903, box 37, CTF Papers.

47. MODC to the Mayor and City Council of Chicago, November 7, 1903, and Secretary M. J. Deutsch, Building Materials Trade Council, to Mayor Harrison and the City Council, November 9, 1903, both filed March 23, 1904, box 271, Council Proceedings.

48. *Tribune*, November 3, 6, 1902.

49. *American*, February 23, *Tribune*, February 24, April 8, 1903; Lloyd to Jessie Bros Lloyd (his wife), March 2, [1903], Ethelbert Stewart to Lloyd, March 2, [1903], reel 14, Lloyd Papers, SHSW; Ginger, *Altgeld's America*, 266–70.

50. *The Book of Chicagoans: A Biographical Dictionary of Leading Men and Women of the City of Chicago* (Chicago: A. N. Marquis, 1917), 550; *Abendpost*, January 30, 1905; *American*, December 2, 1902; Tingley, "Politics 1904."

51. Reid, *Battleground*, 69, 80–81; Ginger, *Altgeld's America*, 254, 289; Richard Schneirov, "Rethinking the Relation of Labor to the Politics of Urban Social Reform in Late Nineteenth-Century America: The Case of Chicago," *International Labor and Working-Class History* 46 (Fall 1994): 97. Quotation from Murray F. Tuley, "Address on the Traction Crisis in Chicago," [January, 1905] in Hooker Collection, UC. See also *Tribune*,

January 17, 1905; Richard E. Becker, "Edward Dunne: Reform Mayor of Chicago, 1905–1907" (Ph.D. diss, University of Chicago, 1971), 20.

52. Hugo Grosser, "The Movement for Municipal Ownership in Chicago," *Annals of the American Academy of Political and Social Science* (November 25, 1905): 81; *Tribune,* March 4, 1905.

53. *Tribune,* January 31, 16, *Abendpost,* January 18, 1905; Hapgood, *Spirit of Labor,* 367–69. There was some speculation that Fitzpatrick might run for alderman in the third ward, but nothing came of it. *Tribune,* March 10, 1905.

54. *Denni Hlasatel,* March 22, 1905, in Foreign Language Press Survey (Bohemian), CHS; *The Public* 8 (April 8, 1905); Becker, "Edward Dunne," 113.

55. Quotation from Reid, *Battleground,* 32. Don T. Davis, "The Chicago Teachers Federation and the School Board," CTF Papers; Ricker, "Unionizing," 397.

56. "The Women's Municipal Ownership League: To the Women of Chicago," *CTF Bulletin* 4 (March 24, 1905); *Book of Chicagoans.* Other members of the league included Dr. Julia Holmes Smith, Miss Leonora Beck, Hanna Solomon, and Winona Fitts. *Abendpost,* March 16, 1905; Becker, "Edward Dunne," 113.

57. *Book of Chicagoans,* 200; "Edward F. Dunne, Mayor of Chicago," *The Public,* April 29, 1905, 53.

58. *The Citizen,* April 1, 1905; *Denni Hlasatel,* March 22, 1905, in Foreign Language Press Survey (Bohemian), CHS; Letter of Florian Holek, March 21, 1906, Hooker Collection, UC; "Jetzt oder nie!" pamphlet; *Abendpost,* February 2, 1905.

59. Becker, "Edward Dunne," 32; College Men's Republican Club, "The Municipal Campaign of 1905: Important Political Issues," Hooker Collection, UC.

60. *Chronicle,* May 1, 1905; E. F. Dunne, Address at the Democratic City Convention, February 25, 1905, Hooker Collection, UC; *Labor Advocate,* April 1905; Rodgers, *Atlantic Crossings,* 130–59, esp. 148.

61. *The Commons* 9 (March 1905): 137–43; *Book of Chicagoans,* 301; Harlan Report.

62. *Abendpost,* January 25, 1905; *The Commons* 9 (March 1905): 137–43; Becker, "Edward Dunne," 30–50. *Economist* quoted from Grosser, "Municipal Ownership," 81. Dunne, "Municipal Ownership."

63. *Tribune,* April 5, 1905; *Chicago Daily News Almanac and Year Book for 1905,* 355; Arthur F. Bentley, "Municipal Ownership Groups in Chicago: A Study of Referendum Votes, 1902–1907," Newberry Library, Chicago; Grosser, "Municipal Ownership," 82; *The Commons* 10 (April 1905): 198; Ginger, *Altgeld's America,* 293.

64. CFL Minutes, November 1, 1903 (my emphasis).

65. E. Franklin Morrow, "Negro Democracy," [1907], Hooker Collection, UC.

66. Hooker, "The March of Municipal Ownership," *Record-Herald,* November 28, 1903.

67. Lloyd, "Chicago Traction," 40. CFL quotation from *Journal of Proceedings,* February 9, 1903.

68. Lloyd Memorial.

69. Hapgood, *Spirit of Labor,* 138.

70. Lloyd, "Chicago Traction," 39. Quotation from *The Commons* (May 1904): 170.

71. Hapgood, *Spirit of Labor,* 210–11.

72. Lloyd, "Chicago Traction," 40.

4—THE 1905 TEAMSTERS STRIKE

1. For the epigraph, Fitzpatrick is quoted from Margaret Dreier Robins (MDR) to Margaret E. Robins (MER), May 9, 1908, in Margaret Dreier Robins Papers, *Papers of the Women's Trade Union League and Its Principle Leaders* (Woodbridge, CT: Research Publications, 1979; hereafter MDR Papers).

2. Quotation from Grant, "True Story," 172.

3. *The Public* 6 (May 9, 1903).

4. J. P. Richards, head of the Chicago-based National Casket Company, on the *Chicago Chronicle,* in Richards to Horatio W. Seymour, May 23, 1903, box 1, Seymour Papers, Newberry Library, Chicago; *Typographical Journal* 20 (June 15, 1902); *The Economist* 28 (September 20, 1902): 381; *American,* January 26, 1903.

5. E. C. Potter to Seymour, May 18, 1903, in Horatio W. Seymour, Incoming Letters, [1903], box 1, Newberry Library.

6. Ernest Poole, "The Disappearing Public," *World To-Day* 6 (1904): 1056–62, esp. 1062; *Chicago Socialist,* December 12, 1905; *Voice of the Negro,* June 1905; *American,* December 9, 1902; *Book of Chicagoans.*

7. David Montgomery, *Workers' Control in America* (Cambridge: Cambridge University Press, 1979), 57–63; D. Montgomery, *Fall of the House,* 269–75; Witwer, *Corruption and Reform,* 26–27; Daniel R. Ernst, *Lawyers against Labor: From Individual Rights to Corporate Liberalism* (Urbana: University of Illinois Press, 1995), esp. 110–12, 124–46; William Forbath, "The Shaping of the American Labor Movement," *Harvard Law Review* 102 (1989): 1109–256, esp. 1148–65. See also William Forbath, *Law and the Shaping of the American Labor Movement* (Cambridge, MA: Harvard University Press, 1991).

8. J. Barrett, *Work and Community,* 131–46, 165–82.

9. *World To-Day* 6 (1904): 782–83. Upon learning of the construction of the tunnels, organized labor filed complaints with the city against the Illinois Telephone and Telegraph Tunnel Company and demanded a public investigation as to how the company had managed to secure franchises from city hall. Letters from E. J. Nockels, secretary of CFL, to F. [?] Bender, City Clerk, [undated] and October 15, 1904, W. M. Persons to Haley, July 23, 1905, folder 1, box 38, CTF Papers.

10. CFL Minutes, March 26, 1905; *The Public,* May 6, April 15, 1905; Myers, "Labor Disputes," 560. Quotation from *Labor Advocate,* May 1905.

11. John Cummings, "The Chicago Teamsters Strike," *Journal of Political Economy* 13 (1905): 536–73, esp. 551–52; Grant, "True Story," 173.

12. Commons, "Teamsters"; Leiter, *Teamsters Union,* 24; Myers, "Labor Disputes," 567.

13. Myers, "Labor Disputes," 555; *The Public,* May 4, 1905; Grant, "True Story," 174; Cummings, "Teamsters Strike," 546.

14. *Arbeiterzeitung,* April 10, 1905; "Final Statement of Defense Fund," *Labor Advocate,* September, July 1905. Estimates of the teamsters' strike fund ranged from five hundred to seven hundred thousand dollars. *Tribune,* April 11, 1905; Myers, "Labor Disputes," 569.

15. *Arbeiterzeitung,* May 22, 1905; Bigham, "Chicago Federation of Labor," 78; Cummings, "Teamsters Strike," 547; CFL Minutes, May 7, 1905; *Tribune,* May 8, *Labor Advocate,* June, August 1905.

16. Myers, "Labor Disputes," 581–90; *Arbeiterzeitung,* April 8, 9, 14, 30, 1905; Cummings, "Teamsters Strike," 499, 559; *The Public,* May 13, July 29, 1905; Tuttle, *Race Riot,* 120; *The Economist* 33 (May 6, 1905): 686.

17. *Arbeiterzeitung,* May 11–16, *Tribune,* May 23, 1905. Quotation from CFL Minutes, May 21, 1905; Myers, "Labor Disputes," 575.

18. Tuttle, *Race Riot,* 120–23; Grant, "True Story," 173–74.

19. Quotation from William M. Tuttle Jr., "Labor Conflict and Racial Violence: The Black Workers in Chicago, 1894–1919," *Labor History* 10, no. 3 (Summer 1969): 408–32, esp. 415.

20. *The Public,* May 13, 1905. Quotation from *Labor Advocate,* June 1905.

21. *Voice of the Negro* 2 (June 1905): 375.

22. *The Public,* May 13, *Tribune,* May 8, 1905. Quotation from *Labor Advocate,* June 1905.

23. *The Commons,* June 1905.

24. "Chicago Strike—By a Teamster."

25. *Voice of the Negro* 2 (June 1905). See also *The Public,* June 6, 1905.

26. *The Economist* 33 (May 6, 1905): 686. See also *Tribune,* April 10, May 26, *The Public,* April 15, 1905.

27. *Labor Advocate,* June, September 1905; Mowry, *Era of Theodore Roosevelt,* 102–3.

28. Report by labor attorneys Daniel Cruice and A. S. Langville to CFL, *Labor Advocate,* October 1905; Testimony of [Chicago] employer James A. Miller, Commission on Industrial Relations, *Report,* 8:cviii; Myers, "Labor Disputes," 610.

29. Cummings, "Teamsters Strike," 500; Grant, "True Story," 174.

30. Grant, "True Story," 174; *Tribune,* April 21, 1905; Myers, "Labor Disputes," 610; Cummings, "Teamsters Strike," 552.

31. Forbath, "American Labor Movement," esp. 1148–65; Leon Fink, "Labor, Liberty, and the Law: Trade Unionism and the Problem of the American Constitutional Order," chapter in Leon Fink, *In Search of the Working Class: Essays in American Labor History and Popular Culture* (Urbana: University of Illinois Press, 1994).

32. *The Public,* July 8, 1905. Quotation from *Record-Herald,* May 1, 1905.

33. Department stores provoked the ire of small retail merchants, real estate developers, and organized labor during the late 1890s. Joel A. Tarr, "The Chicago Anti–Department Store Crusade of 1897: A Case Study in Urban Commercial Development," *Journal of the Illinois State Historical Society* 64 (1971): 161–72.

34. D. Montgomery, *Fall of the House,* 269–81; Forbath, "American Labor Movement," 1202–27; L. Fink, "Labor, Liberty, and the Law," 157–59.

35. Addams cited from [Jane Addams], *Twenty Years at Hull-House; with Autobiographical Notes* (New York: New American Library, 1961), 225–26.

36. Grant, "True Story," 173; CFL Minutes, March 5, 26, 1905; *The Public,* May 6, 1905; Myers, "Labor Disputes," 560.

37. *The Public,* April 15, May 6, 13, *Arbeiterzeitung,* April 15, 1905; E. F. Dunne, *Illinois: The Heart of the Nation* (Chicago: Lewis, 1933) 2:268.

38. Quotations from "Chicago Strike—By a Teamster." Victor E. Soares, "Reforming a Labor Union," *World-Today* 10 (1905): 92–97; *Arbeiterzeitung,* June 12, 1905. See also William Z. Foster, *Misleaders of Labor* (Chicago: Trade Union Educational League, 1927).

39. Quotation from John V. Farwell Jr. to Graham Taylor, August 7, 1906, folder "Incoming Letters," Taylor Papers, Newberry Library. See also *The Commons,* September 1905; Witwer, *Corruption and Reform,* 30–35.

40. *Arbeiterzeitung,* April 17, May 1, *Labor Advocate,* March 1905. Quotation from *Chicago Socialist,* June 1905.

41. *Typographical Journal* 27 (September 1905): 320–21; *The Commons* 10 (July 1905). Taylor cited from *The Commons* 10 (September 1905): 487.

42. Cummings, "Teamsters Strike," 571.

43. *Labor Advocate,* June 1905.

44. Graham Taylor, *Chicago Commons through Forty Years* (Chicago: Chicago Commons Association, 1936), 118.

45. *Chicago Socialist,* July 1905; *Tribune,* May 22, 26, 1905.

46. Cummings, "Teamsters Strike," 571; *Typographical Journal* 27 (September 1905), 320–21; also *The Commons,* September 1905.

47. Addams, *Newer Ideals of Peace,* 128.

48. *The Commons,* September 1905.

49. Cummings, "Teamsters Strike," 501, 546; *The Public* May 4, *Tribune,* April 12, *Arbeiterzeitung,* April 24, *Record-Herald,* April 9, 1905; *Economist* 33 (May 6, 1905): 686.

50. Cummings, "Teamsters Strike," 569. Quotation from Leiter, *Teamsters Union,* 25. On CFL's strike-related actions, see Myers, "Labor Disputes," 774; *Tribune,* May 27, *Arbeiterzeitung,* June 19, July 7, 1905; *The Public,* July 29, 1905.

51. *Tribune,* September 10, 13, 1906.

52. Quoted from Witwer, *Corruption and Reform,* 36.

53. *Labor Advocate,* August, September 1905; *Tribune,* March 26, May 1, November 3, 5, 1906. Quotation from John V. Farwell Jr. to Graham Taylor, August 7, 1906, folder "Incoming Letters," Taylor Papers, Newberry Library. Witwer, *Corruption and Reform,* 36.

54. *Tribune,* August 9, September 10, 13, November 26, December 3, 1906, March 22, 1907; Myers, "Labor Disputes," 580; Leiter, *Teamsters Union,* 24–27.

55. CFL Minutes, December 3, 1905.

56. Folder 10, box 228, Pierce Collection, UC. Statistics based on *American Federationist* and *U.S. Senate Report on Condition of Women and Child Wage Earners in the United States,* vol. 10, 61st Cong., 2nd sess. Quotation from Andrews and Bliss, "History of Women," 166.

57. *Record-Herald,* January 8, 1906.

58. *Tribune,* April 16, January 10, 15, 1906. In the aftermath of these disturbances, the CFL decided to hold elections annually instead of biannually. *Tribune,* May 7, 1906.

59. *Tribune,* August 13, 1906. Quotation from ibid., September 4, 1906.

60. *Labor Advocate,* May 1906; CFL Minutes, February 4, 1906.

61. *Tribune,* February 6, 15, July 16, 30, August 8, September 14, 1906; *Labor Advocate,* July, December 1905, May 1906; *Record-Herald,* July 16, 1906.

62. *Typographical Journal* 30 (March 1907): 235, and 31 (November 1907): 548. Quotation from Myers, "Labor Disputes," 580.

5—THE POLITICS OF STREETCAR REGULATION

1. The epigraph is from MDR to MER, March 23, 1907, MDR Papers. Quotations from Woodruff, "Municipal Progress," 201.

2. MDR to MER, November 7, 1906, MDR Papers.

3. *Tribune,* April 3, 1907.

4. Lloyd, "Chicago Traction," 35. See also Edwin Burritt Smith, "Street Railway Legislation in Illinois," *Atlantic Monthly,* January 1904, 109–18.

5. John H. Hamline, "A prophecy by John Hamline and its fulfillment by the supporters of the Mueller Bill," January 9, 1904, 23–24, 32, 35, Hooker Collection, UC; Ruth F. Necheless, "Assistant's Report" and essay in box 228, Pierce Collection, UC; A. B. Adair, Representative of Chicago Typographical Union, No. 16, Argument against Traction Grants, addressed to Transportation Committee of Chicago City Council, December 1903; *The Public,* January 24, February 7, 1903.

6. Rodgers, *Atlantic Crossings,* 155.

7. *Economist,* July 8, 1905.

8. Biographical note, Fisher Papers, LC.

9. *Tribune,* April 30, 1905; [undated] letter from [unknown] to Charles Merriam, folder 8, box 71, Charles Merriam Papers, Special Collections, University of Chicago.

10. Quotation from Fisher to "My dear Mr. Roosevelt." [Th. Roosevelt, pres.], February 19, 1904, General Correspondence, also Fisher to John V. Farwell Jr., March 10, 1904, Fisher Papers, LC.

11. Henry Phipps to Fisher, December 15, 1906, Fisher Papers, LC.

12. Arnold, "Report on the Engineering and Operating Features of the Chicago Transportation Problem," 49; *Book of Chicagoans,* 20–21; P. Barrett, *Automobile,* 29.

13. MDR to MER, January 22, 1906, box 20, MDR Papers.

14. Sikes, "Chicago's Struggle"; John Fairlie, "The Street Railway Question in Chicago," *Quarterly Journal of Economics* 21 (1907): 371–404, esp. 394.

15. Tarbell, "Chicago," 125–27; Dalrymple to Dunne, June 29, 1905, Hooker Collection, UC; Fairlie, "Street Railway Question," 391–92. Quotation from *Journal of Proceedings,* January 15, 1906.

16. *Tribune,* April 4, *Economist,* April 7, 1906; Zane L. Miller, "Municipal Ownership," [1960], box 228, Pierce Collection, UC.

17. *Tribune,* March 13, *The Public,* March 17, *Economist,* March 17, September 30, 1906; Fairlie, "Street Railway Question," 392, 394; Willard E. Hotchkiss, "Chicago Traction: A Study in Political Evolution," *Annals of the American Academy of Political and Social Science* 28 (1906): 398; Eugene E. Prussing, "Municipal Ownership and Municipal Operation of Street Railways," [March 24, 1906], Hooker Collection, UC; MDR to MER, March 15, 1906, reel 20, MDR Papers; *World To-Day* 9 (1905): 1152–54. For details, see Committee on Local Transportation, Minority Report, *Journal of Proceedings,* December 4, 1905.

18. Richard Allen Morton, *Justice and Humanity: Edward F. Dunne, Illinois Progressive* (Carbondale: Southern Illinois University Press, 1997), 23, 32; Darrow to Dunne, June 19, 1905, box 1, General Correspondence, Clarence Darrow Papers, LC.

19. Fairlie, "Street Railway Question," 396–98. Quotation from Fisher, untitled, undated manuscript, box 22, Fisher Papers, LC.

20. Dunne to Werno, April 27, 1906, in *Journal of Proceedings,* January 15, 1907; Fairlie, "Street Railway Question," 395; *Economist,* May 5, *The Public,* May 5, 1906; Hotchkiss, "Chicago Traction," 398–401; Victor Yarros, "The Chicago Election and the City's Traction Outlook," *American Monthly Review of Reviews,* 1907; Hotchkiss, Willard E. Hotchkiss, "Recent Phases of Chicago's Transportation Problem," *Annals of the American Academy of Political and Social Science* 31 (1908): 619–29.

21. *The Public,* September 16, 1905, 376.

22. *Labor Advocate,* October 1905. Quotations from MDR to MER, March 22, April 11, 1906, reel 20, MDR Papers. *Revyen,* March 2, 1907, Foreign Language Press Survey (Albanian), CHS; Becker, "Edward Dunne," 115; *Economist,* May 5, 1906.

23. *Tribune,* May 21, 1906; CFL Minutes, January 5, 1905; *Labor Advocate,* April 1905.

24. *Tribune,* December 24, 1906. Quotation from *Record-Herald,* June 18, 1906.

25. *Tribune,* December 10, 1906; CFL Minutes, October 15, 1905; *Labor Advocate,* January 1906.

26. Morton, *Justice and Humanity,* 34–40.

27. CFL Minutes, April 15, 1906.

28. MDR to MER, March 22, April 5, 1906, reel 20, MDR Papers.

29. *Record-Herald,* January 5, 13, 15, March 5, *Tribune,* March 5, 1906; Bigham, "Chicago Federation of Labor," 96.

30. *Labor Advocate,* May 1906; *Tribune,* March 20, 21, April 3, 9, 1906.

31. Greene, *Pure and Simple Politics,* introduction.

32. *Tribune,* May 21, 28, August 20, *Record-Herald,* August 20, 1906.

33. *Tribune,* June 25, August 6, October 22, November 7, *Record-Herald,* October 22, 1906.

34. Flyer, Municipal Ownership Central Committee, Hooker Collection, UC; Morton, *Justice and Humanity,* 41–42.

35. *Tribune,* March 29, 1907; *Economist* 37 (March 2, 1907): 415; *Svenska Kuriren,* April 6, 1907, Foreign Language Press Survey (Swedish), CHS.

36. *Tribune,* July 2, 1906; Morton, *Justice and Humanity,* 41–42; MDR to MER, March 22, 1906, reel 20, MDR Papers.

37. Tarbell, "Chicago," 136–37.

38. *Economist,* March 2, 1907. See also *Economist,* February 23, March 9, 1907.

39. Letter, [author unknown], February 20, 1907, and Citizens Non-Partisan Traction Settlement Committee, letter to [unknown], February 20, 1907, both in Hooker Collection, UC; *Tribune,* March 22, 1906.

40. *The Public,* April 9, 1909; *Tribune,* March 22, 1906; *Economist,* March 9, 1907.

41. Flyer by the Citizens' Non-Partisan Traction Settlement Association, March 29, 1907, Hooker Collection, UC.

42. Quotation from *Tribune,* December 3, 1906. See also *Tribune,* July 30, 1906.

43. Fisher, "The Traction Ordinances," *City Club Bulletin* 1, no. 3 (March 6, 1907): 17–42.

44. *Tribune,* January 7, 1907.

45. Bentley, "Municipal Ownership Groups," in "Chicago: A Study of Referendum Votes, 1902–1907" (undated, probably 1907), Newberry Library; Finegold, *Experts and Politicians,* 178.

46. Cited in Peter Novick, *That Noble Dream: The 'Objectivity Question' and the American Historical Profession* (Cambridge: Cambridge University Press, 1988), 301.

47. Walter Smith, "Pluralism," in *Theory and Methods in Political Science,* ed. David Marsh and Gerry Stoker (London: Macmillan, 1995), 212–18; Leon Fink, *Progressive Intellectuals and the Dilemmas of Democratic Commitment* (Cambridge, MA: Harvard University Press, 1997), 16–19.

48. *Tribune,* March 19, 1906.

49. Ibid., February 5, January 16, 1907.

50. [Anonymous] to R. Robins, May 20, 1907, reel 20, MDR Papers; Flanagan, *Seeing with Their Hearts,* 4–7.

51. Cited in Rowe, "Foreign Experience," 247. See also William H. Brown, "Public Ownership and Popular Government," *American Journal of Sociology* 12 (1906–1907): 328–40.

52. *Tribune,* December 24, 1906, January 7, 1907.

53. L. Fink, *Progressive Intellectuals,* 26–43.

54. *Labor Advocate,* February 1907.

55. CFL Minutes, Report of the Legislative Committee, *Labor Advocate,* February 1907; D. K. Tone, Flyer of Municipal Ownership Central Committee, [1907], Hooker Collection, UC.

56. CFL circular, March 18, 1907, Hooker Collection, UC.

57. Pamphlet by Street Railway Employees Union, Hooker Collection, UC; Nockels to "Gentlemen," January 7, 1907, box 304, Council Proceedings. Quotation from *Labor Advocate,* January 1907.

58. *Tribune,* October 8, 1906. See also John R. Commons, "The Organization of Public Employees into Labor Unions," address before WTUL, Hull House, October 13, 1907; *CTF Bulletin,* October 25, 1907, 6.

59. Prussing, "Municipal Ownership"; Brown, "Public Ownership," 328–40.

60. *Tribune,* February 1, 1907.

61. *Tribune,* October 10, 1906. See also *The Public,* July 28, September 17, November 24, 1906, January 5, March 23, 1907; Morton, *Justice and Humanity,* 34–40.

62. *The Public,* April 14, 1906.

63. MDR to MER, November 7, 1906, March 23, 1907, MDR Papers.

64. MDR to MER, March 22, April 5, 1906, ibid.

65. MDR to MER, November 10, 1906, ibid.

66. *Chicago Daily News Almanac,* 1908, 319–20; Morton, *Justice and Humanity,* 45, 48.

67. *The Economist,* April 6, *Tribune,* April 3, 1907.

68. P. Barrett, *Automobile,* 27, 37–49.

6—THE ECLIPSE OF REFORM IN A FRAGMENTED CITY

1. Hogan, *Class and Reform,* 41–44; Kenneth Finegold, "Busse, Merriam, and the Bureau of Public Efficiency," in Finegold, *Experts and Politicians,* 153–68; Charles E. Merriam, *Chicago: A More Intimate View of Urban Politics* (New York: Macmillan, 1929), 34–67.

2. Busse quoted in Finegold, *Experts and Politicians,* 154.

3. Flanagan, *Charter Reform,* 145–58; Hogan, *Class and Reform,* 44–46; Harold F. Gosnell, *Machine Politics: Chicago Model* (1937; repr., New York: AMS Press, 1969), 126–93; Finegold, *Experts and Politicians,* 156–63. Examples of the revisionist school in the boss-reformer debate include Robert K. Merton, "The Latent Functions of the Machine," Zane L. Miller, "Boss Cox's Cincinnati," and Thomas Lee Philpott, "Settlement House Workers versus the Ward Boss," all in Stave and Stave, *Urban Bosses;* John F. Bauman, "The Philadelphia Housing Commission and Scientific Efficiency, 1909–1916," in Ebner and Tobin, *Age of Urban Reform.*

4. Ralph E. Heilman, "The Chicago Subway Problem," *Journal of Political Economy* 22 (1914): 992–94; Alan Bliss, "Chicago's Government: Form and Function" [1938], 181 (manuscript in Pierce Collection, UC). Quotation from Fisher, box 22 [1930], Fisher Papers, LC.

5. Fairlie, "Street Railway Question"; John Fairlie, "The Chicago Street Railways: A Supplementary Note," *Quarterly Journal of Economics* 22 (1907–1908): 476–79; George Sikes, "Recent Startling Aspects of the Chicago Traction Question," *City Club Bulletin,* April 25, 1913, 4; Hotchkiss, "Recent Phases."

6. Hotchkiss, "Recent Phases," 623; "Reply to an Order by the Chicago City Council for Information Respecting Improvements Made under the 1907 Ordinances in Service, Operation and Equipment of the Chicago Surface Traction Companies, Submitted by the Board of Supervising Engineers, July 13, 1913," in Hooker Collection, UC; Yago, *Decline of Transit,* 156–58. Quotation from Sikes, "Recent Startling Aspects," 4.

7. Harold L. Platt, *The Electric City: Energy and the Growth of the Chicago Area, 1880–1930* (Chicago: University of Chicago Press, 1991), 58–92, 95–138; Forrest McDonald, *Insull* (Chicago: University of Chicago Press, 1962), 82–89; Yago, *Decline of Transit,* 157–58; Sikes, "Recent Startling Aspects," 3–8; Christopher Armstrong and H. V. Nelles, *Southern Exposure: Canadian Promoters in Latin America and the Caribbean, 1896–1930* (Toronto: University of Toronto Press), 1–13.

8. State Public Utilities Commission of Illinois, *Opinions and Orders for the Year Ending November 30, 1915* (Springfield, IL: s.n., 1915), vol. 2; Yago, *Decline of Transit,* 157; Bernard A. Weisberger, *The La Follettes of Wisconsin: Love and Politics in Progressive America* (Madison: University of Wisconsin Press, 1994); Delos F. Wilcox, "Effects of State Regulation upon the Municipal Ownership Movement," in *State Regulation of Public Utilities* (Philadelphia: American Academy of Political and Social Science, 1914), 71–84, esp. 75.

9. Platt, *Electric City,* 95–138. Quotation from Gosnell, *Machine Politics,* 4.

10. "Reply to an Order by the Chicago City Council for Information Respecting Improvements Made under the 1907 Ordinances in Service, Operation and Equipment of the Chicago Surface Traction Companies, Submitted by the Board of Supervising Engineers, July 13, 1913," p. 4; John Ericson [chairman of the Harbor and Subway Commission of Chicago], "Synopsis of an Address to the Irish Fellowship Club, March 2, 1912"; Ralph E. Heilman, "The Transportation Problem of Chicago, Report of the Transportation Committee, Cook County Real Estate Board," 3–15, all in Hooker Collection, UC. Quotation from Heilman, "Chicago Subway Problem," 993. P. Barrett, *Automobile,* 68–69.

11. Tarr, "Anti–Department Store Crusade"; "Urbanism," manuscript in folder B 225/4, Pierce Collection, UC; Benjamin Levering, "The Subway: An Argument against the Proposed Down-Town Subway of Chicago," 7, in Hooker Collection, UC; Yago, *Decline of Transit,* 156. North-West Side Commercial Association of Chicago, *Monthly Bulletin,* November 1913, 2, and "The Transportation Problem of Chicago," esp. p. 13, Report of Transportation Committee, Cook County Real Estate Board, both in Hooker Collection, UC. Subway activists' quotation from P. Barrett, *Automobile,* 68–69.

12. Heilman, "The Chicago Subway Problem," 996; Clarence Oran Gardner, *The Referendum in Chicago* (Philadelphia: University of Pennsylvania Press), 21; David M. Maynard, "The Operation of the Referendum in Chicago" (Ph.D. diss., University of Chicago, 1930), 13–14; Yago, *Decline of Transit,* 152–56.

13. Quotation from "Aldermen Long and McCold Object to Car Line in Kenwood," *Saturday Evening Call,* June 30, 1909. Letter of the Kenwood Residents' Association to the City Council of Chicago, [undated], in Kenwood Protective Association Papers, CHS-Mss.

14. "Essays on Ethnics—Population-Blacks," folder 229/8 in Pierce Collection, UC.

15. *Saturday Evening Call,* June 30, 1909.

16. Chicago Commission on Race Relations, *The Negro in Chicago: A Study of Race Relations and a Race Riot in 1919,* The American Negro: His History and Literature (1922; repr., New York: Arno Press, 1968), 297–309, esp. 298; *Chicago Defender,* January 23, 1915, cited in "Essays on Ethnics—Population-Blacks," folder 229/8 in Pierce Collection, UC; Charles L. Swanson, letter to his wife, November 17, 1918, in Chas. L. Swanson Papers, CHS-Mss; Grossman, *Land of Hope,* 166–67; Spear, *Black Chicago,* 11–23. See also Erik S. Gellman, "'Carthage Must Be Destroyed': Race, City Politics, and the Campaign to Integrate Chicago Transportation Work, 1929–1945," *Labor* 2.2 (Summer 2005): 81–114.

17. P. Barrett, *Automobile,* 46–81.

18. CFL Minutes, December 19, 1912, 4; Yago, *Decline of Transit,* 165.

19. CFL Minutes, October 20, November 3, December 15, 1907, January 5, 1908, April 2, 1916. Quotation from ibid., November 3, 1907. Pamphlets of the Chicago Municipal Ownership League, October 1918, in Hooker Collection, UC, Ms. Division. Quotation from Gellman, "'Carthage Must Be Destroyed,'" 81–114.

20. CFL Minutes, January 5, 19, July 19, August 2, 16, 1908, February 4, 1912, February 1, 1914.

21. Ibid., March 19, 1914; "Labor Night," *City Club Bulletin* 5 (1912): 216.

22. John Fitzpatrick to Hon. Fred A. Busse, Mayor of Chicago, November 3, 1909, CFL Minutes; "City Planning in Justice to the Working Population," *City Club Bulletin* 2 (March 17, 1909): 327–37.

23. Douglas Bukowski, "Big Bill Thompson (1915–1923, 1927–1931)," 63–64, in Green and Holli, *The Mayors;* Marjorie Murphy, "Taxation and Social Conflict: Teacher Unionism and Public School Finance in Chicago, 1898–1934," *Journal of the Illinois State Historical Society* 74.4 (1981): 244–47.

24. "The Story in Brief of the Chicago Newspaper Trouble," May 16, 1912, folder 6, box 1, Fitzpatrick Papers, CHS-Mss.

25. CFL Minutes, March 3, April 7, May 5, 19, October 6, November 3, 1912, September 21, 1913; *Union Progressive* 2 (August 15, 1913).

26. Habermas, *Historia y crítica,* 196–97; Jürgen Habermas, "The Public Sphere," in Seidman, *Society and Politics,* 236; Winkler, *William Randolph Hearst.* For an uncritical appraisal of the Hearst press's contribution to American democracy, see Mrs. Fremont Older, *William Randolph Hearst, American* (New York: D. Appleton-Century, 1936). For an extremely critical account, see Lundberg, *Imperial Hearst.* For an analysis of Hearst's role in the transformation of the public sphere in the context of San Francisco, see Ethington, *Public City,* 312–19.

27. CFL Minutes, November, December 1910, January 1911; Steve Fraser, *Labor Will Rule: Sidney Hillman and the Rise of American Labor* (Ithaca: Cornell University Press, 1991), 40–76; Newell, *Labor Movement*, 220–25; Jentz, "Labor, the Law, and Economics."

28. Foster quoted in J. Barrett, "Ethnic and Racial Fragmentation," 287–309, esp. 294–95; J. Barrett, *Work and Community*, 188–268; Brody, *Steelworkers in America*, 39–46; Wally Hettle, "'Radicalism of the Destructive Type': Anti-Bolshevism, Class Consciousness and Industrial Unionism in Chicago after World War I" (paper presented to Illinois History Symposium, December 1992; manuscript courtesy David Zonderman).

29. CFL Minutes, August 7, 1910; "First National Convention of the Labor Party of the U.S., November 22, 1919," folder 17, box 1997.46, Fitzpatrick Papers, CHS-Mss; J. Barrett, "Ethnic and Racial Fragmentation," 295–97; Wrigley, *Class Politics*, 36–47.

30. Lizabeth Cohen, *Making a New Deal: Industrial Workers in Chicago, 1919–1939* (New York: Cambridge University Press, 1990), 1–52.

31. Paul Adamson, "Looking Back on Our Future: Conflicting Visions and Realities of the Modern American City," in Thomas Deckker, ed., *The Modern City Revisited* (London: Spon Press, 2000), 214–44.

CONCLUSION—CLASS, REFORM, AND DEMOCRACY IN EARLY TWENTIETH-CENTURY AMERICA

1. Habermas, *Historia y crítica*, 94–123; Calhoun, "Introduction: Habermas and the Public Sphere," in Calhoun, *Habermas*, 29–33. Historian Philip Ethington's recent study of San Francisco's political culture during the late nineteenth century confirms these Habermasian shifts. Once group actors such as the workingmen's parties entered the city's public sphere, the pursuit of a singular public interest was abandoned in favor of a pluralist one. Ethington, *Public City*, 41.

2. Robert Park, "Ecología humana," chapter in "Ecología humana," in Mario Bassols et al., *Antología de sociología urbana* (Mexico: UNAM, 1988); Georg Leidenberger, "Nature and the Public: Urban Ecology and the Politics of Transportation in Progressive-Era Chicago," *Revista de Urbanismo*, electronic journal of the Department of Urban Planning, University of Chile, Santiago, September 2000 (http://revistaurbanismo.uchile.cl).

3. Rodgers, *Atlantic Crossings*, 152.

4. Ibid., 153, 157–58, esp. 158.

5. David Brody, *In Labor's Cause: Main Themes on the History of the American Worker* (New York: Oxford University Press, 1993); Leon Fink, "American Labor History," *The New American History*, ed. Eric Foner (Philadelphia: Temple University Press, 1990); Bruce Laurie, *Artisans into Workers: Labor in Nineteenth-Century America* (New York: Noonday Press, 1989); Ira Katznelson and Aristide R. Zolberg, *Working-Class Formation: Nineteenth-Century Patterns in Western Europe and in the United States* (Princeton, NJ: Princeton University Press, 1980); Gary Marks, *Unions in Politics: Britain, Germany, and the United States in the Nineteenth and Early Twentieth Centuries* (Princeton, NJ: Princeton University Press, 1989); Victoria C. Hattam, *Labor Visions and State Power: The Origins of Business Unionism in the United States* (Princeton, NJ: Princeton University Press, 1993); Kim Voss, *The Making of American Exceptionalism: The Knights of Labor and Class Formation in the Nineteenth Century* (Ithaca: Cornell University Press, 1993). See also Selig Perlman's original formulation of labor's political outlook as stated in his *Theory of the Labor Movement* (New York: Macmillan, 1928).

6. Rodgers, *Atlantic Crossings*, 121–23, 125–29.

7. Tocqueville, *Democracy in America*.

SELECT BIBLIOGRAPHY

MANUSCRIPT COLLECTIONS

Bowman Dairy Company Records. Manuscript Division. CHS.

Chicago City Council Proceedings File. Illinois Regional Archives Depository. Northeastern Illinois University, Chicago.

Chicago City Wide Collection. Special Collections. Chicago Public Library, Chicago.

Chicago Federation of Labor Minutes. Special Collections. CHS.

Chicago Single Tax Club. Special Collections. University of Illinois at Chicago Circle.

Chicago Surface Lines. Manuscript Division. CHS.

Chicago Teachers Federation. Manuscript Division. CHS.

City Club of Chicago. Manuscript Division. CHS.

Civic Federation of Chicago. Manuscript Division. CHS.

Darrow, Charles S. Manuscript Division. Library of Congress, Washington DC.

Dever, William E. Manuscript Division. CHS.

Dreier Robins, Margaret. In *Papers of the Women's Trade Union League and Its Principle Leaders*. Woodbridge, CT: Research Publications, 1979.

Eastman, Sidney C. Manuscript Division. CHS.

Fisher, Walter L. Manuscript Division. Library of Congress, Washington DC.

Fitzpatrick, John C. Manuscript Division. CHS.

Foreign Language Press Survey. Manuscript Division. CHS. Microfilm.

Hooker, George. Collection of Pamphlets. Special Collections. UC.

Lloyd, Henry D. State Historical Society of Wisconsin. Microfilm edition.

McDowell, Mary E. Manuscript Division. CHS.

Merriam, Charles E. Special Collections. Joseph Regenstein Library. UC.

Meyne, Gerhardt F., Papers. Manuscript Division. CHS.

Nestor, Agnes. Manuscript Division. CHS. See also *Papers of the Women's Trade Union League and Its Principle Leaders*. Woodbridge, CT: Research Publications, 1979.

Pierce, Bessie L. Collection. Special Collections, Joseph Regenstein Library, UC.

Post, Louis F. Manuscript Division. Library of Congress, Washington DC.

Stewart, Ethelbert, Census. Manuscript Division. CHS.

Taylor, Graham C. Special Collections. Newberry Library, Chicago.

United Brotherhood of Carpenters and Joiners of America. Manuscript Division. CHS.

United States Industrial Commission. *Reports of the United States Industrial Commission.* 19 vols. Washington, DC, 1900–1902.

Willett, H. L., Papers. Manuscript Division. CHS.

NEWSPAPERS AND JOURNALS

The American Journal of Sociology
The American Monthly Review of Reviews
Chicago Abendpost
Chicago American
Chicago Daily News Almanac
The Chicago Economist
Chicagoer Arbeiterzeitung
Chicago Inter-Ocean
Chicago New World
Chicago Record-Herald
Chicago Socialist
Chicago Teachers' Federation Bulletin (CTF Bulletin)
Chicago Tribune
The Commons
The Literary Digest
The Nation
The Outlook
The Public
Scribner's Magazine
Typographical Journal
Union Labor Advocate
The Voice of the Negro
Women's Trade Union League. Biennial Report.
Workers' Call
The World To-Day

UNPUBLISHED WORKS

Becker, Richard E. "Edward Dunne: Reform Mayor of Chicago, 1905–1907." Ph.D. diss., University of Chicago, 1971.
Berlet, Robert E. "Municipal Ownership of Street Railways in Chicago." In Hooker Collection, UC.
Bigham, Truman C. "The Chicago Federation of Labor." M.A. thesis, University of Chicago, 1924.
Dunne, Edward F. "Municipal Ownership: How the People May Get Back Their Own." Address before the Men's Club of the Stewart Avenue Universalist Church of Englewood, January 12, 1904, Municipal Ownership Central Committee pamphlet. Hooker Collection, UC.
Errant, James W. "Trade Unionists in the Civil Service of Chicago, 1895 to 1930." Ph.D. diss., University of Chicago, 1939.
H. W. [probably Harold Woodman]. "Organization of Labor in Chicago, 1893–1914." In folder 10, box 228 (Labor), Bessie L. Pierce Collection, UC.
Heilman, Ralph Emerson. "Chicago Traction: A Study of the Efforts of the City to Secure Good Service." Ph.D. diss., Harvard University, 1912.
Hettle, Wally. "'Radicalism of the Destructive Type': Anti-Bolshevism, Class Consciousness and Industrial Unionism in Chicago after World War I." Paper presented to Illinois History Symposium, December 1992. Manuscript courtesy David Zonderman
Keiser, John. "John Fitzpatrick and Progressive Unionism, 1915–1925." Ph.D. diss., Northwestern University, 1965.
Leidenberger, Georg. "Labor and Reform Politics in Two Metropolis: Streetcar Unions in

San Francisco and Chicago at the Turn of the Century." Conference paper, American Historical Association—Pacific Coast Branch, San Francisco, August 1996.

———. "Reformers and Revolutionists: The Socialist Party in Minnesota, 1910–1919." Honors thesis, Macalester College, 1987.

———. "Working-Class Progressivism and the Politics of Transportation in Chicago, 1895–1907." Ph.D. diss., University of North Carolina at Chapel Hill, 1995.

Malloy, Scott, "Labor Relations on the Street Railways in the 1890s: The Rhode Island Example." Pullman Strike Centennial Conference, Terre Haute, September 1994.

Marks, Donald D. "Evolution of Civic Reform Consciousness in Chicago, 1874–1900." Ph.D. diss., Northwestern University, 1960.

Maynard, David M. "The Operation of the Referendum in Chicago." Ph.D. diss., University of Chicago, 1930.

McCarthy, Michael. "Businessmen and Professionals in Municipal Reform: The Chicago Experience, 1887–1920." Ph.D. diss, Northwestern University, 1971.

Moore, Elizabeth A. "Life and Labor: Margaret Dreier Robins and the Women's Trade Union League." Ph.D. diss., University of Illinois at Chicago Circle, 1981.

Murphy, Marjorie. "From Artisans to Semi-Professionals: White-Collar Unionism among Chicago Public School Teachers, 1870–1930." Ph.D. diss., University of California at Davis, 1981.

Myers, Howard Barton. "The Policing of Labor Disputes in Chicago." Ph.D. diss., University of Chicago, 1927.

Prussing, Eugene E. "Municipal Ownership and Municipal Operation of Street Railways." [March 24, 1906]. Hooker Collection, UC.

Schneirov, Richard. "The Knights of Labor in the Chicago Labor Movement and in Municipal Politics, 1877–1887." Ph.D. diss., Northern Illinois University, 1984.

Stromquist, Shelton. "Reconfiguring Classes: Labor, Politics, and Reform in the 1890s." Pullman Strike Centennial Conference, Terre Haute, September 1994.

Tingley, Ralph R. "From Carter Harrison II to Fred Busse: A Study of Chicago Political Parties and Personages from 1896 to 1907." Ph.D. diss., University of Chicago, 1950.

Weber, Robert D. "Rationalizers and Reformers: Chicago Local Transportation in the Nineteenth Century." Ph.D. diss., University of Wisconsin at Madison, 1971.

Wright, Richard R., Jr. "Industrial Conditions of Negroes in Chicago." 1901. In Main Library, CHS.

Yates, Donatta M. "Women in Chicago Industries, 1905–1915: A Study of Working Conditions in Factories, Laundries, and Restaurants." Ph.D. diss., University of Chicago, 1948.

Zingler, Leonard M. "Financial History of the Chicago Street Railways." Ph.D. diss., University of Illinois at Urbana, 1931.

CONTEMPORARY PUBLISHED REPORTS AND PROCEEDINGS

Andrews. John B., and W. D. P. Bliss. *History of Women in Trade Unions*. Vol. 10 of *Report on Conditions of Women and Child Wage-Earners in the United States*. U.S. Senate Document No. 645, 61st Cong., 2nd sess. Washington, DC: GPO, 1911.

Arnold, Bion J. "Report on the Engineering and Operating Features of the Chicago Transportation Problem." Chicago: City Documents, 1902.

Barnett, George E. "Growth of Labor Organization in the United States, 1897–1914." *Quarterly Journal of Economics* 30 (1916): 780–95.

Bentley, Arthur F. "Municipal Ownership Groups in Chicago: A Study of Referendum Votes, 1902–1907." Undated, probably 1907. Newberry Library, Chicago.

Board of Supervising Engineers. "First Annual Report of Board of Supervising Engineers of Chicago Traction." Chicago, 1908.

The Book of Chicagoans: A Biographical Dictionary of Leading Men and Women of the City of Chicago. Chicago: A. N. Marquis, 1917.

Bureau of Labor Statistics of the State of Illinois. Biennial Reports. Springfield, IL, 1896–1908.

Chicago Charter Convention. *Proceedings*. Chicago, 1905–1907.

Chicago City Council. *Journal of Proceedings*. 1899–1908. Harold Washington Municipal Library, Chicago.

Chicago Daily News Almanac and Yearbook. Chicago, 1900–1908.

Chicago Federation of Labor (CFL). "Organized Labor against the Humphrey Bills." Chicago: Eight Hour Herald Print, 1897. In Newberry Library, Chicago.

Civic Federation of Chicago. "The Street Railways of Chicago." Edited by Milo R. Maltbie. Chicago, 1901.

Hull House Year Book.

Independent Anti-Boodle League. "Listen to the Voice of the People." Chicago: Hollister Brothers, 1898. In Hooker Collection, UC.

National Civic Federation. *Municipal and Private Operation of Public Utilities*.

Special Committee on Transportation of the City Council of Chicago. "Report on the Street Railway Franchises and Operations." Chicago, 1898.

Street Railway Commission of the City of Chicago. "Report." Chicago, December 1900.

United States Census, 1900. Washington DC: U.S. Census Office, 1902.

BOOKS AND ARTICLES

Abu-Lughod, Janet L. *New York, Chicago, Los Angeles: America's Global Cities*. Minneapolis: University of Minnesota Press, 1999.

Addams, Jane. *Newer Ideals of Peace*. New York: Macmillan, 1907.

———. "Problems of Municipal Administration." *American Journal of Sociology* 10 (January 1905): 425–44.

———. *Twenty Years at Hull-House; with Autobiographical Notes*. New York: New American Library, 1961.

Armstrong, Christopher, and H. V. Nelles. *Southern Exposure: Canadian Promoters in Latin America and the Caribbean, 1896–1930*. Toronto: University of Toronto Press.

Barrett, James R. "Ethnic and Racial Fragmentation: Toward a Reinterpretation of a Local Labor Movement." In *African American Urban Experience: Perspectives from the Colonial Period to the Present*, ed. Joe W. Trotter, with Earl Lewis and Tera W. Hunter. New York: Palgrave Macmillan, 2004.

———. *Work and Community in the Jungle: Chicago's Packinghouse Workers, 1894–1922*. Urbana: University of Illinois Press, 1987.

Barrett, Paul. *The Automobile and Urban Transit: The Formation of Public Policy in Chicago, 1900–1930*. Philadelphia: Temple University Press, 1983.

Bemis, Edward W. "Regulation or Ownership." In *Municipal Monopolies: A Collection of Papers by American Economists and Specialists*. New York: Th. Y. Cromwell, 1899.

Bender, Thomas. *Intellect and Public Life: Essays on the Social History of American Intellectuals in the United States*. Baltimore: Johns Hopkins University Press, 1993.

Berlanstein, Lenard R. *Rethinking Labor History: Essays on Discourse and Class Analysis*. Urbana: University of Illinois Press, 1993.

Berman, Marshall. *All That Is Solid Melts into Air: The Experience of Modernity*. New York: Simon and Schuster, 1982.

Bluestone, Daniel M. "'The Pushcart Evil': Peddlers, Merchants, and New York City's Streets, 1890–1940." *Journal of Urban History* 18 (1991): 68–92.

Bobbio, Norberto. *Liberalismo y democracia*. Mexico City: Fondo de Cultura Económica, 1985.

Bottles, Scott. *Los Angeles and the Automobile: The Making of the Modern City.* Berkeley and Los Angeles: University of California Press, 1987.

Boyer, Paul. *Urban Masses and Moral Order in America, 1820–1920.* Cambridge, MA: Harvard University Press, 1978.

Bridges, Amy. *A City in the Republic: Antebellum New York and the Origins of Machine Politics.* New York: Cambridge University Press, 1984.

Brinkley, Alan. *Voices of Protest: Huey Long, Father Coughlin, and the Great Depression.* New York: Knopf, 1982.

Brody, David. *In Labor's Cause: Main Themes on the History of the American Worker.* New York: Oxford University Press, 1993.

———. *Steelworkers in America: The Nonunion Era.* 1960. Reprint, New York: Russell and Russell, 1970.

Brown, William H. "Public Ownership and Popular Government." *American Journal of Sociology* 12 (1906–1907): 328–40.

Browne, Waldo R. *Altgeld of Illinois: A Record of His Life and Work.* New York: B. W. Huebsch, 1924.

Bryant, Keith L., Jr. "Labor in Politics: The Oklahoma State Federation of Labor during the Age of Reform." *Labor History* 11 (1970): 259–76.

Buenker, John D. "Dynamics of Chicago Ethnic Politics, 1900–1930." *Journal of the Illinois State Historical Society* 67 (1974).

———. *Urban Liberalism and Progressive Reform.* New York: Norton, 1973.

Burgess, Ernest W. "The Growth of the City: An Introduction to a Research Project." In Burgess and McKenzie, *The City.*

Burgess, Ernest W., and Roderick McKenzie, eds. *The City.* 1925. Reprint, Chicago: University of Chicago Press, 1967.

Burritt Smith, Edwin. "Council Reform in Chicago: Work of the Municipal Voters' League." *Municipal Affairs* 4 (June 1900): 347–62.

———. "Street Railway Legislation in Illinois." *Atlantic Monthly,* January 1904, 109–18.

Calhoun, Craig, ed. *Habermas and the Public Sphere.* Cambridge, MA: MIT Press, 1992.

Cheape, Charles W. *Moving the Masses: Urban Public Transit in New York, Boston, and Philadelphia, 1880–1912.* Cambridge, MA: Harvard University Press, 1980.

Chicago Commission on Race Relations. *The Negro in Chicago: A Study of Race Relations and a Race Riot in 1919.* The American Negro: His History and Literature. 1922. Reprint, New York: Arno Press, 1968.

"The Chicago Strike—By a Teamster." *Independent* 59 (1905): 15–20.

Christie, Robert A. *Empire in Wood: A History of the Carpenters' Union.* Ithaca: Cornell University Press, 1956.

Chudacoff, Howard P. "Industrialization and the Transformation of Urban Space." In Chudacoff and Smith, *American Urban Society.*

Chudacoff, Howard P., and Judith E. Smith, eds. *The Evolution of American Urban Society.* 4th ed. Englewood Cliffs, NJ: Prentice Hall, 1994.

Cleveland, F. A. "Municipal Ownership as a Form of Governmental Control." *Annals of the American Academy of Political and Social Science* 28 (1906): 359–70.

Cobble, Dorothy Sue. *Dishing It Out: Waitresses and Their Unions in the Twentieth Century.* Urbana: University of Illinois Press, 1991.

Cohen, Lizabeth. *Making a New Deal: Industrial Workers in Chicago, 1919–1939.* New York: Cambridge University Press, 1990.

Commons, John R. "Is Class Conflict in America Growing and Is It Inevitable?" *American Journal of Sociology* 13 (1907–1908): 756–83.

———. "Municipal Monopolies." In John R. Commons, *Social Reform and the Church.* 1894. Reprint, New York: Cromwell, 1967.

————. "The New York Building Trades." *Quarterly Journal of Economics* 18 (May 1905): 409–36.

————. "Types of American Labor Organizations: The Teamsters of Chicago." *Quarterly Journal of Economics* 19 (1904).

Cronon, William. *Nature's Metropolis: Chicago and the Great West.* New York: Norton, 1991.

Cudahy, Brian J. *Cash, Tokens and Transfers: A History of Urban Mass Transit in North America.* New York: Fordham University Press, 1990.

Cummings, John. "The Chicago Teamsters Strike." *Journal of Political Economy* 13 (1905): 536–73.

Darrow, Clarence. "The Chicago Traction Question." *International Quarterly* 7 (August 1905).

————. *Story of My Life.* New York: Scribner's, 1932.

Davis, Allen F. *Spearheads for Reform: The Social Settlements and the Progressive Movement, 1890–1914.* New York: Oxford University Press, 1967.

Davis, James Leslie. *The Elevated System and the Growth of Northern Chicago.* Evanston: Northwestern University Studies in Geography no. 10, 1965.

Dawson, Andrew. "The Parameters of Craft Consciousness: The Social Outlook of the Skilled Worker." In *American Labor and Immigration History, 1877–1920s: Recent European Research,* ed. Dirk Hoerder. Urbana: University of Illinois Press, 1983.

Demastes, William W. *Beyond Naturalism: A New Realism in American Theatre.* New York: Greenwood Press, 1988.

Destler, Chester McArthur. *American Radicalism, 1865–1901.* 1946. Reprint, Chicago: Quadrangle Books, 1966.

Diner, Steven J. *A City and Its Universities: Public Policy in Chicago, 1892–1919.* Chicago: University of Chicago Press, 1980.

Dreiser, Theodore. *Sister Carrie.* 1907. Reprint, Philadelphia: University of Pennsylvania Press, 1981.

————. *The Titan.* New York: John Lane Company, 1914.

————. *Trilogy of Desire: Three Novels.* New York: World, 1972.

Duis, Perry. *The Saloon: Public Drinking in Chicago and Boston, 1880–1920.* Urbana: University of Illinois Press, 1983.

Dunne, E. F. *Illinois: The Heart of the Nation.* Vol. 2. Chicago: Lewis, 1933.

Ebner, Michael H., and Eugene M. Tobin, eds. *Age of Urban Reform: New Perspectives on the Progressive Era.* Port Washington, NY: Kennikat Press, 1977.

Edwards, Jerome. "Government of Chicago, 1893–1915." Bessie L. Pierce Collection, UC.

Einhorn, Robin L. *Property Rules: Political Economy in Chicago, 1833–1872.* Chicago: University of Chicago Press, 1991.

Engels, Friedrich. *The Condition of the Working Class in England.* New York: Macmillan, 1958.

Ernst, Daniel R. *Lawyers against Labor: From Individual Rights to Corporate Liberalism.* Urbana: University of Illinois Press, 1995.

Ethington, Philip J. *The Public City: The Political Construction of Urban Life in San Francisco, 1850–1900.* New York: Cambridge University Press, 1994.

Fairfield, John D. "The Scientific Management of Urban Space: Professional City Planning and the Legacy of Progressive Reform." *Journal of Urban History* 20 (1994): 179–204.

Fairlie, John. "The Chicago Street Railways: A Supplementary Note." *Quarterly Journal of Economics* 22 (1907–1908): 476–79.

————. "Recent Extensions of Municipal Functions in the United States." *Annals of the American Academy of Political and Social Science* 25 (1905): 299–310.

————. "The Street Railway Question in Chicago." *Quarterly Journal of Economics* 21 (1907): 371–404.

Feffer, Andrew. *The Chicago Pragmatists and American Progressivism.* Ithaca: Cornell University Press, 1993.

Fine, Lisa M. *The Souls of the Skyscraper: Female Clerical Workers in Chicago, 1870–1930.* Philadelphia: Temple University Press, 1990.

Finegold, Kenneth. *Experts and Politicians: Reform Challenges to Machine Politics, New York, Cleveland, and Chicago.* Princeton, NJ: Princeton University Press, 1995.

Fink, Gary M. "The Rejection of Voluntarism." *Industrial and Labor Relations Review* 26 (1973): 805–19.

Fink, Leon. "American Labor History." In *The New American History,* ed. Eric Foner. Philadelphia: Temple University Press, 1990.

————. "Labor, Liberty, and the Law: Trade Unionism and the Problem of the American Constitutional Order." In Leon Fink, *In Search of the Working Class: Essays in American Labor History and Popular Culture.* Urbana: University of Illinois Press, 1994.

————, ed. *Major Problems in the Gilded Age and the Progressive Era.* Lexington: D. C. Heath, 1993.

————. *Progressive Intellectuals and the Dilemmas of Democratic Commitment.* Cambridge, MA: Harvard University Press, 1997.

Fink, Leon, and Brian Greenberg. *Upheaval in the Quiet Zone: A History of Hospital Workers' Union, Local 1199.* Urbana: University of Illinois Press, 1989.

Flanagan, Maureen A. *Charter Reform in Chicago.* Carbondale: Southern Illinois University Press, 1987.

————. "Charter Reform in Chicago: Political Culture and Urban Progressive Reform." *Journal of Urban History* 12 (1986).

————. "Gender and Urban Political Reform: The City Club and the Women's City Club of Chicago in the Progressive Era." *American Historical Review* 95 (October 1990): 1032–50.

————. *Seeing with Their Hearts: Chicago Women and the Vision of the Good City, 1871–1933.* Princeton, NJ: Princeton University Press, 2002.

Foner, Philip S. *History of the Labor Movement in the United States.* Vol. 3, *The Policies and Practices of the American Federation of Labor, 1900–1909.* New York: International, 1964.

Forbath, William. *Law and the Shaping of the American Labor Movement.* Cambridge, MA: Harvard University Press, 1991.

————. "The Shaping of the American Labor Movement." *Harvard Law Review* 102 (1989): 1109–256.

Foreman, Milton J. "Chicago's New Charter Movement—Its Relation to Municipal Ownership." *Annals of the American Academy of Political and Social Science* 31 (1908): 639–48.

Foster, Mark S. *From Streetcar to Superhighway: American City Planners and Urban Transportation, 1900–1940.* Philadelphia: Temple University Press, 1981.

Foster, William Z. *Misleaders of Labor.* Chicago: Trade Union Educational League, 1927.

Fraser, Steven. *Labor Will Rule: Sidney Hillman and the Rise of American Labor.* Ithaca: Cornell University Press, 1991.

Friedman, Allen. *Power and Greed: Inside the Teamster Empire of Corruption.* New York: F. Watts, 1989.

Friedman, Gerald. "New Estimates of Union Membership: The United States, 1880–1914." *Historical Methods* 32 (Spring 1999): 75–86.

Garnel, Donald. *Rise of Teamster Power in the West.* Berkeley and Los Angeles: University of California Press, 1972.

Gellman, Erik S. "'Carthage Must Be Destroyed': Race, City Politics, and the Campaign to Integrate Chicago Transportation Work, 1929–1945." *Labor* 2.2 (Summer 2005): 81–114.

Ginger, Ray. *Altgeld's America: The Lincoln Ideal versus Changing Realities.* New York: Funk and Wagnalls, 1958.

Goldfield, David R., and Blaine A. Brownell. *Urban America: A History.* 2nd ed. New York: Houghton Mifflin, 1990.

Gosnell, Harold F. *Machine Politics: Chicago Model.* 1937. Reprint, New York: AMS Press, 1969.

Grant, Luke. "True Story of the Chicago Strike." *The Public,* June 17, 1905.

Green, Paul M., and Melvin G. Holli. *The Mayors: The Chicago Political Tradition.* Rev. ed. Carbondale: Southern Illinois University Press, 1995.

Greene, Julie. *Pure and Simple Politics: The American Federation of Labor and Political Activism, 1881–1917.* Cambridge: Cambridge University Press, 1998.

Grosser, Hugo. "The Movement for Municipal Ownership in Chicago." *Annals of the American Academy of Political and Social Science,* November 25, 1905.

Grossman, James R. *Land of Hope: Chicago, Black Southerners, and the Great Migration.* Chicago: University of Chicago Press, 1989.

Haber, William. *Industrial Relations in the Building Industry.* Cambridge and New York: Cambridge University Press, 1930.

Habermas, Jürgen. *Historia y crítica de la opinión pública. La transformación estructural de la vida pública.* Naucalpan, Mexico: Gustavo Gili, 1994.

Hammack, David C. *Power and Society: Greater New York at the Turn of the Century.* New York: Russell Sage Foundation, 1982.

Hapgood, Hutchins. *The Spirit of Labor.* New York, Duffield, 1907.

Harris, Richard, and Robert Lewis. "The Geography of North American Cities and Suburbs, 1900–1950: A New Synthesis." *Journal of Urban History* 27 (March 2001): 262–92.

Harvey, David. *The Condition of Postmodernity: An Enquiry into the Origins of Cultural Change.* Cambridge, MA: Blackwell, 1989.

Hattam, Victoria C. *Labor Visions and State Power: The Origins of Business Unionism in the United States.* Princeton, NJ: Princeton University Press, 1993.

Hays, Samuel P. "Politics of Reform in Municipal Government in the Progressive Era." *Pacific Northwest Quarterly* 55 (1964): 157–69.

Heilman, Ralph E. "The Chicago Subway Problem." *Journal of Political Economy* 22 (1914): 992–1005.

Hofstadter, Richard. *The Age of Reform: From Bryan to F.D.R..* New York: Knopf, 1955.

Hogan, David John. *Class and Reform: School and Society in Chicago, 1880–1930.* Philadelphia: University of Pennsylvania Press, 1985.

Holdom, Jesse, Hon. "Some Comments on Chicago Strikes and Injunctions." *Open Shop* 4 (1905): 551–56.

Holli, Melvin G. *Reform in Detroit: Hazen S. Pingree and Urban Politics.* New York: Oxford University Press, 1969.

Holt, Glen E. "The Changing Perception of Urban Pathology: An Essay on the Development of Mass Transit in the United States." In *Cities in American History,* ed. Kenneth T. Jackson and Stanley K. Schultz. New York: Knopf, 1972.

Hotchkiss, Willard E. "Chicago Traction: A Study in Political Evolution." *Annals of the American Academy of Political and Social Science* 28 (1906): 385–404.

———. "Recent Phases of Chicago's Transportation Problem." *Annals of the American Academy of American Political and Social Science* 31 (1908): 619–29.

Hough, Leslie S. *The Turbulent Spirit: Cleveland, Ohio, and Its Workers, 1877–1899.* New York: Garland, 1991.

Howe, Frederick C. *The City: The Hope of Democracy.* 1905. Reprint, Seattle: University of Washington Press, 1967.

———. *The Confessions of a Reformer.* Kent, OH: Kent State University Press, 1988.

Hoyt, Homer. *One Hundred Years of Land Values in Chicago.* Chicago: University of Chicago Press, 1933.

———. *The Structure and Growth of Residential Neighborhoods of American Cities.* Washington, DC: U.S. Federal Housing Administration, 1939.

Hughes, Thomas. *Networks of Power: Electrification in Western Society, 1880–1930.* Baltimore: Johns Hopkins University Press, 1983.

Huthmacher, J. Joseph. "Urban Liberalism and the Age of Reform." *Mississippi Valley Historical Review* 49 (1962): 231–41.

Hyman, Colette. "Labor Organizing and Female Institution Building: The Chicago Women's Trade Union League, 1904–1924." In *Women, Work, and Protest: A Century of U.S. Women's Labor History,* ed. Ruth Milkman. Boston: Routledge, 1985.

"In Memoriam. Henry Demarest Lloyd." Typescript. Newberry Library, Chicago.

Issel, William, and Robert W. Cherny. *San Francisco, 1865–1932: Politics, Power, and Urban Development.* Berkeley and Los Angeles: University of California Press, 1986.

Jackson, Kenneth T. *Crabgrass Frontier: The Suburbanization of the United States.* New York: Oxford University Press, 1985.

Jentz, John B. "Labor, the Law, and Economics: The Organization of the Chicago Flat Janitors' Union, 1902–1917." *Labor History* 38 (Fall 1997): 413–31.

"Jetzt oder nie!" (Now or never). Pamphlet, 1905. Hooker Collection, UC.

Johnston, Robert D. *The Radical Middle Class: Populist Democracy and the Question of Capitalism in Progressive Era Portland, Oregon.* Princeton, NJ: Princeton University Press, 2003.

Kantowicz, Edward R. *Polish-American Politics in Chicago, 1888–1940.* Chicago: University of Chicago Press, 1975.

Karson, Marc. *American Labor Unions and Politics, 1900–1918.* Carbondale: Southern Illinois University Press, 1958.

Katznelson, Ira. *City Trenches: Urban Politics and the Patterning of Class in the United States.* New York: Pantheon, 1981.

Katznelson, Ira, and Aristide R. Zolberg. *Working-Class Formation: Nineteenth-Century Patterns in Western Europe and in the United States.* Princeton, NJ: Princeton University Press, 1980.

Kazin, Michael. *Barons of Labor: The San Francisco Building Trades and Union Power in the Progressive Era.* Urbana: University of Illinois Press, 1987.

———. "The Great Exception Revisited: Organized Labor and Politics in San Francisco and Los Angeles, 1870–1940." *Pacific Historical Review* 55 (1986): 371–402.

———. *The Populist Persuasion: An American History.* New York: Basic Books, 1995.

Keating, Ann Durkin. *Building Chicago: Suburban Development and the Creation of a Divided Metropolis.* Columbus: Ohio State University Press, 1988.

Keil, Hartmut, and John B. Jentz, eds. *German Workers in Chicago: A Documentary History from 1850 to World War I.* Urbana: University of Illinois Press, 1988.

Kennedy, John Curtis. "Socialistic Tendencies in American Trade Unions." *Journal of Political Economy* 15 (1907): 470–88.

Kessler-Harris, Alice. "The Wage Conceived: Value and Need as Measures of a Woman's Worth." In *A Woman's Wage: Historical Meanings and Social Consequences.* Lexington: University of Kentucky, 1990.

Kimeldorf, Howard, and Robert Penney. "'Excluded by Choice': Dynamics of Interracial Unionism on the Philadelphia Waterfront, 1910–1930." *International Labor and Working-Class History* 51 (Spring 1997): 50–71.

Kolko, Gabriel. *The Triumph of Conservatism: A Reinterpretation of American History, 1900–1916.* New York: Free Press of Glencoe, 1963.

Lash, Christopher. "Work and Loyalty in the Social Thought of the 'Progressive' Era." In *The True and Only Heaven: Progress and Its Critics.* New York: Norton, 1991.

Lash-Quinn, Elizabeth. *Black Neighbors: Race and the Limits of Reform in the American Settlement House Movement, 1890–1945.* Chapel Hill: University of North Carolina Press, 1993.

Laurie, Bruce. *Artisans into Workers: Labor in Nineteenth-Century America.* New York: Noonday Press, 1989.

Lawson, George W. *Organized Labor in Minnesota.* St. Paul: Minnesota State Federation of Labor, 1955.

Lefebvre, Henri. "Industrialization and Urbanization." In Henri Lefebvre, *Writings on Cities,* ed. and trans. Eleonore Kofman and Elizabeth Lebas. Cambridge, MA: Blackwell, 1996.

Leidenberger, Georg. "Nature and the Public: Urban Ecology and the Politics of Transportation in Progressive-Era Chicago." *Revista de Urbanismo* 3 (September 2000). Department of Urban Planning, University of Chile, Santiago, Chile. http://revistaurbanismo.uchile.cl.

———. "Proximidad y diferenciación: el manejo del concepto del espacio en la historia urbana." *Historia y Grafía* (Ibero-American University) no. 22 (2004).

———. "'The Public Is the Labor Union': Working-Class Progressivism in Turn-of-the-Century Chicago." *Labor History* 36 (Spring 1995): 187–210.

Leiter, Robert D. *The Teamsters Union: A Study of Its Economic Impact.* New York: Bookman, 1957.

Lewis, Lloyd, and Henry J. Smith. *Chicago: The History of Its Reputation.* New York: Harcourt, Brace, 1929.

Lindholm, S. V. "Analysis of the Building-Trades Conflict in Chicago: From the Trades-Union Standpoint." *Journal of Political Economy* 8 (1900): 327–46.

Lloyd, Henry Demarest. "The Chicago Traction Question." [1903]. At Newberry Library, Chicago.

Lundberg, Ferdinand. *Imperial Hearst: A Social Biography.* New York: Equinox Cooperative, 1936.

Marks, Gary. *Unions in Politics: Britain, Germany, and the United States in the Nineteenth and Early Twentieth Centuries.* Princeton, NJ: Princeton University Press, 1989.

Mason, Mary Ann. "Neither Friends Nor Foes: Organized Labor and the California Progressives." In *California Progressivism Revisited,* ed. William Deverell and Tom Sitton. Berkeley and Los Angeles: University of California Press, 1994.

Mattson, Kevin. *Creating a Democratic Public: The Struggle for Urban Participatory Democracy during the Progressive Era.* University Park: Pennsylvania University Press, 1998.

Mayer, Harold M., and Richard C. Wade. *Chicago: Growth of a Metropolis.* Chicago: University of Chicago Press, 1969.

McCarthy, Michael P. "New Metropolis." In Ebner and Tobin, *Age of Urban Reform.*

McCormick, Richard L. "The Discovery that Business Corrupts Politics: A Reappraisal of the Origins of Progressivism." *American Historical Review* 86 (1981): 247–74.

———. "Progressivism: A Contemporary Assessment." *In The Party Period and Public Policy: American Politics from the Age of Jackson to the Progressive Era.* New York: Oxford University Press, 1986.

McDonald, Forrest. *Insull.* Chicago: University of Chicago Press, 1962.

McDonald, Terrence J. "The Burdens of Urban History: The Theory of the State in Recent American Social History." *Studies in American Political Development. Vol. 3.* New Haven: Yale University Press, 1989.

———. "Comment." Review essay. *Journal of Urban History* 8 (August 1984): 454–62.

McDowell, Mary E. "At the Heart of the Packingtown Strike." *The Commons* 9 (1904): 397–406.

McKillen, Elizabeth. *Chicago Labor and the Quest for a Democratic Diplomacy, 1914–1924*. Ithaca: Cornell University Press, 1995.

Merriam, Charles E. *Chicago: A More Intimate View of Urban Politics*. New York: Macmillan, 1929.

Meyerowitz, Joanne J. *Women Adrift: Independent Wage Earners in Chicago, 1880–1930*. Chicago: University of Chicago Press, 1988.

Miller, James A. "Coercive Trade-Unionism as Illustrated by the Chicago Building-Trades Conflict." *Journal of Political Economy* 9 (1901): 321–50.

Mittelman, Edward B. "Chicago Labor in Politics, 1877–1896." *Journal of Political Economy* 28 (1920): 407–27.

Mollenkopf, John H., ed. *Power, Culture, and Place: Essays on New York City*. New York: Russell Sage Foundation, 1988.

Monkkonen, Eric H. *America Becomes Urban: The Development of U.S. Cities and Towns, 1780–1980*. Berkeley and Los Angeles: University of California Press, 1988.

Montgomery, David. *The Fall of the House of Labor: The Workplace, the State, and Labor Activism, 1865–1925*. New York: Cambridge University Press, 1987.

———. *Workers' Control in America*. Cambridge: Cambridge University Press, 1979.

Montgomery, Royal E. *Industrial Relations in the Chicago Building Trades*. Chicago: University of Chicago Press, 1927.

Morton, Richard Allen. *Justice and Humanity: Edward F. Dunne, Illinois Progressive*. Carbondale: Southern Illinois University Press, 1997.

Mowry, George E. *The Era of Theodore Roosevelt and the Birth of Modern America, 1900–1912*. New York: Harper and Row, 1958.

Murphy, Marjorie. *Blackboard Unions: The American Federation of Teachers and the National Education Administration, 1900–1980*. Ithaca: Cornell University Press, 1990.

———. "Taxation and Social Conflict: Teacher Unionism and Public School Finance in Chicago, 1898–1934." *Journal of the Illinois State Historical Society* 74.4 (1981): 242–60.

"Negro Pioneers in the Chicago Labor Movement." A. P. Randolph Educational Fund. In Main Library, CHS.

Nestor, Agnes. *Women's Labor Leader: An Autobiography of Agnes Nestor*. Rockford, IL: Bellevue Press, 1954.

Newell, Barbara W. *Chicago and the Labor Movement: Metropolitan Unionism in the 1930s*. Urbana: University of Illinois Press, 1961.

Nicholes, Anna. "Women and Trade Unions." *The Commons* 9 (June 1904): 268–73.

Norton, Samuel Wilber. *Chicago Traction: A History, Legislative and Political*. Chicago, 1907.

Norwood, Stephen H. *Labor's Flaming Youth: Telephone Operators and Worker Militancy, 1878–1923*. Urbana: University of Illinois Press, 1990.

Novick, Peter. *That Noble Dream: The 'Objectivity Question' and the American Historical Profession*. Cambridge: Cambridge University Press, 1988.

Oestreicher, Richard. *Solidarity and Fragmentation: Working-People and Class Consciousness in Detroit, 1875–1900*. Urbana: University of Illinois Press, 1986.

———. "Urban Working-Class Political Behavior and Theories of American Electoral Politics, 1870–1940." *Journal of American History*, 1987, 1257–86.

Older, Mrs. Fremont. *William Randolph Hearst, American*. New York: D. Appleton-Century, 1936.

Park, Robert. "Ecología humana." In *Antología de sociología urbana*, ed. Mario Bassols et al. Mexico: UNAM, 1988.

Partridge, Newton A. "Suggestions on the Chicago Street Railway Problem." Chicago: R. R. Donnelley & Sons, 1898.

Payne, Elizabeth A. *Reform, Labor and Feminism: Margaret Dreier Robins and the Women's Trade Union League.* Urbana: University of Illinois Press, 1988.

Pegrem, Thomas R. *Partisans and Progressives: Private Interest and Public Policy in Illinois, 1870–1922.* Urbana: University of Illinois Press, 1992.

Perlman, Selig. *A Theory of the Labor Movement.* New York: Macmillan, 1928.

Pierce, Bessie Louise. *A History of Chicago.* Vol. 3, *1871–1893.* New York: Knopf, 1937.

Platt, Harold L. *The Electric City: Energy and the Growth of the Chicago Area, 1880–1930.* Chicago: University of Chicago Press, 1991.

Poole, Ernest. "The Disappearing Public." *World To-Day,* 1904, 1056–62.

———. "How a Labor Machine Held Up Chicago and How the Teamsters' Union Smashed the Machine." *World To-Day* 7 (July 1904): 896–905.

———. "Packingtown during the Strike: Photographs without a Camera." *World To-Day* 7 (1904): 1271–74.

Porter Benson, Susan. "'The Customers Ain't God': The Work Culture of Department Store Saleswomen, 1890–1940." In *Working-Class America: Essays on Labor, Community, and Society,* ed. Michael H. Frisch and Daniel J. Walkowitz. Urbana: University of Illinois Press, 1983.

Reid, Robert L., ed. *Battleground: The Autobiography of Margaret A. Haley.* Urbana: University of Illinois Press, 1982.

Ricker, David Swing. "Unionizing the Schoolteachers." *World To-Day* 8 (1905): 394–402.

Robbins, Hayes. "Public Ownership versus Public Control." *American Journal of Sociology* 10 (1904–1905): 787–813.

Rodgers, Daniel T. *Atlantic Crossings: Social Politics in a Progressive Age.* Cambridge, MA: Harvard University Press, 1998.

———. "In Search of Progressivism." *Reviews in American History* 10 (1982): 113–32.

Roediger, David R. *Towards the Abolition of Whiteness: Essays on Race, Politics, and Working-Class History.* New York: Verso, 1994.

Rogin, Michael. "Voluntarism: The Political Functions of an Antipolitical Doctrine." *Industrial and Labor Relations Review* 15 (1962).

Ross, Dorothy. *The Origins of American Social Science.* Cambridge: Cambridge University Press, 1991.

Rowe, L. S. "Municipal Ownership and Operation: The Value of Foreign Experience." *American Journal of Sociology* 12 (1906–1907): 241–53.

———. "Municipal Ownership and Operation of Street Railways in Germany." *Annals of the American Academy of Political and Social Science* 27 (1906): 37–65.

Salzman, Neil V. *Reform and Revolution: The Life and Times of Raymond Robins.* Kent, OH: Kent State University Press, 1991.

Sandburg, Carl. *Chicago Poems.* New York: Dover, 1994.

Sawislak, Karen. *Smoldering City: Chicagoans and the Great Fire, 1871–1874.* Chicago: University of Chicago Press, 1995.

Schmidt, John R. *The Mayor Who Cleaned Up Chicago: A Political Biography of William E. Dever.* DeKalb: Northern Illinois University Press, 1989.

Schneirov, Richard. *Labor and Urban Politics: Class Conflict and the Origins of Modern Liberalism in Chicago, 1864–1897.* Urbana: University of Illinois Press, 1998.

———. "Rethinking the Relation of Labor to the Politics of Urban Social Reform in Late Nineteenth-Century America: The Case of Chicago." *International Labor and Working-Class History* 46 (Fall 1994): 93–108.

Schneirov, Richard, and Thomas J. Suhrbur. *Union Brotherhood, Union Town: The History of the Carpenters' Union of Chicago, 1863–1987.* Carbondale: Southern Illinois University Press, 1988.

Scott, Leroy. *Walking Delegate.* 1905. Reprint, Upper Saddle River, NJ: Literature House, 1969.

Seidman, Steven, ed. *Jürgen Habermas on Society and Politics: A Reader.* Boston: Beacon Press, 1989.

Shover, John L. "The Progressives and the Working Class Vote in California." *Labor History* 10 (Fall 1969): 584–601.

Sikes, George C. "Chicago's Struggle for Freedom from Traction Rule." *Outlook* 82 (March 31, 1906): 748–53.

———. "The Chicago Traction Tangle." *World To-Day* 8 (1905): 515–18.

———. "Observations on the Street Car Strike." *The Voter,* December 1903.

———. "Public Policy Concerning Franchise Values—A Problem in Taxation." *Journal of Political Economy* 9 (1900–1901): 527–39.

———. "Recent Startling Aspects of the Chicago Traction Question." *City Club Bulletin,* April 25, 1913, 4.

———. "The Relation of Chicago to Public Service Corporations." *Annals of the American Academy of Political and Social Science* 31 (1908): 689–702.

———. *The Street Railway Situation in Chicago.* Harrisburg, PA: Mount Pleasant Press, 1902.

Sinclair, Upton. *The Jungle.* 1905. Reprint, New York: Signet Classics, 1960.

Sklar, Martin J. *The Corporate Reconstruction of American Capitalism, 1890–1906: The Market, the Law, and Politics.* New York: Cambridge University Press, 1988.

Skocpol, Theda. "Theories of the State and the Case of the New Deal." *Politics and Society* 10 (1980).

Skocpol, Theda, and John Ikenberry. "The Political Formation of the American Welfare State in Historical and Comparative Perspective." *Comparative Social Research* 6 (1983).

Smith, Walter. "Pluralism." In *Theory and Methods in Political Science,* ed. David Marsh and Gerry Stoker. London: Macmillan, 1995.

Soares, Victor E. "Reforming a Labor Union." *World-Today* 10 (1905): 92–97.

Soja, Edward W. *Postmodern Geographies: The Reassertion of Space in Critical Social Theory.* London and New York: Verso Press, 1989.

Spear, Allan H. *Black Chicago: The Making of a Negro Ghetto, 1890–1920.* Chicago: University of Chicago Press, 1967.

Staley, Eugene. *History of the Illinois State Federation of Labor.* Chicago: Chicago University Press, 1930.

Stave, Bruce M., and Sandra A. Stave, eds. *Urban Bosses, Machines, and Progressive Reformers.* Rev. ed. Malabar: R. E. Krieger, 1984.

Stead, William T. *If Christ Came to Chicago: A Plea for the Union of All Who Love in the Service of All Who Suffer.* Chicago: Laird & Lee, 1894.

Stephenson, Carl. "Altgeld and the Progressive Tradition." *American Historical Review* 46 (July 1941): 813–31.

Stevens, Harry R. "Some Aspects of the Standards of Living in Chicago, 1893–1914." Bessie L. Pierce Collection, UC.

Stromquist, Shelton. "The Crucible of Class: Cleveland Politics and the Origins of Municipal Reform in the Progressive Era." *Journal of Urban History* 23 (January 1997): 192–220.

Taft, Philip. *Labor Politics American Style: The California State Federation of Labor.* Cambridge, MA: Harvard University Press, 1968.

Tamayo Flores-Alatorre, Sergio. "Una revisión de las principales corriente teóricas sobre el análisis urbano." *Anuario de Estudios Urbanos* (Universidad Autónoma Metropolitana—Azcapotzalco, Mexico) no. 1 (1994): 73–118.

Tarbell, Ida M. "How Chicago Is Finding Herself." *American Magazine* 67 (November, December 1908).

Tarr, Joel A. "The Chicago Anti–Department Store Crusade of 1897: A Case Study in Urban Commercial Development." *Journal of the Illinois State Historical Society* 64 (1971): 161–72.

————. "From City to Suburb: The 'Moral' Influence of Transportation Technology." In *American Urban History: An Interpretive Reader with Commentaries,* ed. Alexander B. Callow Jr. 2nd ed. New York: Oxford University Press, 1973.

————. *Transportation Innovation and Changing Spatial Patterns in Pittsburgh, 1850–1934.* Chicago: Public Works Historical Society, 1978.

Tarr, Joel A., and Josef W. Konvitz. "Patterns in the Development of the Urban Infrastructure." In *American Urbanism: A Historiographical Review,* ed. Howard Gillette Jr. and Zane L. Miller. New York: Greenwood Press, 1987.

Taylor, Graham. *Chicago Commons through Forty Years.* Chicago: Chicago Commons Association, 1936.

Thelen, David P. *The New Citizenship: Origins of Progressivism in Wisconsin, 1885–1900.* Columbia: University of Missouri Press, 1972.

————. "Social Tensions and the Origins of Progressivism." *Journal of American History* 56 (September 1969): 323–41.

Tocqueville, Alexis de. *Democracy in America.* New York: Vintage Classics, 1990.

Tolman, Edgar B. "Chicago's Traction Question." *World To-Day* 10 (1905–1906): 637–45.

Tomlins, Christopher L. *The State and the Unions: Labor Relations, Law, and the Organized Labor Movement in America, 1880–1960.* Cambridge: Cambridge University Press, 1985.

Trachtenberg, Alan. "Leyendo la ciudad de la edad dorada: del misterio al realismo." In *Nuevas perspectivas en los estudios sobre historia urbana latinoamericana,* ed. Jorge E. Hardoy and Richard P. Morse. Buenos Aires: Grupo Editor Latinoamericano, 1989.

Turner, Frederick Jackson. "Social Forces in American History." In *The Frontier in American History.* New York: H. Holt, 1920.

Tuttle, William M., Jr. "Labor Conflict and Racial Violence: The Black Workers in Chicago, 1894–1919." *Labor History* 10, no. 3 (Summer 1969): 408–32.

————. *Race Riot: Chicago in the Red Summer of 1919.* New York: Atheneum Press, 1985.

Voss, Kim. *The Making of American Exceptionalism: The Knights of Labor and Class Formation in the Nineteenth Century.* Ithaca: Cornell University Press, 1993.

Wacker, Charles H. "The Plan of Chicago." *American City* 1 (October 1909): 49–58.

Wade, Richard. "Urbanization." In *The Comparative Approach to American History,* ed. C. Vann Woodward. New York: Basic Books, 1968.

Walling, William E. "The Building Trades Employers and the Unions." *World's Work,* August 1903.

————. "Can Labor Unions Be Destroyed?" *World's Work,* May 1904.

Warner, Sam Bass, Jr. *Streetcar Suburbs: The Process of Growth in Boston, 1870–1900.* Cambridge, MA: Harvard University Press, 1962.

————. *The Urban Wilderness: A History of the American City.* New York: Harper and Row, 1972.

Weber, Harry P. *An Outline History of Chicago Traction.* [Chicago]: s.n., [1936].

Weber, Max. "In Chikago." In *Max Weber: Ein Lebensbild,* ed. Marianne Weber. Tübingen, Germany: J. C. B. Mohr, 1926.

Weinstein, James. *The Corporate Ideal in the Liberal State, 1900–1918.* Boston: Beacon Press, 1968.

Weisberger, Bernard A. *The La Follettes of Wisconsin: Love and Politics in Progressive America.* Madison: University of Wisconsin Press, 1994.

Wiebe, Robert. *The Search for Order, 1877–1920.* New York: Hill and Wang, 1967.

Wilcox, Delos F. *The American City: A Problem in Democracy.* New York: Macmillan, 1904.

Winkler, John K. *William Randolph Hearst: A New Appraisal.* New York: Hastings House, 1955.

Wish, Harvey. "Altgeld and the Progressive Tradition." *American Historical Review* 46 (July 1941): 813–31.

Witwer, David. *Corruption and Reform in the Teamsters Union.* Urbana: University of Illinois Press, 2003.

———. "Unionized Teamsters and the Struggle over the Streets of the Early-Twentieth Century City." *Social Science History* 24 (Spring 2000): 183–222.

Wolman, Leo. "The Extent of Labor Organization in the United States in 1910." *Quarterly Journal of Economics* 30 (May 1916): 486–518.

Woodruff, Clinton Rogers. "Practical Municipal Progress." *American Journal of Sociology* 12 (1906–1907): 190–215.

Wright, Carroll D. "The Ethical Influence of Invention." *Social Economist* 1 (September 1891): 338–47.

Wrigley, Julia. *Class Politics and Public Schools: Chicago, 1900–1950.* New Brunswick, NJ: Rutgers University Press, 1982.

Yago, Glenn. *The Decline of Transit: Urban Transportation in German and U.S. Cities, 1900–1970.* New York: Cambridge University Press, 1984.

Yarros, Victor S. "The Chicago Election and the City's Traction Outlook." *American Monthly Review of Reviews,* May 1907.

———. "Chicago's Significant Election and Referendum." *American Monthly Review of Reviews* (1904): 584–87.

Yellowitz, Irvin. *Labor and the Progressive Movement in New York State, 1897–1916.* Ithaca: Cornell University Press, 1965.

Yudelson, Sophie. "Women's Place in Industry and Labor Organizations." *Annals of the American Academy of Political and Social Science* 24 (1904): 343–53.

Zunz, Olivier. *The Changing Face of Inequality: Urbanization, Industrial Development, and Immigrants in Detroit, 1880–1920.* Chicago: University of Chicago Press, 1982.

INDEX